FROM ATHENS TO MELBOURNE

Athens, Paris, St. Louis, London, Stockholm, Antwerp, Amsterdam, Los Angeles, Berlin, Helsinki—and now, in 1956, Melbourne. It is a striking record of accomplishment and adventure.

This is the story Colonel Grombach tells. From 1200 B.C. down through history he traces the Olympic pageantry—the rivalries, the triumphs, the color and excitement of the world's greatest athletic contests. The development of each sport is traced from its origins to its present-day stars—from Hermogenes of Xanthos to Bob Mathias of California.

Here is a complete history of the Olympic games—fascinating reading for every follower of every sport.

This is an original publication—not a reprint—published by
BALLANTINE BOOKS, INC.

by John V. Grombach

OLYMPIC
CAVALCADE
OF
SPORTS

BALLANTINE BOOKS • NEW YORK

CONTENTS

The important thing in the Olympic games is not to win, but to take part; the important thing in life is not the triumph but the struggle; the essential thing is not to have conquered but to have fought well.

To spread these precepts is to build up a stronger and more valiant and above all more scrupulous and more generous humanity.

—Baron de Coubertin

CHAPTER I

Origin of the Ancient Olympics and first efforts to revive them in modern times

THE CAVALCADE of Olympic games is the oldest show on earth. Although revived by popular request in modern times, in 1896, the Olympics ran continuously every four years for at least 1200 years in ancient Greece. The first recorded Olympic games were in 776 B.C. and the last recorded Olympics were in 394 A.D., at which time Roman Emperor Theodosius suspended the games. According to modern historical research, however, the games actually began long before 776 B.C.—began, in fact, sometime between 1253 B.C. and 884 B.C.

The Olympic pageant of sports, which started with one foot race, a sprint, therefore covers approximately 3000 years and 309 definitely recorded Olympics, and has encompassed practically every competitive sport known to man. In fact, the Olympics is the greatest single factor behind the development of every one of the sports which form part of the current daily peaceful fare of activity, interest, conversation and entertainment of the peoples of the world. The 16th modern Olympics at Melbourne, Australia, in 1956 is actually the 310th recorded Olympiad in the history of competitive athletics.

Let us go back to the earliest times among the green-wooded slopes and grassy plains through which flowed two rivers in ancient Hellas, now Greece. The banks of the Alpheus and the Cladeus were overshadowed by willow trees, mirrored in the clear sparkling waters. As the first settlement of Olympia, the ancient site of the Olympics, belongs to mythical times and legend, so do the fables which historians and poets tell of the origin of the greatest and oldest series of athletic competitions on earth.

According to one version, Heracles, as a penance for his misdeeds, was given the difficult problem and unpleasant chore of quickly cleaning the stables in which Augeas, King of Elis, maintained a great herd. Heracles accomplished his job with the greatest of ease by simply turning the river Alpheus from its course through the stables, but not before making a friendly bet with the King that if he accomplished

1

his task he would be due, as a commission, a ten-percent cut of the herd. Augeas refused to pay up, claiming that Heracles' method was all wet. Heracles then killed Augeas and took over the herd, the property, and the throne of Augeas. To salve his guilty conscience and at the same time to celebrate his accomplishments and the acquisition of his new properties, Heracles then instituted the first Olympic games—*circa* 1253.

Another version would have us believe that Lycurgus, the great Spartan formulator of law, joined with Iphitus of Elis on the alleged bidding of the oracle to "restore" the festival in 820 B.C. This at least would indicate that the games had been run before, as there is some historical basis for this story and definite evidence points to the word "restore."

Greek mythology seems to claim that the Olympics began as religious celebrations and games in commemoration of Zeus's having defeated Kronos in a mighty wrestling match of the gods for possession of the earth.

Another rather stubborn story is given by the natives of Greece interested in the Olympics—the legend of Pelops. Here the river Alpheus is again the background for a story, this time of a King of Elis, Oenomaus, with a beautiful daughter named Hippodamia. This girl was offered to any suitor who could successfully kidnap her in a chariot. The catch, of course, was that the King gave pursuit, had light chariots, fast horses, and was handy with the spear or javelin. According to legend, thirteen young men got away with Hippodamia, but all were caught up with and promptly transfixed with a royal spear. This may be the origin of our modern superstition about the number thirteen. At any rate, one day a young man named Pelops showed up, studied the situation carefully, took certain precautions, and made certain preparations. Shortly thereafter Pelops left his amiable royal host, taking the daughter with him. Oenomaus gave chase, but Pelops had bribed the King's charioteer to tamper with the kingly car's axle, and the result was the ancient counterpart of a blowout. Thus Pelops won a bride and a throne with a bribe and instituted the games and religious ceremonies on the hallowed ground of Olympia in Elis. The date generally ascribed to this episode is 884 B.C.

No matter which one of these uncertain legends or dates we accept, one thing is certain—that the first recorded Olympics occurred in 776 B.C., and that thereafter the Greeks began to reckon time by Olympiads, the four-year intervals at which the games were held. From the first Olympiad to the 310th is history, and what came before is legend. However, archeologists assert that the ruins of Olympia reveal the fact that many of the great buildings within the enclosure for games and religious celebrations of the Olympics were built hundreds of years before the first recorded Olympiad in 776 B.C.

The games were conducted on the highest plane—almost a religious one. At first only pure Greeks could compete, and for centuries the moral standards were carefully upheld. No one with a police record, or even related to anyone with a police record, could be a contestant.

At first, only the sprint or foot race—one length of the stadium (approximately 200 yards)—was involved. At the games of the 14th Olympiad, a second race of two times around the stadium (less than one-half mile) was added; at the 15th, a long-distance race of twelve times around the stadium (approximately 2½ miles). In the 18th, a five-event pentathlon (broad jumping, javelin throw, 200-yard dash, discus throw, and wrestling), obviously for the soldier-athlete, was added. This was the first appearance of wrestling in the Olympics, although it was later added as a separate event. Boxing began at the 23rd Olympics; equestrian events came in with the four-horse chariot in the nearby hippodrome at the 25th games; and the pancratium, a combination of boxing, wrestling, and modern waterfront brawling, was added in the 33rd Olympics. Running with full military equipment, including shields, and jumping were also added in the earlier games.

Many field events closely resembling our modern events, such as javelin and discus throwing, were added to the ever-increasing cavalcade of Olympic sports. However, the jumping events differed from our modern jumping in using weights which contestants carried in their hands and tossed backward at the moment of take-off. Even the tug of war, football, gymnastics and weight lifting can be traced back to the ancient Olympics. From the earliest Olympics, separate but similar events for boys were added.

Interest in all forms of athletics made the Olympics the greatest event in the known world. The Olympic athletic program was expanded from one morning to five days, with two additional days for religious ceremonies. Tourists and sports fans as far back as the fifth century B.C. trooped to Olympia from communities along all shores of the Mediterranean—France, Spain, Africa, Sicily, Italy, Asia Minor. These regions also sent their athletes and representatives to compete and erect sanctuaries and treasure houses at Olympia.

The world looked to peace and cooperation and "good will to man" through the Olympic games.

Although wars did occur, it was evident that the Olympic games had achieved an importance far above that of any other institution or idea of the period. Today, in the twentieth century and in the atomic age, the Olympics once again present a hope to all nations and races that friendly competition hand in hand with freedom and tolerance can make a better world.

Olympia, the center of the ancient Olympics, where the Alpheus and the Cladeus converge, must be described. The reports of contemporary writers and poets, together with the comparatively recent excavation of its ruins, make it possible to visualize the setting. The Altis, or sacred grove of Zeus, was in the shape of a rectangle. Hills surrounded Olympia on the north, the rivers were on the south and the west. The eastern side was formed by the tremendous hippodrome, or race track, site of the equestrian events. The marble stadium was fairly well centered but against the sloping hillsides of the north. The sides or spectator part of the stadium had a capacity of approximately 60,000, and the field was approximately 214 yards long and 32 yards wide. (Yankee Stadium is approximately 180 yards long and 98 yards wide with a seating capacity of 67,000.) No spectators were ever allowed on the field, nor were bleachers ever built to increase the paid attendance. Only judges, competitors and announcers were allowed in the field or enclosure.

The hippodrome was a marble edifice, large even by modern standards. The field or amphitheatre where equestrian events—chariot and mounted races—were run off was 806 yards in length by 405 yards in width. (Delaware Park in Wilmington, Delaware, the largest mile-track race course in the United States, measures 720 yards in length and 280 yards in width, and could neatly fit into the ancient Olympic hippodrome with a little left over.) No Hollywood set ever built could compare with the actual marble splendor of Olympia.

There were numerous treasure houses, temples, and religious buildings in Olympia. The most important building was the Olympium, which housed one of the seven wonders of the world—a huge ivory statue of Zeus with robes of solid gold. The figure of the Greek god was forty feet high.

The most important building for the athletes was the gymnasium with its long colonnade-covered track. The main floor of the gymnasium, called the palaestra, was about 250 feet square and was like our present-day gyms except that it had sand as flooring. Here the wrestlers, boxers, gymnasts, and pancratium contestants practiced under the supervision of

4

trainers and judges for the month preceding the actual games.

The Greek thoroughness in athletics in antiquity may have surpassed even that in England in the early part of the twentieth century or that in the United States today. According to written records which have come down to us, all the athletes followed a strict regimen which began early and ended late. After a breakfast of fermented bread and grape juice, a morning of punishing exercises was followed, with no stop for lunch, by more training in the afternoon and a mighty dinner. In the earlier Olympics, vegetables, fruits and plenty of cheese was the menu. Later, fish and meat appeared. According to some original sources, Milo of Crotona and Theagenes of Thasos, the greatest wrestler and boxer of antiquity respectively, each ate a broiled ox at one sitting. Although there may be some exaggeration in this story, there is evidence that the Olympic athletes of ancient Greece averaged over six pounds of meat per man per dinner. From the earliest days, alcoholic beverages and cold drinks were taboo.

The ancient Olympics started, according to the records that have come down to us, with the Olympic Oath taken by the athletes and judges before the statue of the god Zeus. The athletes swore to observe the rules, the judges swore to be fair, and all prayed for personal success and the success of the games. Then came the parade around the stadium, the contestants grouped by city or country. Trumpets were blown at the beginning and at the end of each event. A branch from a palm tree was placed in the hands of the winner and a wreath made from the leaves of the wild olive trees was put on his head. A closing ceremony at the end of the games always featured prayers of thanks.

Although Olympic athletes had their expenses paid and winners received great favors from their communities and rich neighbors and were marked, if not favored, for life and certainly aided if they desired to train for another Olympics, the spirit behind the ancient Olympics was basically one of amateurism. In other words, various types of subsidies were provided to enable qualified athletes to compete, just as they are today. The crux of the problem was then, as it is today, whether the athlete was basically an amateur at heart or whether he was a professional performing solely for actual payment. Some countries today that are advanced economically can, like the United States, send Olympic teams and maintain the apparatus to operate competitive athletics by voluntary contributions from educational, athletic and recreational organizations. Other nations less fortunate must support their Olympic teams by government subsidy.

The question of professionalism is a serious one and that is why the Olympic Committee and the AAU in the United States have leaned over backward to be strict on any issues involving excessive expenses. Every country, according to the Olympic spirit in both the ancient and modern games, should satisfy itself on athletic purity and adhere to the moral principle that two wrongs never make one right. Each must keep its own amateur sports clean. It was the issue of professionalism of the Romans that caused the discord, scandal and free-for-all fighting that made the ancient Olympics a public nuisance and resulted in their suspension.

While it is admitted the ancient Olympic games deteriorated after a thousand years or so and the real Olympic spirit was lost after some ten centuries, the disintegration may be laid to human frailty and the decline of civilization and morals rather than to any weakness in the ideals or in the organization of the Olympic games. As long as the high moral and religious nature of the participants and officials continued, the games were both successful and popular. When bribery, corruption, and dishonesty crept in, the games lost both their success and their popularity. They became a battlefront instead of a gathering for peaceful competition to bind peoples together.

Shortly after the suspension of the games in 394 A.D., Olympia was sacked and looted by barbaric invaders from the north, and the Romans further destroyed the Greek temples. Thereafter, two earthquakes not only completed the destruction of Olympia but, by changing the course of the Alpheus and Cladeus rivers, soon buried the city beneath twenty-five feet of sand and silt.

Over 1300 years later, in 1829, the French government and later, in 1875, the German government, began to dig Olympia out. In 1881 the ruins, still projecting a golden era in history, were completely uncovered, and there is no doubt that the scientists and historians dug up not only the secrets of the site of the ancient Olympics but their spirit and glory as well, and that the renewal of this spirit led to the many efforts toward a renaissance of the Olympics, first by the Greeks in 1859 and 1870—which failed—and then by the French in 1892.

Notwithstanding the full credit usually given the French and the French father of the modern Olympics, Baron de

Coubertin, for reviving the games (described in Chapter II), the real story is that the Greeks and a man named Zappas began working toward the revival of the Olympics long before Coubertin and the French succeeded. The two modern Olympics forgotten in history as efforts which did not restore the glory or the existence of the games occurred in Greece in 1859 and 1870.

They failed essentially because the world was not quite ready and because Greece was not a powerful enough country or a rich enough country at the time to put over the idea. Another even more important reason was that the individual sponsor involved was naive and inexperienced in both promotion and amateur athletics. Unlike Baron de Coubertin, he did not first seek out the leaders of school, college, and amateur athletic organizations throughout the world and solicit their help.

Thrilled by the romance and glory of old Greece and by the Olympic spirit of drawing people together through sports, Evangelios Zappas, a Greek living in Rumania, first contributed and, on his death, following the failure of his first Olympics, willed money to re-establish the Olympic games in Greece. The Greek government supported Zappas and accepted the money, but ineffectively organized the games. Both the resulting games were good examples of what not to do. The 1859 games were held in a square—Place Louis—and in the streets of Athens, as no stadium was available. Confusion and chaos resulted. Although the king and queen and many dignitaries attended, spectators were trampled on and injured by mounted police trying to keep the streets open for contestants, and athletes were arrested for acting like spectators. Boys and old men entered the competitions at the last minute and actually ran in some of the preliminary heats in order to get through the police lines. A blind man presented himself to the officials for one of the events, using the opportunity to sing a song to the multitude, for which he was not unrecompensed. One of the long-distance runners dropped dead in the two-mile race. Events in the 1859 Olympics were the equivalent of a 200-yard dash, a two-mile run, a triple jump (our present hop, step and jump), and the discus throw. In the 1870 competition, wrestling and a tug-of-war competition were added. It must be remembered that the 1859 Olympics were held thirty-seven years before the first officially recognized modern Olympiad. Though unsuccessful, they were a logical connection between the dim past and the uncertain future.

CHAPTER II

Origin, Management, and Spirit of the Modern Olympic Games

At the beginning of the twentieth century, when the rebirth of the Olympics and the Olympic spirit took place, the world was again particularly conscious of the principles of freedom and peace and appreciative of the equality and dignity of man as a result of so many unsuccessful centuries of dictators, wars, and despotism.

"Olympia and the Olympics symbolize an entire civilization, superior to countries, cities, military heroes or even the ancient religions." So wrote a young French nobleman, Baron Pierre de Coubertin. A cadet at St. Cyr, the French West Point, Coubertin resigned to study political science and later became interested in education and sociology. He traveled all over the world and was particularly impressed by the "Anglo-Saxon" (British and American) interest in sports. Alerted by the discoveries at Olympia and by the abortive efforts to recreate the Olympics in 1859 and 1870 and believing that friendly international athletic competitions might teach youth international understanding as it had done once before, he became obsessed with the ambition to revive the Olympics on a world basis.

"The Olympics—the entire planet is its domain—all sports —all nations," he wrote. French soldiers had found and restored the temple of Zeus at Olympia. Germans had uncovered the entire site of the ancient games after six years of work. Greece retained and glorified every single piece of marble recovered from her Olympic glory. European youth was stirring and demanding athletic competition. Throughout the British Empire, known for its sports and games, and in the United States, a young nation, there was widespread participation in competitive athletics.

Coubertin presented his plan to the Athletic Sports Union in Paris, late in 1892, after a sound public-relations preparation. "Let us export oarsmen, runners, fencers; there is the free trade of the future—and on the day when it shall take its place among the customs of Europe, the cause of peace will have received a new and powerful support . . . so please help me re-establish the Olympic games," begged Coubertin.

8

Coubertin was persistent and soon had the opportunity to sound out other countries for support when the French Sports Union held an International Congress on Amateurism. Mr. C. Herbert, representing the Amateur Athletic Association of the British Empire; Professor William Sloane of Princeton, representing amateur athletics in the United States; and Baron de Coubertin, representing France and the rest of Europe made the original preparations not only to present the amateur issue but also to propose re-creating the Olympic Games. In 1894 the Congress was held and Coubertin obtained surprising and strong support from the United States, Great Britain, and Sweden, and from prominent people such as the Duke of Sparta, the Prince of Wales, the Crown Prince of Sweden, the King of Belgium, and the Prime Minister of the British Empire. Delegates from France, England, the United States, Greece, Russia, Sweden, Belgium, Italy, and Spain were present. Interest was indicated in official letters from Hungary, Germany, Bohemia, Holland, and Austria. The enthusiastic delegates decided not to wait for 1900, heretofore considered a likely basic year to start recomputing Olympiads, but to have the first modern Olympics in 1896 and to hold it in Athens, near the site of the ancient Olympics. It was decided that the games would move every four years to major cities of the world and that an International Olympic Committee should be selected to have full authority over the games. The Baron's dream had become a reality.

Another Frenchman with another idea based on history was responsible for the modern Olympics' most dramatic and spectacular event—the marathon. Michel Bréal, one of the French delegates, wanted to do much more than help the Congress initiate the modern Olympics. He wanted to contribute toward a trophy to top all others and to inspire help and enthusiasm. Shortly after the Congress, he wrote to Coubertin announcing his trophy for a foot race to outdo all others—a race based on the legendary feat, and feet, of Pheidippides.

About 490 B.C. Darius of Persia sent Hippias, former tyrant of Athens, and an army to overrun and enslave Athens and its ally Eretria. Eretria was captured after a long siege, and Hippias then landed at Marathon, a plain approximately twenty-six miles from Athens. Pheidippides, an Olympic champion, was sent as a courier to try to get help from Sparta. According to the story, he ran, swam rivers, climbed mountains for days without rest and succeeded in persuading the Spartans to come to the aid of Athens. He later got back as fast as he could to deliver the good news and join the Athenian Army. As the Persians tried to take Athens by a surprise sea attack, the Greeks, under their great general, Miltiades, marched down from the mountain upon a large force left by Hippias at Marathon and killed approximately 20,000 warriors, discouraged Hippias and Darius, and saved Athens.

With the victory won, the Athenian general again sent his Olympic champion, exhausted from his trip to Sparta and his participation in the great battle, to bring the good news to the worried city. The legend goes on to tell how Pheidippides ran the twenty-six miles between Marathon and Athens and on arriving home cried, "Rejoice—we conquer," then fell dead. To Mr. Bréal this was a great reminder of the glory and spirit of the Olympic games, so he proposed the marathon race in the modern Olympics to commemorate this historical event. Today most people believe the marathon was part of the ancient Olympics, and the name and contribution of Michel Bréal are universally unknown. Often nations, races, and large segments of people go mad with pride when one of their contestants wins this, the greatest event in the track and field competitions or perhaps in the entire schedule of the Olympics. An indication of the spread and influence of the marathon is the fact that eighty-one countries at some time have adopted this event temporarily or permanently. Some years ago American G.I.'s in Korea contributed enough money to pay the expenses of a trip by several Koreans to the United States to participate in an American marathon run off in Boston, Massachusetts. This year a Finn visited the United States from another direction, was welcomed by the people of Boston and won the 1956 Boston marathon.

The marathon had another and far-reaching contribution to make to the modern Olympics which has been neglected by both sportsmen and historians. Just before and even during the first Olympics in 1896 in Athens, the usual jealousies and nationalism crept in to make Greece and the Greeks antagonistic to the games. The unexpected regularity with which championships were won by Americans discouraged other countries and was particularly galling to Greece, the host nation, with its ancient Olympic memories. However, when a Greek peasant named Spiridion Loues, after fasting and prayers, won the marathon, the Crown Prince of Greece and his brother carried Loues on their shoulders to the royal box to receive the Breal trophy. This was not only a fitting climax to the first modern Olympics but also swept away all jealousy of foreign victories in other events. Loues was overwhelmed with presents, from money and rare jewels to the offer of a shoe-shine boy to take care of his shoes for life. The Greeks, and in fact all nations present, became enthusiastic supporters of the Olympic idea and Breal had scored a valuable assist in making Baron de Coubertin's revival of the modern Olympics possible.

Unfortunately, although the Athens 1896 Olympics were successful and the Olympic idea had been sold to the world, there was trouble ahead. The Greek government and the Zappas brothers (the inheritance of Zappas had been used to help sponsor the Athens games) were adamant on taking over from Coubertin and his Olympic committee. Had not the Greek government spent $100,000 in addition to the Zappas money to make possible the first Olympics? George Averoff, a rich Greek merchant in Alexandria, had been the donor of $390,000 with which to restore the Panathenaic Stadium in which the 1896 games had been held. Had not the ancient Olympics been celebrated at Olympia for over a thousand years? In the words of the King of Greece: "May Greece be destined to become the peaceful meeting ground of all nationalities, and may Athens become the permanent seat of the Olympic games." At the King's dinner after the games, America's athletes, not knowing they were undermining the plans of the man responsible for it all, unwittingly helped the Greeks by circulating a petition to hold the games permanently in Athens.

Coubertin, however, was firm in keeping the Olympic games strictly international. The next Olympic Congress met at Le Havre, with France, Russia, and Hungary officially represented and Sweden, the United States, England, Italy, and Germany represented by individuals from educational institutions or athletic organizations. Félix Faure, President of France, acted as President. Greece, involved in a war with Turkey, had to abandon her ideas of taking over the management of the Olympics and retaining them permanently in Athens. A well-thought-out and detailed plan for the future of the modern games was submitted and approved. Competitions were to be in three categories: 1) Ancient sports of Egypt, India, Greece, and Rome; 2) Sports of the Age of Chivalry; and 3) Sports of the modern period.

The Olympics were on the march everywhere and Henri Desgranges offered the use of his seven-acre Parc des Princes and 666-meter track in Paris to the Olympic Committee headed by Coubertin. Desgranges stated, "It is only the Seine that I cannot give you." Newspapers all over the world offered free space for promotion, and the Scotch and the Irish rushed representatives to Paris in a wild dash to be the first to enter. Everything seemed in fine shape when suddenly the French government stepped in and took over and,

11

just as all governments and politicians do, appointed a whole host of committees and groups of politicians, most of whom knew nothing about the Olympics or athletics. The result was that the take-over by government bureaucrats almost ruined the 1900 Olympics and almost ended the modern Olympics.

The Olympic Committee's control over the Olympics was actually strengthened as a result of the many difficulties and disappointments of the "bureaucratic" Paris 1900 games. Coubertin had no difficulty regaining the wheel and helping the United States and the St. Louis Exposition of 1904 to get the III Olympiad.

The 1904 Olympics, while generally successful, were not too well attended by athletes because of the difficulty of traveling great distances. The outstanding feature of the actual competition was the great number of wins by American college athletes. These Olympics suffered, as the 1900 Olympics had, by being staged as part of a world's fair. The side-shows and extraordinary events presented may have succeeded as entertainment, but they certainly did not stimulate any great progress in competitive sports, and the St. Louis games featured the worst hoax and the most curious cramp story of any Olympics. The hoax was perpetrated by Fred Lorz, who dashed into the stadium looking as fresh as when he had started, and appeared to be the winner of the classic marathon. After he had been applauded and photographed with Alice Roosevelt, the daughter of the President, it was discovered that he had traversed most of the course in a newfangled affair called an autotruck.

The cramp story also concerns the marathon. Felix Caravajal of Cuba, who led after eighteen miles, was so far ahead that he stopped along the road and picked and ate a few apples. The apples were green. Felix got violent cramps which cost him the race and Cuba her first and only marathon victory.

At the end of 1905 King Leopold of Belgium, one of the original supporters of Baron de Coubertin, agreed to accept the honorary presidency of the next Olympic Congress. Cities now battled for the award. Rome was originally selected for 1908, but Greece and her claim for the Olympics—or for Panhellenic Olympics every four years between the world Olympics—had to be satisfied. Athens insisted on holding "Olympic Panhellenic" games in 1906.

Along about this time another great organizer, Olympic diplomat, and leader stepped into a more important position to aid Baron de Coubertin—Count Henri de Baillet Latour of Belgium. The first Panhellenic games in 1906 in Athens, al-

12

though officially not a modern Olympiad, nevertheless have come to be accorded a listing with the modern Olympics. The 1906 games resolved many problems raised by the Greeks and sort of packed down everyone and helped make possible the truly international Olympics that had originally been planned. The Greeks were happy to have the 1906 games, but since demands for facilities, services, and money increased as the Olympics expanded, they afterward abandoned —as de Coubertin had expected—their insistence that the Olympics be held every four years at Athens. During this period the Italians lost some of their enthusiasm and fell down in their preparations, and London was awarded the 1908 games.

The London or IV Olympics were highly successful and settled the question of which events and sports to include in the future—as many sports as practicable, but only those that were genuinely international. It was a happy compromise between the restrictions of the French in 1900 and the honky-tonk additions of the St. Louis World's Fair in 1904.

King Edward VII was the patron and the games were held in a huge bowl near London with a capacity of over 70,000. Although the British were guilty of some questionable enthusiasm in assuring themselves an overall unofficial win, and there were some unpleasant incidents, friendly feelings and sportsmanship prevailed and the Olympics were "home" or had reached the plateau where their continuation was assured. Not even two world wars stopped the Olympics, although they caused the cancellation of three Olympiads (1916, 1940, 1944). Baron de Coubertin continued personally to lead and dominate the Olympics until 1925, when he practically ceded the presidency to Latour.

The only major addition was the Olympic winter games, to be held the same year as the Olympic games, but being designated by number beginning with 1924. The International Olympic Committee, it was decided, was to designate the site, giving the right of first refusal to the country holding the main Olympic games.

China finally entered the games in 1932, although it sent but one contestant to represent 400,000,000 people. Russia, for the first time since the days of the Czar, entered a full team in 1952 which did extremely well. Soviet athletes have started auspiciously in 1956 by winning the unofficial winter games team championship. Seventy-two nations have officially entered the 16th Olympiad to be held in Melbourne, Australia, in November, 1956.

In every country in the world, the various amateur sports

organizations hold a series of eliminations and competitions in each sport and send the best athletes to the Olympics. All expenses are paid by voluntary contributions to Olympic funds or by subsidies from the government involved. The only eligibility requirements of the successful athlete are: first, that he be a citizen of the country he represents; second, that he never have represented any other country at previous Olympic games; and third, that he be an amateur.

CHAPTER III

BOXING

BOXING WAS born before the earliest Olympics. It was born probably when a prehistoric man was surprised in a defile by a saber-toothed tiger. He picked up a stone and swung desperately. The first blows of primitive boxing were swings. This is proved by Egyptian hieroglyphics dating back before 4000 B.C. showing soldiers of the Pharaohs boxing with primitive cestus or leather taping, not brass knuckles. To prove the swing of primitive African boxing, these leather, bark, or primitive cloth wrappings covered not only the fists and hands of the Egyptian boxers, but their forearms to the elbows. The clublike punches of these primitive boxers required protection for the whole arm rather than just for the fist. Boxing spread from Egypt, via Crete, to Greece. However, the first development of the art of self-defense and the first golden age of competitive boxing are definitely identified with the Olympics.

Boxing as a competitive sport, like so many others, received its main impetus from Olympic competition and the tremendous rivalry and training brought on by the greatest ancient or modern objective—an Olympic or World's Championship. Through the Olympics, boxing spread first throughout Greece, then over the Greek Empire and later, with the help of Rome and the Roman legions, to the entire known world.

The early Olympics gave us our present-day sport, and evidence shows that there is hardly anything new in modern boxing. Boxers of the Olympic era had boxing gloves of leather, which they kept in good condition by rubbing animal fat on them. The gloves, generally speaking, were used for the same purpose that gloves are used for today. Even the light striking bag and the heavy punching bag are not new. In the fifth century B.C., Olympic boxers trained in gymnasiums just as they do today and used punching bags made of leather and canvas filled with fig seeds and sand.

Today boxers in training and intercollegiate boxers in actual competition have adopted a special headguard of padded leather to protect them against being cut over the eyes, to prevent cauliflower ears and serious head injuries. Even this was not unknown to the Olympic boxers of antiquity, who wore a leather cap called an *amphotide* for the same purpose. Even mouthpieces were used; they were not made of rubber, like those of today, but were made of leather.

There were, nevertheless, some major differences between boxing then and boxing now, both in and out of the Olympics. In those days there were no rounds or regular rest periods, nor were there any weight divisions. Boxing contests lasted until one of the men was knocked so cold he could not continue, or one of the contestants gave up (which was allowed), or until either one or both fighters were too exhausted to stand up.

The Greeks had some unfair rules, too. For instance, if, after hours of fighting, both boxers were too exhausted to continue, each was given a free punch at the other, like a free throw in basketball. Lots were drawn for the privilege of taking the first punch, and naturally the boxer fortunate enough to win the draw had a tremendous advantage. This ancient practice gave us our modern fight term "draw" for an inconclusive decision.

Boxing, although one of the main events in the ancient Olympics for hundreds of years, was not an event in the first recorded Olympics in 776 B.C., but was first introduced as a regular championship event in the 23rd Olympiad (688 B.C.) when a Greek named Onomastus won the first boxing crown and later established the first official Olympic boxing rules. Boxing for boys was added in the 41st Olympiad (616 B.C.).

In these early games, the contestants were exclusively Greeks; later they came from all over the Greek Empire. The games continued after the conquest of Greece by the Romans until the Greco-Roman athletic rivalry degenerated into so many brawls, especially in the boxing contests, that Emperor Theodosius abolished the games in 394 A.D. The last recorded winner of an Olympic boxing championship is Varasdates, who later became King of Armenia.

Boxing contests in the ancient Olympics featured the cestus, the Grecian boxing glove. It was not loaded with metal or spikes, as its later Roman gladiatorial counterpart was, but was made of heavy leather strips wrapped around the hand and arm, with a harder, thicker leather surface over the knuckles. In addition to the regular boxing contests, the Greek Olympic games included a rough-and-tumble contest called the pancratium, in which wrestling as well as boxing was allowed. There were similar events for boys, with about the same rules.

The athletic uniform of Olympic contestants was complete nudity. No women were allowed at the Olympics even as spectators in the beginning on the penalty of being thrown to certain death from a nearby rocky cliff called the Typaean Rock. Later, however, this rule was changed, and eventually girls' events were actually included in the games.

The tradition of fair play and sportsmanship in the Olympics was significantly demonstrated in boxing. Hitting below the waist was a foul and not countenanced by the Greeks. This rule was observed so carefully in Greece that no protectors were ever worn at the Olympics; although they were known and used in Crete. Even accidental fouls were unlikely, since ancient Olympic boxing rules made the head the only target for punches. Body punching was illegal.

The ancient Olympic Games (776 B.C. to 394 A.D.) did more for the development of modern boxing technique than any other single factor, with the possible exception of the contributions of fencing and of fencing masters during the so-called English renaissance period of boxing from 1700 to 1800. The Olympic champions of antiquity and the first world heavyweight bare-fist or prizefighters of England, James Figg and John Broughton, who were also fencing masters, made the major contributions toward the development of the modern sport. However, there is no question that the basic development of the so-called "manly art of self-defense" came from the Olympics. Few people realize it, but most sports today owe the same debt to the Olympic games.

Even the straight hitting of the boxers was often not sufficient to win in combination boxing-and-wrestling matches. Kreugas, a great Olympic boxing champion, was killed by the wrestler Deoxenos in the finals of the pancratium championship at the Nemean games. Generally speaking, both in Greek and modern times, wrestlers have beaten boxers in free-for-all contests. In the entire history of the Greek Olympics only two boxing champions, Theagenes and Cleitomachus, are recorded as winning both boxing and the pancratium in the same Olympics, while seven Greek wrestling champions doubled up with Olympic wins in the pancratium.

Although the swing and not straight punching is instinctive to man, there is certain proof that the technique of straight punching was developed by the Greeks in Olympic competition. The proof is found in the evolution of the cestus. The first cestus, originally used in Egypt, Crete, and at the outset in Greece, consisted merely of leather strips or bands wrapped around the hand, fist, thumb, wrist, and arm to the elbow, with no special hitting surface. This was replaced in the Homeric period and the beginning of the Hellenic or Olympic period by what is called the "soft glove" cestus, which was very close to our present-day gauze-and-adhesive-tape wrappings except that leather was used, and the wrapping was continued halfway up the forearm. In the later Olympic period, when boxing became more important and vast crowds saw men fight with their fists for "world" championships, the cestus underwent another change. It became what is referred to as the "hard glove." The wrappings around the thumb, hand, wrist, and forearm became simply protective and defensive bindings to prevent bruises and broken bones. A close-fitting glove covered the hand, leaving the upper joints of the fingers free and the palm open. The modern feature of this "hard glove" was the hitting surface, three thick rings or bands of leather joined together, one alongside of the other over the four fingers and between the second joint and knuckle, giving the appearance of a sort of doughnut, the edge of which was the hitting surface. The fingers, in closing to make a fist, grasped the other side of this leather doughnut.

The rules of the pancratium did not allow the use of gloves or cestus, and boxers, deprived of their hard glove as an offensive adjunct and as a protection for their hands, were generally defeated by wrestlers. With the hard glove and its hitting edge, the boxers would undoubtedly have knocked most of the wrestlers bowlegged. With unprotected hands, the boxers broke their fists on the wrestlers' heads before being dumped on their backs.

The ancient Olympics gave us our modern boxing glove. John Broughton, the English "pro" who was buried in Westminster Abbey and has been called the "father of modern boxing," created the design of our present glove from drawings and photographs of the Olympic hard glove.

With the left hand the boxer in ancient Olympic competition held off his opponent or pushed him "off set" or off balance and thereby broke up his offense and his right-hand

17

punches. Olympic boxers also with the straight left measured their opponents for their own right-hand follow-through or knockout swing. The ancient pugilist, by hitting or pushing his opponent with the left hand at the moment the latter was about to throw a punch, threw him off balance and thereby prevented him either from starting the blow, or, if the blow was already started, prevented it from landing with any great force. Much of our present-day defensive technique comes from experience gained in hundreds of years of Olympic boxing.

The absence of rounds and regular rest periods led to stalling, to lulls in the fighting during which both contestants took it easy. Defensive stalling occurred in both the ancient Greek and the more modern English era. In Greece, even in the Olympics and other great games, contestants could by mutual consent take a rest during the progress of a fight. The most famous statue of an Olympic boxer (now in a museum in Rome) is believed to show Cleitomachus sitting down during a rest period in his fight against a handsome Egyptian named Aristonikos in the finals of an Olympic boxing championship. Before the rest period Cleitomachus was behind on points, but after the rest he knocked out his opponent and won the Olympic crown.

An interesting rule in all early boxing was the one which permitted any boxing competitor to indicate his desire to give up and end the bout by merely holding up his right or left hand with a forefinger pointed upward. In early Greece there were no neutral corners and no rules against hitting a man who was partially down but still showed fight.

The Greeks used their feet as well as their heads and fists. There was continuous maneuvering for position. Hundreds of pictures, statues, and friezes show beyond doubt that the Greeks used a stance approximating our own and requiring the same basic footwork. In addition, there is evidence that Greek boxing developed the human figure to the proportions of the typical boxer of today—early Olympic boxers had thin legs, large shoulders, and long muscles, indicating both speed and hitting power.

The winners of each of the events at the Olympics were announced by a herald who proclaimed the victorious entrant's name, his father's name, and the name of the city or country from which he came, and each victor was then privileged to erect a statue of himself in the sacred Altis.

There were other games during the golden age of boxing in Greece, though none so famous as the Olympics. However,

18

the boxing events were just as popular and just as closely contested at the Pythian, Nemean, and Isthmian games. After 573 B.C., the Olympics were held in July or August of every fourth year, both the Isthmian games and the Nemean games in the summer or spring of every second and fourth year, and the Pythian games in August of every third year, making a total of six championships in the four "great games" every four years. According to the records, the various games, including all preliminaries, semifinals and finals in all events, usually lasted five days.

Since the winners of all contests in all sports were virtually certain to be subsidized or supported in some way by their city-states or countries for the rest of their lives, and since most competitors had their expenses paid by their sponsors or city-states, contestants were attracted from every corner of the Greek and Roman Empires, so that at no time in the world's history was a consistent winner more truly entitled to be called "World's Champion."

When one examines the records that have been preserved and sees the startling accomplishments and consistency of championship performance of some of the ancient boxers, one wonders why more has not been written about them. For instance, a boxer named Tisander won four Olympic boxing championships, over a span of more than twelve years. Boxing as an art and science has progressed technically to such a degree that a modern pugilist should have an advantage over the boxer of antiquity. However, basing a comparison on cunning, experience, endurance, speed, agility, and strength, it is very questionable if the great Olympic boxers of ancient Greece could have been beaten by the best of today. How, for instance, does any boxer's record today compare with that of the man who in twenty years won 1400 championships, each representing many fights in series of eliminations, often involving as many as ten fights in a single day? This is the record of Theagenes of Thasos, the greatest of all ancient Olympic boxers.

Theagenes is believed to have been born in Thrace about 505 B.C. At the age of nine he is said to have carried away a huge bronze statue which stood in a square or agora in his city, simply because he took a childish fancy to it. Instead of being punished, he was made to return it to its place and thereupon became famous for his tremendous strength. Upon coming of age, he began competing in boxing and in the pancratium and, when he was older, in long-distance running. He won twenty-five or thirty major championships in boxing and as many more in the pancratium, some in the same games, and had about 1400 olive wreaths placed upon his head during his lifetime.

To prove his championship caliber further, Theagenes defeated another of the great boxers of ancient Greece. This boxer, Euthymus, had won many boxing championships, including the 74th Olympics, and probably would have achieved a greater stature in the history of boxing if he had not been contemporary with Theagenes. In the 75th Olympics Theagenes decided to enter both the boxing and the pancratium events. The two greats met in the boxing final. Theagenes won, but was so badly cut up by Euthymus that, while he had also qualified for the final in the pancratium, he had to forfeit the final bout in this event and consequently the championship. Euthymus was not entered in the pancratium.

The officials took a very arbitrary view of the situation, probably out of love for Euthymus, who was the older champion. They ruled that if Theagenes had been able to defeat Euthymus and also win the pancratium, he would have been a competitor worthy of the best Greek tradition. However, the judges felt that in depriving Euthymus of his boxing title but in having then to default in the pancratium final, Theagenes had shown a flaw in his character by biting off more than he could chew, so they fined him, claiming he had spoiled the Olympic show and wronged Euthymus by being too greedy in wanting two titles. Part of his fine had to be paid to the Olympic gods and part to Euthymus. Theagenes paid his Olympic fine, but settled his debt to Euthymus by not entering the boxing event in the next, or 76th Olympics. As a result, Euthymus won, although he couldn't really be considered boxing champion. Theagenes won the pancratium and at a later Olympiad, probably the 77th, won the double victory. Only one other boxer—Cleitomachus—ever accomplished this feat. When Theagenes died, he became almost a deity and for centuries his statues were thought to have the power to heal the injuries of athletes.

Next in line for fistic immortality are Glaucus of Carystus, Polydamus of Scotussa and Cleitomachus. Although they won their Olympic crowns some 2100 years before modern boxing got its start in the early eighteenth century, these champions should be classed with the best of the modern era, even among such of our professionals as Figg and Broughton, Sullivan and Jeffries, Dempsey and Louis.

Glaucus of Carystus was a farm boy. One day, according to the legend, while he was working with his father, the ploughshare fell out of the plough. He fitted it into place, using his bare hand as a hammer. His father, on seeing this, decided his son should become a boxer, and entered him in the Olympics. The story goes that in spite of his inexperience and lack of boxing knowledge, Glaucus got through the preliminaries by virtue of sheer strength and his good right hand. However, he took lots of punishment and in the finals was so faint from exhaustion and loss of blood that it looked as though he were through. Fortunately for him, it was not then illegal to coach from the sidelines, and his father shouted from the gallery: "Remember the ploughshare!" and Sonny came through with a quick knockout.

After this, Glaucus made a thorough study of the science of boxing as it was understood in those days and, as a great champion, took very little further punishment for many years. His boxing style was considered so fine that statues of him in sparring or "on guard" positions were made. His acquired science, added to an unusual natural punch, earned him several Olympic, two Pythian, eight Nemean, and eight Isthmian boxing championships, as well as hundreds of minor championships.

Polydamus, who lived about 380 B.C., though certainly not in a class with Theagenes, Glaucus, Cleitomachus, or even Euthymus, was nevertheless very colorful and the subject of great contemporary ballyhoo and publicity. While he was a boxer and pancratic performer who won many championships in addition to several Olympics, he is more famous for his accomplishments outside the realm of boxing.

He was the giant of the Hellenic amphitheatres—an Olympian Primo Carnera, standing 6 feet 8 inches tall and weighing 300 pounds. Our other four champions of that period varied from 6 feet to 6 feet 4 inches and from 190 to 235 pounds. The means by which we have been able to figure out the measurements of these fighters may be of interest. In many cases the victory statues had at their bases the actual imprint of the athlete's foot: a sort of Olympian Grauman's Chinese Theatre. As the imprint of a movie star's hands or feet in Hollywood may tell generations to come their stature in the field of the cinema, the imprints of the Olympic athletes' feet, next to their perfectly proportioned statues, allow us, centuries later, to determine rather closely their height and weight. Also, the Greek measurements of some have come down to us in cubits and fingers: 18.25 inches and 0.7 inches respectively.

Polydamus, with his tremendous size, weight, and strength, did some phenomenal things, if we can believe the original sources. He could stop a chariot drawn by three horses by

21

holding on to the back of it. In a battle royal against three men, he killed all three. In various exhibitions he pulled a bull's leg off and killed a lion with his bare hands. Overconfidence caused Polydamus' death. He and some friends were in a cave when a cave-in started. The others ran out, but Polydamus tried to hold the roof up and perished when the hill fell in on him.

Cleitomachus was neither colorful nor a performer of spectacular stunts, but in the ring or in the stadium he was second only to Theagenes. He was the only other man to win both the boxing and pancratium crowns at the same Olympics —the 141st, in 216 B.C. But boxing was his specialty, and, like Theagenes, he was undefeated in hundreds of championship contests over many years. Unfortunately for him, however, his competitive career overlapped that of one of the greatest wrestlers of all time, Caprus, who also competed in the pancratium event. In the 142nd Olympics the two men met in the pancratium finals, but the wrestler won, not the boxer. However, Cleitomachus retained his boxing crown, and his reputation through the ages makes him seem a challenger worthy of any one of our best heavyweights.

With the arrival of the barbarian tribes, wars, dictators, and the Dark Ages, boxing first degenerated into gladiatorial boxing with brass knuckles and the cruel and deadly myrmex, called the "limb piercer," and then disappeared completely. The myrmex was a bronze, spurlike instrument which the gladiatorial boxer strapped to his cestus in order to make the blows from his fist fatal. Although the Roman legions carried the sport of boxing all over the known world, boxing, like most athletics and the Olympics, was doomed and did not reappear until some twelve centuries later, when civilization once more began to recognize the dignity of man and to hope for a world of peace and democracy. As both a means and symbol, man sought out and brought back the Olympics.

The first modern Olympics, in 1896, ought logically to have included boxing, but because boxing had become almost exclusively American and English, it was thought best to omit it in the program for fear of discouraging many nations which would have no entries in this sport. Boxing, therefore, was not featured in the modern Olympics until, mainly through the efforts of the United States, it was included in the third modern Olympiad in 1904 at St. Louis. The individual winners in seven classes are listed in the appendix. O. L. Kirk starred in winning titles in both the bantamweight and featherweight classes. The 1904 games did not attract many foreign entries, and as a result the United States had little or no competition in boxing. Every title was won by an American. However, boxing began to spread fast, as it had once before through the Olympics.

The 1906 unofficial Olympics at Athens did not have boxing competition, but the regular IV Olympiad in London in 1908 featured boxing competition in five weights. The British made a clean sweep—H. Thomas winning the bantam title, and 38-year-old R. K. Gunn winning the featherweight title with a perfect exhibition of the old British straight-up boxing with the straight left jab developed by the fencing masters and boxing champions, James Figg and John Broughton. Grace won the lightweight title, and the great British cricket star, J.W.N.T. Douglas, won the middleweight title. A.L. Oldham, a London policeman, won the heavyweight class. No competition was held in the flyweight class, nor in the welterweight division. The United States did not enter a team, as the British had not decided to add boxing until the last minute.

The 1912 Olympics did not have any boxing because the laws of the host nation, Sweden, did not permit it. Although World War I interrupted the Olympics, it spread the sport of boxing as it was a popular pastime and conditioner in the armed services of all the warring countries.

By 1920 truly world-wide interest in boxing led for the first time to real competition, with entries from many countries. The United States boxing team, selected after eliminations and competitions throughout the United States, included the best boxers from the army, navy, the colleges, and the amateurs of AAU competitions. The New York police force was also well represented. Among the Americans who boxed for the United States in 1920 was Joe Cranston of West Point, later to become a combat general in the United States Army in World War II. Still another member of the 1920 United States team was Eddie Egan of Colorado and Harvard, who was to become a lieutenant colonel in the United States Air Force in World War II and later chairman of the New York State Boxing Commission. Unfortunately, although the caliber of boxing exhibited at this Olympic championship was quite high indeed, the contestants, and particularly the American team, were handicapped by the fact that the quality of the officiating had not kept pace with the spread of the sport. However, sportsmanship won out, and although there is no question that the United States was deprived of some few victories through the inexperience of the officials, no disagreeable incident marred the competition for long.

The United States won more first places than any other nation, but finished second to Great Britain in the unofficial team score. For the United States, Frank Genaro won the flyweight title. He later went on to become the professional flyweight champion of the world. Samuel Mosberg won the lightweight title and Edward Egan the light-heavyweight Olympic championship. Fred Kolberg, another United States entry, was third in the welterweight class. The other champions were L. Walter of South Africa in the bantamweight division, Fritsch of France in the featherweight, Schneider of Canada in the welterweight, H. Mallin of the London police in the middleweight class, and R. R. Rawson, also of Great Britain, in the heavyweight division. The coach of the United States team was Spike Webb, boxing coach at the United States Naval Academy. His efficiency and sportsmanship made a deep impression on the entire Olympic fraternity. Jack and Pete Zivic, who later became well known in professional boxing, were both members of this United States boxing team.

Twenty-nine nations had representatives in the boxing competition at the next Olympics in 1924 in Paris. The United States boxing team won the unofficial team championship. Again, the competition was marred by inexperience in judging and refereeing, and a novel and unusual experiment particularly handicapped the British and American boxers. The referee, who according to custom in British and American boxing is always in the ring, was stationed outside of the ring, following a custom established in some European countries where boxing had just begun. Sometimes the referee's order to break from a clinch was heard by the contestants in the ring, and sometimes it was not. This system was extremely ineffective and led to at least one very unfair decision.

Joe Lazarus, a bantamweight from Cornell University, knocked out his opponent but lost the fight because the referee ruled that he had hit his opponent on a break. The referee claimed he had yelled "Break" from outside the ring a split-second before the K.O. punch, but ringside spectators hadn't seen a clinch or heard the referee. Hector Mendez of Argentina, now an ambassador in the Foreign Service of his country, also received an inexcusably bad decision in the finals of the welterweight class. And an outstanding middleweight from France was disqualified, after being awarded a decision, for biting his opponent during one of the clinches. Although the bite mark was in evidence, it went unnoticed until after the contestants had left the ring.

Nevertheless, the general caliber of boxing exhibited in these Olympic championships was good. Three members of the United States team became professional world's champions, and a number of contestants from other countries later fared well in the professional boxing field.

The particular stars of the 1924 Olympic boxing competition were Fidel La Barba of the United States, who later became the professional flyweight champion of the world, and Jackie Fields of the United States, who later became professional welterweight champion of the world. H. Mallin, a lieutenant in the London police force, was the first and only repeat winner in boxing in sixty years of modern Olympics; he had previously won the Olympic middleweight title in 1920. Hector Mendez of Argentina, even though deprived of an Olympic title by a poor decision, impressed everyone with his boxing, punching power, and sportsmanship.

The most dramatic feature of the 1924 Olympic competition was the story of Jackie Fields and Joe Salas. Joe Salas had won the national amateur featherweight boxing championship of the United States in Boston in 1924 to become a member of the Olympic boxing team. Featherweight Jackie Fields had an off day, and was eliminated by a decision in the same tournament. Both boys came from Los Angeles, went to school together, took up boxing together, boxed for the same club and were coached by the same man. Both had the same ambition—to win an Olympic championship. Jackie Fields, because of his past record, was added to the Olympic team as an extra but official member, as were several others, since in 1924 each nation could enter two men in each weight class. Salas and Fields were chosen by Coach Spike Webb as the two United States contestants in the welterweight class. They both fought and won five fights and met in the final. For three rounds in the Olympic ring in Paris, thousands of miles from home, the two fought toe-to-toe. The fact that they were close friends made no difference. At the end both were punched out. After a tense moment the officials awarded the bout and the Olympic championship to Fields. The two friends ran across the ring and fell into each other's arms as the band played "The Star Spangled Banner." As two American flags were hoisted to the first- and second-place flagpoles, two California boys in tears stood locked in each other's arms. Jackie Fields later turned professional and became the world's welterweight champion.

As an indication of the increasing popularity of boxing throughout the world, it is interesting to note that points were made for first, second, or third place in 1924 by eleven countries: the United States, Great Britain, Denmark, Argentina, Holland, Belgium, Norway, Sweden, South Africa, France and Canada. The International Amateur Boxing Association was organized at the 1924 Olympics with Mr. Cuddy, the manager of the United States team, as its first president and the writer, who was a member of the 1924 team, as secretary.

In the 1928 Olympics, the number of nations competing in boxing increased to thirty. Once again the officiating, although improving, left much to be desired, but the poor decisions were evenly distributed and handicapped all the teams more or less equally. For the third time, the United States coach was Spike Webb, and Benny Levine of the AAU was manager.

The unofficial team title for boxing in 1928 went to Italy. Individual titles were won in the flyweight class by Anton Kocsis of Hungary, in the bantamweight class by Vittorio Tamagnini of Italy, in the lightweight class by Carlo Orlandi of Italy, in the welterweight class by Edward Morgan of New Zealand, in the middleweight class by Piero Toscani of Italy, in the light-heavyweight class by Victoria Angel Pedro Avendano of Argentina, and in the heavyweight class by Jurado Arturo Rodriguez of the Argentine.

Once again the referee sat outside of the ring, which was a great disadvantage to boxers accustomed to having the referee inside the ring. The only places the United States was able to gain were second in the bantamweight class with John L. Daly, second in the lightweight class with Stephen Holaiko, and third in the featherweight class with Harry Devine. Thomas Lawn, a welterweight, and Harry Henderson, intercollegiate middleweight champion from the Naval Academy, did not live up to the advance expectancy of becoming title winners.

Spike Webb, for the fourth time as coach, piloted the boxing team at the X Olympiad in Los Angeles in 1932, and for the second time saw the United States win the unofficial team title—the last team title, however, which the United States was to win in this sport until 1952. The final standings of the 1932 Olympic boxing were as follows:

Flyweight — 1st: Stephen Enekes, Hungary; 2nd: Francisco Cabanas, Mexico; 3rd: Louis Salica, United States; 4th: Thomas Pardoe, Great Britain.

Bantamweight — 1st: Horace Gwynne, Canada; 2nd: Hans Ziglarski, Germany; 3rd: Jose Villanueva, Philippines; 4th: Joseph Lang, United States.

Featherweight —	1st: Carmelo Ambrosio Robledo, Argentina; 2nd: Joseph Schleinkofer, Germany; 3rd: Carl Allen Carlsson, Sweden; 4th: Gaspare Alexandri, Italy.
Lightweight —	1st: Lawrence Stevens, South Africa; 2nd: Thure Johan Ahlqvist, Sweden; 3rd: Nathan Bor, United States; 4th: Mario Bianchini, Italy.
Welterweight —	1st: Edward Flynn, United States; 2nd: Eric Campe, Germany; 3rd: Bruno Valfred Ahlberg, Finland; 4th: David Edward McCleave, Great Britain.
Middleweight —	1st: Carmen Barth, United States; 2nd: Amado Azar, Argentina; 3rd: Ernest Pierce, South Africa; 4th: Roger Michelot, France.
Light-Heavyweight —	1st: David E. Carstens, South Africa; 2nd: Gino Rossi, Italy; 3rd: Peter Jorgensen, Denmark; 4th: James J. Murphy, Ireland.
Heavyweight —	1st: Santiago Alberto Lovell, Argentina; 2nd: Luigi Rovati, Italy; 3rd: Fred Feary, United States; 4th: George Maugham, Canada.

According to most experts, the outstanding boxer of the tournament was Edward Flynn of New Orleans and Loyola University, who is the only man in the history of United States amateur boxing to win a national intercollegiate championship, a National AAU championship, and an Olympic championship. In addition to welterweight titles, he won many middleweight titles, although he was a natural welterweight. The refereeing and judging in this Olympic competition was, for the first time, really satisfactory.

At the next Olympics, in 1936, the host nation, Germany, won the unofficial boxing title. The individual winners are listed in the appendix. Louis Lauria of Cleveland, Ohio, placed third in the flyweight class, and Jack Wilson, also of Cleveland, a boxer 6 feet 2 inches tall who only weighed 117 pounds, placed second in the bantamweight class.

The next Olympics were held in 1948, after an interruption of twelve years occasioned by World War II. The 1948 boxing teams did the best they could to pick up where Olympic boxing had left off before the war. The competition in London was highly successful from the standpoint of the number of nations entered and the number of spectators attracted. The officiating was not as good as in 1932 or 1936 and a score of judges were relieved early in the tournament, being adjudged incompetent by the International Jury of Appeal. The unofficial team championship was shared by Italy and South Africa. The individual winners are listed in the appendix. Only one American, Horace Herring, a United States Navy entry, reached the final round. In fact, his second place in the welterweight class scored the only points made by the United States in the entire tournament. It was one of the worst showings made by a United States boxing team in any Olympics.

United States prestige in Olympic boxing bounced back fast in 1952 with coach Peter E. Mello, assisted by Joseph T. Owen, and a resolute management group intent on getting a well-balanced boxing team. The boxing championship at the Helsinki Olympics featured more contestants from more countries than any other modern Olympic games. The United States team was considered by many to be the finest ever to represent the United States, and won five individual Olympic championships as well as the unofficial team championship. Our Olympic champions were flyweight Nate Brooks of Cleveland, Ohio; light-welterweight Charles Adkins of Gary, Indiana; middleweight Floyd Patterson of Brooklyn, New York; light-heavyweight Norvel Lee of Washington, D.C. and heavyweight Edward Sanders of Los Angeles, California. Archie Slaten of Chattanooga, Tennessee, who was our number-one man in the lightweight class, was not able to compete, due to an attack of appendicitis. Norvel Lee was awarded the "most proficient performer" trophy, and Floyd Patterson won in impressive style. Patterson, now a professional, is a leading contender for the world's heavyweight championship.

The outlook for the 1956 boxing competition in Australia is promising. More contestants from more nations than ever before are expected. The host nation is experienced in boxing, and there should be no difficulties with the officiating. Fifty years ago the United States, Great Britain, and, to a lesser degree, France were the only countries with experience in boxing, but the sport has spread throughout the world and today there is no boxer anywhere in the world who cannot have the ambition of qualifying to represent his country in the Olympic games. It would not be surprising if some country new to boxing started winning not only the individual titles but also the team championship. Friendly fists can become salesmen for democracy, tolerance, and peace throughout the world.

CHAPTER IV

CANOEING

CANOEING IS, of course, the sport of paddling a canoe. The word "canoe" is applied to a wide variety of primitive boats, from the hollowed log of the Iroquois Indians of North America to the kayak of the Eskimo. The history of canoeing, like that of rowing, extends back to the dugout boat of the Stone Age. Its modern popularization dates back to 1865, when a British barrister, John MacGregor, developed the Rob Roy type of canoe and wrote extensively of his canoe voyages throughout Europe, Scandinavia, and the Holy Land. That same year, he organized the Royal Canoe Club. Within three years, other types of canoes had been developed, and over three hundred kinds crowded the waterways around London and Oxford. In 1871 a canoeing club was first organized in the United States at what is now St. George, Staten Island. In 1880, the American Canoe Association was formed at Lake George, N. Y., and the Canadian Canoe Association was formed shortly thereafter. At about the same time, the British Canoe Association, now known as the British Canoe Union, came into being. The canoe is now standardized— sharp at both ends, without counter or transom. Because of the low freeboard a canoe cannot be rowed but must be paddled.

International canoeing competition was practically created by the Olympics which spread the sport and the standard canoes used in the Olympics all over the world.

The VIII Olympiad, held at Paris in 1924, featured demonstration events in canoeing, which Canada won, but the first formal competitions in canoeing were not held until 1936. The winner of the first canoeing competition in the Olympic Games was Austria, with Germany second and Czechoslovakia third. Although the United States did not win, the very inclusion of canoeing in the Olympics was an event for which an American could take some credit. W. Van B. Claussen of Washington, D. C., who was the manager of the first United States Olympic canoe team, had in the early 1920's begun a correspondence with foreign canoe clubs that eventually led to the formation of the I.R.K., or International Canoeing Association. It was through this organization that nineteen nations first organized and then participated in the nine events of the Berlin Olympics, at distances ranging from 1000 to 10,000 meters.

The canoeing events at the Berlin Olympics were conducted at the site of the rowing course at Grünau, a suburb on the River Spree. Canoeists from Austria took three first, three second, one third, and two fourth places. The Germans won two firsts, three seconds, two thirds, and two fourths. The United States finished in sixth place in the general team rankings, with one third, one fourth, and three fifth places. Twenty-one nations were affiliated with the International Canoe Federation and all of them, except Brazil, were represented at the Olympics. Ernest Riedel of Teaneck, New Jersey, made the best showing of the American canoeists, finishing third in the 10,000-meter kayak single and fourth in the 1000-meter kayak single. Joseph and Walter Hasenfus of Needham, Mass., paired together to finish fifth in the Canadian double event of 10,000 meters. Joseph Hasenfus was fifth in the Canadian single event at 1000 meters while Clarence R. McNutt and Robert Graf of Philadelphia were fifth in the Canadian double over the 1000-meter course. The 10,000-meter two-seater folding kayak was won by a team from Sweden, with Germany second, Holland third, Austria fourth, Czechoslovakia fifth, Switzerland sixth, and the United States seventh. The one-seater folding kayak was won by Gregor Hradetzky of Austria, with Henri Eberhardt of France second and Zaver Hormann of Germany third. The first American to finish, Burr Folks, was tenth. The two-seater rigid kayak was won by a team from Germany, followed by Austria, Sweden, Denmark, Holland, Switzerland, and the United States. One-seater rigid kayak was won by Ernst Krebs of Germany, with Fritz Landertinger of Austria second, and Ernest Riedel of the United States third. The tandem Canadian canoe was won by a team from Czechoslovakia, with Canada second, Austria third, Germany fourth, and the United States fifth. The 1000-meter two-seater rigid kayak was won by a team from Austria, with Germany second and Holland third. Tandem Canadian canoe was won by a team from Czechoslovakia, with Austria second and Canada third. And the one-man Canadian canoe was won by Francis Amyot of Canada; B. Karlik of Czechoslovakia was second, Eric Koschik of Germany third.

Between 1936 and the postwar 1948 Olympics the I.R.K. was reorganized as the International Canoe Federation, I.C.F., with J. Asschier of the Swedish Kayak Association as

President. In 1948, seventeen nations competed in eight events. Olympic competition has brought about a change in the racing equipment of canoeists, especially in the United States. The I.C.F. supplied for the 1948 competitions several types of racing kayaks never used in this country before. The single-seater (K-1) is 17 feet long, with a 20-inch beam, while the K-2 is about 21 feet long and has a 21½-inch beam. The old 16 footer with a 30-inch beam, which was called a "peanut" and was used for one-man and tandem competition, was replaced by an I.C.F. racing canoe 17 feet long and 29½ inches wide. The K-4 is gaining a place in this country. It is a four-man racing kayak about 36 feet by 23½ inches.

The 14th Olympiad at London presented canoeing competitions, with more competitors and better performance than that of the preceding Olympiad. The unofficial team championship was won by Sweden, with Czechoslovakia a close second, Denmark third, France fourth, the United States fifth. The American team was again managed and coached by W. Van B. Claussen. Seventeen nations participated in canoeing —Austria, Belgium, Canada, Czechoslovakia, Denmark, Finland, France, Great Britain, Holland, Hungary, Yugoslavia, Luxembourg, Norway, Poland, Sweden, Switzerland, and the United States. Upon arrival at Henley-on-Thames, it was discovered that the C-1 canoes brought by Sweden, Czechoslovakia, Belgium, and France were in violation of the I.C.F. building rules. A protest was immediately drawn up by the United States and signed by Britain, Canada and Finland. Although this protest was formally lodged and argued to the bitter end, it was rejected in so far as it applied to the London Olympics. Although the Czech representatives definitely promised that their C-1 canoes would immediately be straightened to meet the United States demands, this promise was only partly kept.

The kayak singles 1000-meter was won by G. Fredriksson of Sweden; second was J. Andersen of Denmark, third H. Eberhardt of France. Kayak singles for women, a new event at 500 meters, was won by K. Hoff of Denmark, with A. G. Van de Anker Doedans of Holland second and F. Schwingl of Austria third. The kayak singles 10,000 meter was won by G. Fredriksson of Sweden; second was K. O. Wires of Finland, third E. Skabo of Norway. Riedel, the first United States entrant to finish, was twelfth. Kayak pairs 1000 meter was won by a team from Sweden, followed by Denmark, Finland, and Norway. Kayak pairs 10,000 meter was won by a team from Sweden, with Norway second and Finland third. The United States finished thirteenth. The Canadian singles 1000 meter was won by J. Holecek of Czechoslovakia, with D. Bennett of Canada second and R. Boutigny of France third. F. Havens of the United States came in fifth. Canadian singles 10,000 meter was won by F. Capek, Czechoslovakia; F. Havens of the United States was second and N. D. Lane of Canada third. Canadian pairs 1000 meter was won by a team from Czechoslovakia, with the United States second and France third. The Canadian pairs 10,000 meter was won by the American team of S. Lysak and S. Macknowski; second was Czechoslovakia, third France. The Olympics were spreading interest in this sport all over the world, and American performance was improving.

At the 1952 Olympics at Helsinki, Finland, being an enthusiastic supporter of canoeing, presented an outstanding program. With the help of various associations, clubs, and the U. S. Army, successful trials in the United States produced 69 entries in the finals and an outstanding team. The manager of the team was Walter Hanner, Jr. The canoeing events of these Olympics brought together a number of nations in close cooperation and good fellowship and an unusual amount of fraternization. The nations involved were Belgium, Great Britain, Canada, Italy, Finland, Norway, France, Holland, Germany, Denmark, Luxembourg, Yugoslavia, Hungary, Sweden, Russia, Switzerland, the Saar, Rumania, Austria, and Czechoslovakia. It will be noted that for the first time Russia entered the canoeing competitions. The unofficial canoeing team championship was won by Finland, with Sweden, Hungary, Germany, and Czechoslovakia in close pursuit.

Just before the Olympics a one-man kayak purchased by the United States from Sweden a month before was found to be one-eighth inch too narrow and was therefore disqualified from competition. With true Olympic sportsmanship seven different countries offered to lend a K-1 to the United States team immediately after the news got out. The Americans accepted the K-1 from Sweden, because it was most like the one in which the men had trained for the past two years. The United States team, incidentally, did better than ever before in the canoeing competition in these Olympics. Kayak singles 1000 meter was won by G. Fredriksson of Sweden, repeating his previous victory in this event at the 1948 Olympics; second was T. Stromberg of Finland, third L. Gantois of France. The kayak pairs 1000 meter was won by a team from Finland, with Sweden second, Austria third, and Germany fourth. The kayak singles 10,000 meter was won by T. Stromberg of Finland; second was G. Frediksson of Sweden (who narrowly missed repeating the double win he had scored in

1948), and M. Scheuer of Germany was third. Kayak pairs 10,000 meter was won by a team from Finland, with Sweden second and Hungary third. Russia was tenth in this event and the United States fourteenth. Kayak singles for women was won by S. Saimo of Finland; second was G. Liebhart of Austria, third N. Savina of Russia. Canadian singles 1000 meter was won by J. Holecek of Czechoslovakia, repeating his 1948 win, with J. Parti of Hungary second and O. Ojanpera of Finland third. F. Havens of the United States finished fourth. Canadian pairs 1000 meter was won by a team from Denmark, followed by Czechoslovakia and Germany. The United States team came in seventh. Canadian singles 10,000 meters was won by F. Havens of the United States, the first gold medal ever won by an American in canoeing; G. Novak of Hungary was second and A. Jindra of Czechoslovakia was third. Canadian pairs 10,000 meter was won by a team from France, followed by Canada, Germany, Russia, and the United States, in that order.

It is expected that the canoeing events at the 1956 Olympic games in Melbourne will spread this sport to New Zealand and Australia and to the countries of Asia and Africa and South America, where canoeing has existed for centuries but not as a competitive sport. There is no doubt that canoeing will receive greater world recognition in forthcoming Olympiads.

CHAPTER V

CYCLING

CYCLING IS a clipped term for the sport of riding a bicycle, which in the United States is at least a way to get up an appetite. However in France, where the bicycle is alleged to have been invented by a Parisian, M. de Sivrac, back in 1690, it is still considered a means of transportation. Strangely enough, suggestions for having wheeled vehicles propelled by the effort of the rider or riders date back to earliest times; they have been found in bas reliefs of Egypt and Babylon and frescoes of Pompeii. Leonardo da Vinci later drew up a plan for a flying bicycle, and recently the French have claimed a modern Parisian has developed a flying bicycle, which may be featured in the 1964 Olympics.

Although the French may have invented the first bicycle, it took a Scottish blacksmith named Kirkpatrick McMillan to evolve pedals with connection rods working on the rear axle of a tricycle with wooden wheels and iron tires in 1834. The first prototype of our present bicycle appeared in both England and France after 1850, and the first two-wheel bicycle was brought to America in 1866 by Pierre Lallement of France.

Amateur and professional bicycle riding was organized in both Europe and America by 1878. The Amateur Bicycle League of America has controlled amateur racing in the United States through some hundred clubs in most states from the early days to the present. The first national bicycle championship of the United States was held in 1883, and marked the beginning of the great era of bicycle riding and touring. In the United States, road contests became popular and then arenas were built so that races could be held indoors. Some of the tracks were built like saucers. It was not long before the bicycle became a menace to the pedestrian, the race driver often using the sidewalks for his training, and laws were passed against the "scorchers," as they were called. Six-day bicycle races were held in the old Madison Square Garden in New York, where pairs of drivers rode continuously day and night and ate while cycling the track.

The French being noted as a race of people who never throw anything away, there are still more bicycles in France than automobiles. In 1896, with new bicycles and believing they would win, the French persuaded Baron de Coubertin to make a special plea for the inclusion of this sport at the first modern Olympics in 1896. The Olympic games thereafter helped initiate and maintain international and world's championships run by the International Cyclists' Association and also spread the sport throughout the world.

The bicycle matches of the first modern Olympics were held in the velodrome in New Phaleron, a suburb of Athens. Crown Prince Constantine of Greece officiated. Only ten competitors took part in the match, three of them Greeks. The distance of the race was 100 kilometers, or 300 times around the track. While the interest of the public was very great at the start of the match, after a number of laps the spectators grew bored. Flamand, a Frenchman, won the event, completing the course in three hours, eight minutes, nineteen and one-fifth seconds. Coleitis of Greece, who came in second, was eleven laps behind. The French flag was immediately hoisted to honor the first Olympic champion in cycling. Cycling was so popular at that time that the winner received an ovation from the crowd and special congratulations from the King of Greece. The French won the all-around team championship, as they had expected.

The two-kilometer race had four competitors—one from Greece, one from Germany, and two from France. There were six laps in this race—all contestants starting at the same time. Masson of France won. The third event was the ten-kilometer race, which Masson of France also won. The sprint of 1000 meters was the main attraction. This was also won by Masson of France, with Nicolopoulos of Greece second. The road race from Marathon, which was a cycling equivalent of the famous marathon race in the track and field meet, stirred up great interest. Goedrich of Germany, Battel from England, and Constantinidis from Greece were the three favorites. According to the rules, the riders were to start from the first kilometer stone outside of Athens on the Kethissia Road, then to race as far as the fortieth kilometer stone at Marathon, where they were to sign their names on a parchment in the presence of a special commissioner of the Olympic games. They were then to return by the same road to Athens, cycling through the boulevard called Herodes Atticus and finishing at the velodrome. The total length of this course was 87 kilometers. Umpires were stationed at different points along the road to see that the rules were obeyed. Constantinidis arrived at Marathon first, hastily signed his name, turned his bicycle around, and raced back to Athens. However, his trip back was not as successful as his trip out, for he began to have trouble with his bicycle and this gave Battel of England a chance to overtake him, but as soon as repairs were made on his bicycle Constantinidis got on and away he went. He managed to catch up with Battel, pass him, and win, even though he ran into a carriage on the streets and fell. Constantinidis' time for the 87 kilometers was 3 hours, 22 minutes, and 31 seconds. He became a hero to his fellow Greeks second only to the Greek winner of the marathon foot race.

At the 1900 Olympics, in Paris, the 1000-meter scratch race was won by Taillendier of France, and a Frenchman named Sanz was second. Lake of Great Britain was third. For some reason this was the only event recorded, giving the unofficial team championship to France.

The 1904 Olympic games at St. Louis had a new attraction in cycling. Due to the fact that the public in the United States did not seem to be interested in amateur cyclists, there were competitions for professional cyclists in St. Louis. There were, of course, Olympic or amateur competitions too, the 880-yard race being the most popular, with no less than 124 cyclists competing. Marcus Hurley, Teddy Billington, and Burton Down, all of the United States, finished first, second, and third. Practically no foreign entries in cycling appeared at St. Louis. Because there was no real international competition, and because professionals were included in the program, many sources do not record any official cycling in the 1904 games.

Between the 1904 Olympics and the 1908 Olympics great progress was made in bicycle racing and new world's records were established, some made by racers paced by motorcycle. There were cycling events in the 1906 "extra" or unofficial games in Athens. An English team of Matthews and Rushen won the 2000-meter tandem. Francisco Verri of Italy won the short 333⅓-meter sprint and repeated in the 1000 and 5000 meter. W. J. Petti of Great Britain won the 20-kilometer paced race. Italy won the unofficial team championship.

While the Olympics were still going on in St. Louis, the Olympic Committee was making preparations for the 1908 Olympics in London. Each sport federation, including the Bicycle Association, was given the opportunity to consolidate its own rules, make up its own program of events, arrange its own methods, and choose its own officials. Booklets containing all this information were then printed in different languages and sent all over the world. Further clarification and standardization of rules and events came out of the 1906 Panhellenic games—a beneficial effect these "extra" games had on many other sports as well.

In 1908, the French team of M. Schilles and A. Auffray won the 2000-meter tandem race, although the British made a clean sweep of all other events and won the unofficial team championship.

The 1912 Stockholm Olympics were held in an impressive double-deck stadium built of gray-violet Swedish brick. The Swedes had engaged a Mr. Hjertberg, a famous athlete, formerly from Sweden, who was living in the United States, to make his scientific training methods available to the Swedish athletes. He had a great deal to do with arranging and running the cycling events. The individual road race was won by R. Lewis of South Africa, with the team road race going to the Swedes. C. O. Schutte of the United States came in third in the individual road race. The unofficial team championship in the cycling events went to the host nation.

The 1920 Olympic games were held at Antwerp. Warswept Belgium had overcome great handicaps to present a stadium where it was possible to compete. With the tremendous increase in the importance of the automobile in the United States and the resulting disappearance of bicycle racing, the United States had a very poor team with very few experienced riders. The unofficial overall team cycling championship was won by Great Britain. The 1000-meter race was won by Maurice Peeters of Holland, the 2000-meter tandem race by Ryan and Lance of England, the 4000-meter race by Italy. The 50-kilometer race was won by a Belgian, Henry George. In 1920 events and rules were becoming standardized, and there was a great improvement in performance.

The 1924 Olympiad, in Paris, presented one of the greatest competitions in cycling of any Olympics up until that time. The United States had made considerable effort to field a strong team for this Olympiad. Every state in the Union was combed for cyclists, with the final tryout in New Jersey. The final road race in the United States was held in Paterson, New Jersey, over the full Olympic distance of 188 kilometers, or 116.8 miles. The United States team consisted of six cyclists. Ernest Ohrt, the coach, had lived in France and was familiar with the road race course—some of the roads and streets were five hundred years old—and with the French bicycle. He had a French manufacturer build six bicycles, of the latest French model—one for each member of the United States team. Each bicycle was made to the measurements of the man who was to ride it. In spite of all this preparation, the tailor-made bicycles and hard training, the Americans did not win.

Lucien Michard of France won the 1000-meter scratch. The 2000-meter tandem was won by a French team, J. Cugnot and L. Choury. The 4000-meter team pursuit was won by Italy, and the individual road race, the event that the Americans had pointed for, was won by a Frenchman, Armand Blanchonnet. The team road race was also won by France. The 4000-meter team pursuit was won by a team from Italy. The 50-kilometer race was won by Jacobus Willems of Holland. The over-all winner was France.

The 1928 Olympic games were held in Amsterdam, and Holland won the unofficial cycling championship. The Danes, however, captured the most first places. The manager of the United States cycling team was Emil Fraysse, and the team consisted of but four cyclists—Henry O'Brien, Chester Nelson, Peter Smessaert, and Charles Westerholm. While the team did not win a single event, they deserve some credit for effort, for part of their training regimen en route to the Olympics on the *S.S. President Roosevelt* was a spin around the deck on their bicycles from five until seven in the morning.

The 1932 Olympics, at Los Angeles, again included cycling

events. Emil Fraysse, again acting as manager of the United States team, was not satisfied with the system that had been used before in selecting the American team, and therefore introduced another method. Entry blanks and invitations to the Olympics were sent to every state where district trials were to be held. Ten per cent of those entered qualified for sectional trials. Then the fastest riders in each section qualified for the finals, which were to be held in San Francisco. In previous trials for previous Olympics there had been fewer than 100 cyclists participating. In 1936, thanks to Mr. Fraysse's idea, 346 contestants competed in the state trials, 63 in the sectional, and 17 in the national finals. As a result, there was considerable improvement in the performance of American cyclists. The United States road team finished sixth—a great improvement over 1928. France, a great cycling country, finished fifth. The Italians won the unofficial team championship, with Attilio Pavesi winning the individual road race and an Italian team winning the team road race. Jacobus van Egmond of Holland won the 1000-meter scratch, Edgar L. Gray of Australia won the 1000-meter time trial, France won the 2000-meter tandem, and Italy won the 4000-meter team pursuit.

At the 1936 Olympiad the cycling competition was extremely close. Toni Merkens of Germany defeated Arie Gerrit van Vliet of Holland in the 1000-meter scratch race. These two racers were the great favorites, and Merkens won each of the two finals. However, his performance was marred by a very definite foul which should have resulted in his disqualification. Instead, he was fined 100 marks but declared the winner. One hundred riders started in the 100-kilometer road race and only half that number finished. The men were started in one group, and the road was narrow; there were many mean spills. The American entrants were familiar with three-speed gears, but the riders from Peru were not and caused a spill in which twenty riders went down at one time. Robert Charpentier of France won the 100-kilometer road race and played an important part in France's triumph in the 100-kilometer team race and 4000-meter pursuit race. France's representatives captured three championships, two seconds, and two thirds.

The cycling events were held on the specially banked wooden track in the cycling stadium, while the road race started and finished on the Alvis speedway over a practically flat course. Germany had a strong combination in the 2000-meter tandem race, defeating Holland. Van Vliet of Holland won the 1000-meter standing stock time trial race. This was a grueling contest, and many of the competitors finished in very bad physical shape. Albert Sellinger of the United States finished tenth. The United States team was coached and managed by Walter Grenda.

The 1948 Olympic cycling competitions in London brought together a great many nations and competitors. The unofficial overall championship was again won by France.

Notwithstanding the complaints that had been made after the 1936 pile-up, the Olympic road race retained its original form—the riders all starting and racing together. The road race at these Olympics was a circuit of roads in Windsor Great Park, by permission of the king. The riders had to cover the course 19 times, for a total of 135 miles.

In the first modern Olympic games, in 1896, three of the five cycling events varied only in the distance to be covered, and it was found that one good man could dominate them all, which is what Masson of France did in that year, scoring three wins. In later Olympics the contests were varied to cater to all types of cyclists, and the 1948 events included, in addition to the road race, four races on the track, each offering scope to a different type of rider.

The classic event is the sprint, a distance of 1000 meters. The riders are matched in twos, on a knockout basis from preliminary heat through to the final of two riders. This event was won by Mario Ghela of Italy, and Reg Harris of Great Britain, who had been, before the race, the world's amateur sprint champion, was second. Axel Schandorff of Denmark was third, Charles Bazzano of Australia fourth. The 1000-meter unpaced trial from a standing start was won by J. Dupont of France. J. Heid of the United States finished seventh. The 2000-meter tandem match race for teams was won by Italy, with Great Britain second, France third, and Switzerland fourth. The 4000-meter team pursuit was won by France, with Italy second, Great Britain third, and Uruguay fourth. The team road race was won by Belgium, followed by Great Britain, France, Italy, Sweden, Switzerland, and Argentina. Individual road race winners were: J. Beyaert of France, first; G. Voorting of Holland, second; and L. Wouters of Belgium, third.

The United States team suffered a number of injuries and accidents. In the 1000-meter tandem event, Marvin Thomson and Alfred Stiller, both from Chicago, reached the top eight in their series of match races, and but for an accident coming down the home stretch might have reached the top four. In the 4000-meter pursuit four-man team race, Robert

Travani of Detroit suffered a broken wrist in a spill, and a substitution for him was not allowed. The three remaining men made a very creditable showing against the Belgian team of four riders, and in losing made better time than some of the other countries that had started four riders.

At the 1952 Olympic games at Helsinki, the team cycling was won by Italy. Six of the ten members of the United States team, interestingly enough, were from the armed forces. The Amateur Bicycle League of America, the governing body of amateur bicycle racing in the United States, hopes that even though there are no longer many bicycle tracks in the United States and there are many in almost every foreign city, we can do better in future Olympics.

An indication of the spread of cycling throughout the world was given in the 1952 Olympic games, when European cyclists, who usually have dominated velodrome races, were forced to concede several places to contestants from points outside the European continent. Australian riders and riders from South Africa proved that the Europeans are not invincible, for they won no less than six of the coveted place medals. United States coaches and managers believe that this should prove to United States contestants that European riders can be beaten. Herbert Hoffman was the manager of the United States cycling team and Raymond Smith the team coach. Again the United States was disappointed. American riders are handicapped by the fact that the United States has not built velodromes similar to those on which the Olympic competitions are run, and will continue to be handicapped until such courses are built. The 100-meter time trial was won by R. Mockridge of Australia, followed by M. Morettini of Italy, R. Robinson of South Africa, and C. Cortoni of Argentina. The 1000-meter sprint was won by E. Sacchi of Italy, with L. Cox of Australia second and W. Putzernheim of Germany third. The 2000-meter tandem was won by the Australian team; South Africa was second, Italy third. The 4000-meter team pursuit was won by Italy, with South Africa second and Great Britain third. The famous road race, this time over 118 miles, was won on an individual basis by A. Noyelle of Belgium, followed by R. Grondelaers of Belgium, E. Ziegler of Germany, and L. H. Victor of Belgium. The teams were ranked in the following order: Belgium, Italy, France, Sweden, Germany, Denmark, Luxembourg, the Netherlands, Switzerland, Norway, Great Britain, Rumania, Uruguay. The Russians, for the first time in a long while, participated in the cycling championships at these Olympics.

The Amateur Bicycle League of America and members of

the United States Olympic Association expect that they will finally have medalists in the 1956 Olympic cycling events. One thing certain is that better performances, as well as greater interest, are expected at future Olympiads.

CHAPTER VI

EQUESTRIAN EVENTS

EQUITATION, WHICH comes from the Latin word for horse, is the art or sport of riding. It is the only Olympic sport which requires, in addition to the effort of man, the effort of another living animal. That living animal—the horse—antedates man himself. The evolution of the horse from a dog-sized animal is difficult to trace before 5000 B.C., but John Trotwood Moore, in a tribute to the horse, once wrote that "wherever man has left his footprint in the long ascent from barbarism to civilization, we will find the hoofprint of the horse beside it." Strangely, at the present time the country with the greatest number of different species of horse is Russia, a country that is just beginning to make its mark in Olympic equestrian events and in the modern pentathlon, another Olympic event involving riding.

When the horse was originally domesticated, he was the size of a pony. His size was increased by man through selective breeding, for throughout the Dark Ages larger horses were needed to carry knights in full armor. Horsemanship or equitation as we currently consider it was founded in the sixteenth century by an Italian named Pignatelli, who started a school at Naples which sent "masters of the horse" to all parts of the known world. Later, the exported art or sport and its finest techniques were further developed and spread by the Austrians of the Imperial stables and by the French at their cavalry school at Saumur. Horsemanship formed part of a gentleman's education.

Prehistoric drawings establish the fact that for a long period men did not mount on the back of horses, but used them as draft animals. Horses were used by the Assyrians about 4000 B.C. as the steeds of war chariots. By 1500 B.C. both man and the horse had progressed greatly, the horse from the dog stage and the man to the gambling stage, and Assyrian kings were maintaining racing stables and making bets on the outcome of mounted races. There is also evidence that the Persians were playing polo with ponies or horses at about the same time.

Although there is every reason to believe that there were competitions involving horses in the earlier unrecorded Olympics, our first recorded equestrian event is the four-horse chariot race introduced in the 25th Olympics in 680 B.C. The first actual recorded race with mounted horses was in the 33rd Olympiad, 648 B.C. The jockeys rode bareback, and there is evidence that the horse was sufficiently large to carry a man on his back at considerable speed for reasonable distances. The Grecian or Olympic race horse was the ancestor of our present-day racing thoroughbreds. We are, therefore, indebted first to the Assyrians and later and more importantly to the ancient Olympic games for our "Sport of Kings" as well as for the current equestrian competitions in the modern Olympics.

We know that on the fourth day of the ancient Olympic games the tremendous crowds moved from the stadium to the hippodrome (from the Greek *hippos,* meaning horse, and *dromos,* meaning course) to witness contests of horses and chariots. Homer, Sophocles, Pindar, and Pausanias have described these races. Pagondas, a Theban, is the first great Olympic equestrian winner whose name has come down to us. He won many chariot races with his own horses in the Olympics and in other games around 408 B.C. In the horse and chariot races, the prize was not awarded to the riders or the drivers, but to the horses and to the owners. That is why sometimes women were crowned with the wild olive of Olympia for owning winning horses.

Notwithstanding the glory of the horse in the ancient Olympics, the organizers of the first modern Olympics in Athens in 1896 could not include him because they had enough difficulties in building a stadium and coping with a thousand details of the various other sports. The transportation, care, and feeding of horses was deemed too great an effort on top of all the other problems. As a result, even though there was great pressure by the Greeks and French to include riding and equestrian events, they were passed up. The only horse present at the 1896 Olympics was the one used in gymnastics, which required a minimum of care and no feeding.

While there was great agitation to add equestrian events to the modern Olympic games in 1900, 1904, 1906, and 1908, none were included. The game of polo, generally considered an equestrian event, was picked up by the British Army in India, where it had been played since the days of the Persians, and became an Olympic event in 1900. The British won in 1900 and 1908. Polo was not included in the 1904 or 1906 games because of the expense of transporting polo ponies. In 1908, Prince Carl of Sweden made the suggestion that the world's military equestrian championship, which had been held annually for many years in Brussels, be transferred and made part of the Olympic games. Although a number of people favored the proposal, nothing came of it at that year's Olympics. However, the Olympic organizers and the host nation, Sweden, made certain that equestrian events would be included in the official program at the 5th Olympic games in Stockholm in 1912. (There were some unofficial competitions in riding as well as polo at the 1908 Olympic games in London, which the British claimed as additional victories.)

The first equestrian events in the modern Olympic games in 1912 included as competitors some of the pioneers in the re-creating of the Olympics: Sweden, Germany, Belgium, Denmark, Great Britain, France, and Russia. Sweden won the unofficial team title. All of the contestants were officers of the armies of the various countries participating. There was no polo.

The 1920 or VII Olympiad at Antwerp again presented an equestrian competition, after an interruption caused by World War I. The war, incidentally, in great part eliminated the cavalry as the elite corps of the armies of the world and dealt an indirect but serious blow to equestrian sports. The 1920 competition included Belgium, Denmark, the United States, France, Italy, Finland, and Sweden, with Sweden again winning the unofficial over-all title. The events were held over a period of six days. The 50-kilometer cross-country race was won by Lt. Johansen of Norway, with Capt. Vidart of France second and Lt. D'Emars of Belgium third. The 20-kilometer race had twenty-four starters, of whom nine finished within the allotted time, and was won by Lt. Misonna of Belgium, with Capt. Bert Santigues of France second and Lt. Bonvalet of Belgium third. The show jumping individual competition was won by Lt. Demowner of Sweden, with Lt. Lundstrom of Sweden second and Major Caffarati of Italy third. The team competition in show jumping was won by Sweden, followed by Italy, Belgium, and the United States. The individually trained horse event was won by Capt. Lundblatt's Uno of Sweden, followed by L. Sandstrom's Sabel and Lt. Count de Resen's Running Sister, all four of the leading places in this training event going to Sweden. A vaulting

43

competition, limited to enlisted men of the armies involved, was won by Trooper Bonckaert of Belgium, with Private Field of France second and Trooper Finet of Belgium third. The jumping competition was won by Lt. Lequio of Italy, who took all the jumps with no faults; second was Major Vallerie, with three faults; third was Capt. Lowenhaupp of Sweden, with four faults. The team results for this event were: first, Sweden; second, Belgium; third, Italy; fourth, France; and fifth, the United States. In polo Spain defeated the United States, 18-3, while England defeated Belgium, 8-3. England then defeated Spain for the championship.

The United States Olympic riding team in 1920 was actually the United States Army riding team, with Colonel W. C. Short as Commandant. Officers and men came directly from Fort Riley. Some of them had previously participated in the Inter-Allied games in Paris in 1919, and two of the competitors had represented the United States at Stockholm in 1912. Eight officers and sixteen horses were selected to go to the games. One of the members, realizing the poor quality of the United States horses, obtained permission to go to Virginia to buy a horse, which he paid for out of his private funds, at a cost of over $3,000. Unfortunately, the horse did not win a medal at the Olympics, nor was he even able to go, as he contracted distemper upon reaching New York. Colonel Short, in his report of the games, makes the interesting statement that "in all the competitions not an American rider was thrown without his horse going down and only one horse refused, the first time that particular horse had ever refused." The most outstanding United States rider at these Olympics was Major H. D. Chamberlin.

The 1924 Olympics at Paris marked the first time that there was no complaint from any participating nation about the selection of events or the officiating or the courses. Eighteen countries participated, a new high. The unofficial team championship went to Sweden, with Holland second, Switzerland third, and Italy fourth. The United States and France tied for tenth place. The United States team was managed by Major J. A. Barry, United States Cavalry, and consisted of ten United States Cavalry officers. Major Sloan Doak was our only medalist, placing third in the individual three-day competition. Holland distinguished herself not only by coming in second on the over-all unofficial team championship, but also by winning more first places than any other country, collecting three gold medals. The polo was won by Argentina, beating the second-place United States team and the third-place British team, which included some of

44

the greatest stars in the game. Supremacy in polo has shifted all over the world—as supremacy in many sports has—in this case from Persia to India to the British to the United States to Argentina.

At the IX Olympiad, held in 1928 at Amsterdam, twenty-one nations participated in the equestrian events. There were more competitors and more nations, but fewer events—only three. Two of the three events were won by Dutch army officers, and the third by a German. For the first time, there were a number of civilians in this championship; in future Olympics there were to be more. Holland won the unofficial team championship. There was no polo at this Olympiad.

Major General Guy V. Henry, in opening his report on the Olympic equestrian competition, wrote, "The equestrian events differ from all other Olympic events in that they are the only events in which success does not depend solely on human ability or the mastery of inanimate objects, but depends on a combination of the best horses and the most skillful riders." The United States, after so many disappointments in riding, decided that it would, as European countries do, concentrate its riders and horses and train them together over a long period of time, and preparations for the 1932 Olympics were begun early in 1929. In the fall of 1931, after a series of tryouts, twelve riders and forty horses were moved to Fort Rosecrans, California, and their training continued until the Olympic games began. The manager of the United States team was Lt. Colonel Charles E. Scott, and the finest men and horses that could be turned out by the United States Cavalry were on hand. The result was never in doubt.

In 1932, for the first time, the United States equestrian team won the unofficial championship in the modern Olympics. The dressage competition was won by François Lesage of France, with Charles Marion of France second and Capt. Hiram E. Tuttle of the United States third. In the team ratings, France was first, Sweden second, the United States third. In the three-day event, encompassing discipline, endurance, and jumping, the winners were: Charles F. Pahud de Mortanges of Holland, first; First Lt. Earl F. Thomson, United States Cavalry, second; Clarence von Rosen, Jr. of Sweden, third; and Major Harry D. Chamberlin of the United States Cavalry, fourth. In the team event, the United States was first and Holland was second. It is interesting to note that de Mortanges won six medals in the 1924, 1928, and 1932 Olympic games, four gold and two silver, all in the three-day event individual and team, to set an all-time record. The all-around jumping championship was won by Capt. Takeichi

Nishi of Japan, with eight faults; second was Major Harry D. Chamberlin, United States Cavalry, with twelve faults; third was Clarence von Rosen, Jr. of Sweden, with sixteen faults. In the team competition, no nation had three riders who completed the course, and therefore there were no team awards. The equestrian championships at these Olympics attracted tremendous crowds. There was no polo, because there had already been an international competition between the United States and Argentina in 1932.

The 1936 or XI Olympiad in Berlin featured equestrian events. Due to the military nature of the host nation a great deal of importance was placed upon the equestrian event, the reception of the equestrian teams—which consisted in most cases of army officers—and the effective running off of the competition in such a manner as to permit the greatest number of spectators. The host nation, who had apparently concentrated on winning this event; namely, Germany, won the unofficial all-around championship, with Holland second, Portugal third, the United States fourth, Switzerland fifth, Japan sixth, and France seventh. Twelve other nations participated, the other countries being Italy, Poland, Great Britain, Belgium, Bulgaria, Norway, Sweden, Turkey, Hungary, Rumania, Austria, and Czechoslovakia—a great increase in the number of competitors. Out of a total of six gold, six silver, and six bronze medals, Germany won six gold and one silver, with the other eleven medals scattered among eleven different countries. Capt. Earl F. Thomson of the United States won a silver medal in the three-day competition. The team jumping was won by Germany, with Holland second, Portugal third, the United States fourth. The individual results in this event were: first, a tie between Kurt Hasse of Germany, with Tora (four faults) and Henry Rang of Rumania with Delfis (four faults); third, Joseph von Platthy of Hungary, with Sello (eight faults). The team scoring of the three-day test was Germany first, Poland second, Great Britain third. On an individual basis, first was Ludwig Stubbendorff of Germany, on Nurm; second, Earl Thomson, the United States, on Jenny Camp; and third, Hans Lunding of Denmark, on Jason. The dressage team was won by Germany, with France second, Sweden third, Austria fourth, Holland fifth, and Hungary sixth. The United States was ninth. Dressage individual was won by Heinz Pollay of Germany, on Kronos; second was Frederick Gerhard of Germany, on Absinth; third was Alois Podhajsky of Poland, on Nero. The highest-ranking American in this event was Captain C. Stanton Babcock, in 23rd place.

The polo competition was won by Argentina, with Great Britain second, Mexico third, Hungary fourth, and Germany fifth. Once more the superiority of the Argentinians, and more particularly of their ponies, seemed to discourage many countries from entering, as did the tremendous costs involved in breeding, developing, training, caring for, and transporting sufficient animals.

The manager of the United States team for the 1936 Olympics was again Major General Guy V. Henry. After the 1936 Olympic games another world war broke the Olympic sequence and also threatened to destroy the Olympic spirit, and as far as the equestrian events were concerned indirectly dealt more damage in the fact that World War II further de-emphasized the cavalry, particularly in the United States. In fact, the horse was completely eliminated from the United States Army and the United States Military Academy, although not necessarily from other armies throughout the world. However, General Eisenhower authorized the temporary reactivation of the United States Army equestrian team at the former Cavalry School at Fort Riley, Kansas, in the spring of 1946. From an Olympic standpoint, this was an important step, for United States Olympic equestrian teams have always been composed of army personnel—although civilian riders have become more and more interested.

The equestrian competitions in the London Olympics were held at the stadium at Aldershot. Nine nations entered the dressage competition, sixteen the three-day individual and team competition, and fifteen the *Prix des Nations* show jumping.

It might be interesting to describe here the several events which formed part of the Olympics in 1948 and have been standardized and should be the basis for equestrian competition in future Olympics. The three competitions are dressage, the three-day riding test, and show jumping.

The dressage competition is essentially an exhibition of the art of riding, following the principles of the classical school. Each rider has to perform a set of test exercises of an academic character calculated to display balance, suppleness, brilliance, obedience, and ease of control. The test has to be ridden from memory and in thirteen minutes.

The complete riding competition, also known as the military or three-day test event, is a searching series of tests of practical riding. There are three tests to be performed by the same rider on the same horse. A dressage test takes place the first day. Each competitor has to perform a set test to be ridden from memory in twelve minutes. The exercises are designed to show that the horse is balanced, supple, free-going, and obedient and that the rider possesses the fluency, the ease of control, and the lightness of touch that are expected of an educated horseman. The second day is devoted to the endurance test. This grueling competition consists of five sections to be carried out by each competitor singly and consecutively, without a break and with certain time allowances and time limits. Two sections are over roads and tracks; one over a steeplechase course, one across country with many fixed obstacles, and one on the flat. The total distance is just over twenty miles. The jumping competition comes on the third day, over a course of twelve obstacles to be taken at a speed of 440 yards per minute. The object of this competition is to determine whether the horses still possess, after their previous two days' effort, the necessary reserve of energy.

The third over-all competition is a jumping one for the *Prix des Nations* and is show jumping over a course including from sixteen to twenty jumps over obstacles formidable in height or width and arrangement.

Each of these three competitions is open to three riders and three horses from each competing country. All riders must, of course, be amateurs. There are three individual prizes in each competition and three team awards. No team prize is awarded unless all three members complete the course.

The equestrian events at the London Olympiad of 1948 were won by the United States. The team dressage competition was won by Sweden, with France second, the United States third, Portugal fourth, and Argentina fifth. Unfortunately Sweden was disqualified because of the ineligibility of one of its team members. The individual dressage was won by Captain Moser of Switzerland, with Colonel Jousseaume of France second, Captain Boltenstern of Sweden third, and Lt. Borg of the United States fourth. The three-day competition team award was won by the United States; Sweden was second, Mexico third, Switzerland fourth. The individual three-day test results were: first, Captain Bernard Chevalier of France; second, Lt. Colonel F. S. Henry, the United States; third, Captain J. R. Selfelt of Sweden; fourth, Lt. Charles Howard Anderson of the United States. The show jumping or *Prix des Nations* team event was won by Mexico; Spain was second, Great Britain third, with no other teams finishing. The individual placings were: first, General Mariles of Mexico; second, Captain Uriza of Mexico; third, M. D'Orgeix of France; fourth, Colonel Franklin F. Wing, Jr. of the United States.

Well though the United States did in these Olympics, the future of American teams in this sport was clouded by uncertainty. The abandonment by the United States Army of polo, equestrian sports, and horses left a large hole to be filled. Unselfishly, a group of sportsmen undertook to correct this deficiency by organizing and incorporating The International Equestrian Competitions Corporation in New York State on June 2, 1950. Colonel John W. Wofford, United States Army (Retired), of Milford, Kansas, was elected president. A member of a former Olympic team, he was ready to donate practically all of his time, energy, and equestrian experience to the development, training, and technical management of future Olympic teams. As a non-profit organization, the corporation raised funds and in 1950 selected its first team of six horses and three riders—two men and one woman—which in November represented the United States in equestrian competition at the Pennsylvania Horse Show at Harrisburg, Pennsylvania, the National Horse Show at New York, and the Royal Winter Fair at Toronto. The success of the team provided an incentive and a demand to continue with a view toward the Olympics. The name of the corporation was changed to The United States Equestrian Team, Inc.

The corporation leased from the United States Government some of the veteran horses from the defunct United States Army Horse Show Team. It also leased premises at Fort Riley and maintained for a while a stable of up to 35 horses. It had the services of Captain Robert J. Borg, of the 1948 Olympic team, in helping train the competitors. This organization finally selected competitors for the 1952 Olympic team—eighteen horses, ten men, and one girl, Miss Marjorie B. Haynes, the first woman member of the United States equestrian team. The team manager was Colonel Wofford.

The 1952 Olympic competitions were won on an all-around basis by Sweden. The dressage individual went to Henri St. Cyr of Sweden, on Master Ruffus; second, Mrs. Lis Hartel of Denmark, on Jubilee; third, Colonel A. Jousseaume of France, on Harpagon; fourth, Gosta Boltenstern of Sweden, on Krest. The team competition was won by Sweden, with Switzerland second, Germany third, France fourth, Chile fifth, the United States sixth, Russia seventh, Portugal eighth. The three-day event was won by H. von Blixen-Finecke of Sweden, on Jubal; second, Captain G. Le Frant of France, on Verdun; third, W. Busing of Germany, on Hubertus; and fourth, P. Mercado of Argentina, on Nambinga. The team results in this event were: first, Sweden; second, Germany; third, the United States; fourth, Portugal; fifth, Denmark; sixth, Ireland. No other team of three finished. The *Prix des Nations* was won by Great Britain, with Chile second, the United States third,

49

Brazil fourth, France fifth, Germany sixth, Argentina seventh, Portugal eighth, Mexico ninth, Spain tenth, Sweden eleventh, Egypt twelfth, Rumania thirteenth, and Russia fourteenth. Italy and Finland were eliminated. On an individual basis this competition was won by P. J. D'Oriola of France, on Ali Baba; second, O. Cristi of Chile, on Bambi; third, F. Thiedemann of Germany, on Meteor; fourth, O. de Memezes of Brazil, on Bigua. There was, amazingly, a five-man tie for first place, and a five-man jump-off was held which resulted in the placements above, the man placing fifth in the jump-off being W. White of Great Britain, on Nize Fella. Sixth place went to General H. Mariles of Mexico, on Petrolero—only three-fourths of a fault behind the five who tied for first place. On an over-all basis, Sweden won by a very large margin, and France was second. Considering the tremendous reorganization job done by the United States, they did not do badly at all, with two third places, both in team events. Eighty thousand people witnessed these Olympic equestrian events.

The XVI Olympiad, in 1956, presented equestrian events for the first time as a separate show. This was done because, while Australian hospitality is extended to all human beings, strict quarantine laws so limit animal visitors that horses are not welcome. The equestrian events were, therefore, held in June by agreement between the Olympic Committees of all nations in Stockholm, in the old brick stadium especially built for the 1912 games. The reaction of the riding fraternity throughout the world seemed to be that having a separate show along the lines of the Olympic Winter Games, in a host country enthusiastic about horsemanship, might have great advantages over pooling the riding events in the large Olympic over-all program.

Twenty-nine nations sent contestants: Argentina, Australia, Austria, Belgium, Brazil, Bulgaria, Cambodia, Canada, Denmark, Egypt, Finland, France, Germany, Great Britain, Holland, Hungary, Eire, Italy, Japan, Norway, Portugal, Rumania, Russia, Spain, Sweden, Switzerland, Turkey, the United States, and Venezuela. Over 25,000 persons, a capacity crowd, were on hand for the impressive opening ceremonies. King Gustaf of Sweden, Queen Elizabeth of England with the Duke of Edinburgh and Princess Margaret, Prince Bernhard of Holland, all enthusiastic and experienced equestrians themselves, opened the competition; there were three military bands and a 260-voice choir. Prince Bertil of Sweden, as President of the Swedish Organizing Committee for these games, was host to Avery Brundage, President of the International Olympic Committee. The competition was outstanding, although because of rain and soggy footing there were many falls and accidents.

The dressage was won by Major Henri St. Cyr of Sweden, on Juli, with Mrs. Lis Hartel of Denmark, on Jubilee, second. These two repeated exactly their placement in the 1952 Olympic games. Third was another woman, Liselott Linsenhoff of Germany, on Adular. The top six teams in this event were Sweden, Germany, Switzerland, Russia, Denmark, and France, in that order. The highest-placed United States entrant was Major Robert Borg, on Bill Biddle, in 17th place. This horse and rider finished eighth in this event in 1952. Bill Biddle is a 15-year-old chestnut gelding who was competing in the Olympics for the third time, and, by the rules, is now ineligible for further Olympic competition. Although human beings may compete in as many Olympics as nature will allow, horses, who do not live as long as men, are restricted to three Olympics. This is to prevent a nation from taking too great an advantage of a superior animal competitor.

The three-day test was won by Lt. Petrus Kastenman of Sweden, on Illuster; second was August Lütke-Westhues of Germany, on Trux von Kamax; third was Lt. Colonel Frank Weldon of Great Britain, on Kilbarry; fourth was Lev Baklychkine of Russia, on Guimnast. The team results were: first, Great Britain; second, Germany; third, Canada; fourth, Australia. None of the American contestants finished. The *Grand Prix* jumping results were: (Team) 1. Germany, 2. Italy, 3. Great Britain, 4. Argentina, 5. the United States; (Individual) 1. Hans Winkler of Germany, 2. Raimondo D'Inzeo of Italy, 3. Piero D'Inzeo of Italy. Pierre D'Oriola of France, the 1952 winner, came in sixth. The American who finished highest was Seaman Hugh Wiley, of the United States Navy, who tied for 11th place.

The unofficial over-all equestrian team scoring—which will, of course, together with the Winter Games points, be added to the scoring at Melbourne to determine the over-all winner of the XVI Olympiad—was as follows: Germany, 37½ points; Sweden, 33; Great Britain, 25; Italy, 16; Denmark, 7; Russia, 6. The United States scored 2 points. The final medal tally was: gold—Sweden 3, Germany 2, Great Britain 1; silver—Germany 3, Italy 2, Denmark 1; bronze—Great Britain 2, Canada 1, Switzerland 1, Germany 1, Italy 1.

The modern Olympics have brought lovers of equestrian sports and of the horse together from all over the world; thirty-one nations participated in 1956, as against only seven in 1912, an increase that augurs well for the future. It is to be hoped, however, that the United States—once known for its cowboys, pony express, and wide open spaces, for bluegrass and fast horses—will someday come back to win the Olympic equestrian events as it did in 1932 and 1948.

CHAPTER VII

FENCING

HISTORIANS HAVE estimated that swords have been used for about 5,000 years. The most treasured, if not the oldest, sword in the world was located in Japan, and according to many, the nearest thing to modern fencing originated in Japan over 4,000 years ago. A sort of Japanese fencing in which contestants whaled away at each other with two-handed bamboo sticks is alleged to be thousands of years old.

No one can prove that spears were not used in the early Olympics, not only in throwing contests similar to the modern javelin event but hand-to-hand in fencing sessions. However, everyone agrees that no matter when the sword was first thrust into man's hand, the development of the button (a soft cover for the point of a sword), the foil (a thin, harmless practice sword), and the fencing mask were necessary before competition in swordsmanship was practicable as a part of religious ceremonies or peaceful sports gatherings. Therefore, fencing is one of the very few sports that cannot be proved to be directly tied in with the ancient Olympics, although it owes much of its present popularity and spread throughout the world and its technical development in a major part to the modern Olympics and to the world's fencing championships annually contested between Olympics and inspired by them.

The cruel and dangerous, if not deadly, art of swordsmanship became of vital importance in Europe and later all over the world during the 16th, 17th and 18th centuries. But swordsmanship as a sport became popular in Europe in the first half of the 19th century. In the United States there was such great interest in fencing that an independent group, the Amateur Fencers League of America, was formed in 1891 and took over the general supervision of the sport. This same group, incidentally, controls this sport in the United States to this day, and selects and trains United States fencing teams and sends them to the Olympic games.

While fencing is a major sport in Europe and in many countries in Latin America, United States interest in fencing is secondary but not exactly small, for there are today perhaps 400,000 fencers in the United States, and an expanding interest in fencing in schools, colleges, clubs, and in the Air Force and Navy. There is fencing in some 600 colleges in the United States.

Because this sport is not known generally in the United States, an outline description of it is in order. In fencing the object is to touch the opponent with a certain part of the weapon and at the same time prevent him from scoring a touch. Three types of weapons are used. The foil is the direct descendant of the short dress sword, and has a flexible rectangular blade, a blunt point, and a small guard. Touches must be made with the point on a target, which is the trunk of the body from the collar to the groin lines in front and to the hip-bone line. The épée is the modern counterpart and almost exact replica of the duelling sword and has a rigid triangular blade, a large bell guard; the point is covered by a small cone with barbed points. A touch can be scored on any part of the body, even a finger or a toe. There are no conventions—the first touch from a standpoint of time is scored whereas in the other weapons an attack has the right of way and should be parried. The saber is a flexible, thin, triangular blade with a dull cutting edge along the entire front and one-third of the back edge, and a blunt point; it has a large guard with one section curved from the end of the pommel to the weapon in front of the hand. It is the counterpart of the deadly sharp-bladed weapon of the same name. Both the point and the cutting edges of the blade are used to score touches. Valid touches must land on the body above the waist, including the arms and head. Masks, gloves and protective clothing are used in all fencing events.

In some sports, such as boxing and the track and field events, the United States has contributed improved techniques, training methods, coaching, teaching, and equipment to other nations all over the world. In fencing, however, Italian and French, and later Hungarian competitors, teachers, and coaches have made the major contribution, and many have come to the United States and have gradually built up great interest and unusual performance in America.

The very first modern Olympic games featured fencing as one of the major events. In fact, contrary to American belief, the fencing in the 1896 Olympic games at Athens was considered every bit as important by the Europeans as any other event, including track and field, where United States interest was concentrated.

The three men's events of the 1896 Olympic games represented the three weapons of the sport. (Women's foil competition, an important fencing event today, was not officially started in the Olympics until 1924, after women had begun to win the right to vote.) E. Gravelotte, one of the greatest earlier fencers of France, won both the foil and épée championships in 1896, while a Greek, I. Georgiadhis, to the great pleasure of the host nation, won the saber title.

In fencing, experience, mental poise, and maturity, together with a delicate sense of time, are so important that the average age of great competitors is far above that in other sports. Great fencers reach their peak between the ages of 28 and 35, and the average competitive life of a fencer covers a span of almost 25 years. Quite a few fencers have competed in four or five Olympiads. Imagine an all-American college football player or even an amateur boxer actively competing with young men of another generation at the age of 55. Fencers, like old soldiers, fade but never die. Baron de Coubertin, the founder of the modern Olympic games, who was a fencer, went to his *Salle d'Armes* for frequent workouts in his seventies, as did Colonel Graeme Hammond, one-time United States Olympic fencer and former President of both the Amateur Fencers League of America and the New York Athletic Club.

The 1900 Olympics saw for the first time one of the great fencers of all time—a man who was to leave a great mark in the annals of modern swordsmanship. Ramon Fonst was a Cuban who lived in Paris and became an ardent and enthusiastic fencer. With great teachers and competition, and great natural skills, he soon became one of the greatest swordsmen in Europe, especially with the épée, and in 1900 won the world's épée championship. E. Coste of France won the foil, and Comte de la Falaise, a dashing French cavalry officer, won the saber. Robert Ayat won the special individual sword event.

The 1904 Olympic fencing, however, was a Cuban and a Fonst show. These were the Olympics which gave Fonst immortality among modern fencers. He won the individual foil, the individual épée and led his teammates to a Cuban win in the first fencing team competition in the Olympics— team foil. There was only one discordant note in the Cuban victory. Most of the European countries did not send their best fencers to the St. Louis Fair in distant Missouri, almost a month's travel away. Few of the best fencers in France and Italy made the trip.

Fonst also won the individual sword championship, an event discontinued thereafter. M. de Diaz, inspired by Fonst, won the saber for Cuba. Only one man—Nedo Nadi of Italy—has come near equaling Fonst's record in the sixty-year history of the modern Olympics. An added event never again contested—the single sticks made famous by Robin Hood and Little John in English legend—was won by V. Z. Post, an American living in Cuba. This is the only Olympic title in any fencing event ever won by the United States of America. Post won five assorted United States national championships in foil, épée, or saber between 1896 and 1903.

By 1906 fencing in the Olympics had become so popular that for the first time regular team competitions in all three weapons, in addition to the individual championships, were begun. An Irish-Frenchman named Dillon-Cavanagh won the foil for France. France won the team foil. In épée, Comte de la Falaise won the individual honors and France the team event, while I. Georgiadhis of Greece, winner of the individual saber, won this event again. Germany won the team saber and Gustav Casimir the three-cornered saber event, never before and never after contested.

The 1908 Olympic fencing produced its quota of fine champions. The épée individual was won by G. Alibert of France, and the épée team by France. Hungary began her grip on saber handles and title as a result of the work of the great Italo Santelli, an Italian fencing master who started coaching saber in Budapest and created a style to fit the national character and spirit of the Hungarians. His Hungarian pupils and his Hungarian pupils' pupils have pretty well dominated saber fencing throughout the world since then. To show what transplanted and adapted genius in athletic coaching can do, Hungarians have won every Olympic saber championship from 1908 through 1952, except one, and 23 out of 29 world's championships. The Olympics, it is interesting to note, have given the world such an appetite for sports competition that in many international sports, including fencing, world championships are now held separately in the years between the Olympics. Hungarians have also won national competitions wherever they have emigrated. Dr. Tibor Nyilas and George Worth, Hungarian-Americans, have won the United States saber championships for four out of the past five years, coached by Georgio Santelli, Hungarian-American son of Italo Santelli.

E. Fuchs won the 1908 Olympic saber title for Hungary and Hungary won the saber team title. Hungarians were to win seven of the following nine Olympic saber titles.

The 1912 Olympics in Stockholm presented the most hotly contested international fencing competition ever held up until that time. During the period between 1908 and 1912, several countries met in international competitions, especially the fencing leaders of the world: France and Italy. Thanks to the Olympics the sport was improving and spreading rapidly, with more and better competition. When 1912 rolled around, top fencing contestants from many nations were ready to do or die for Olympic championships.

Another all-time great appeared on the Olympic fencing strips of Stockholm—Nedo Nadi of Italy. Nadi won the individual foil in 1912, to begin a brilliant career. Paul Anspach of Belgium won the individual épée and helped Belgium win the épée team honors. E. Fuchs of Hungary repeated in individual saber, and Hungary again won the saber team.

World War I interrupted the Olympics, but two sports made great advances notwithstanding the war—in fact, as a result of it. Boxing and fencing competitions were held in the military services of many countries, to provide recreation and build morale. The Inter-Allied games after World War I pitted the greatest amateurs against the greatest professional athletes in many sports. In fencing the greatest amateurs and professionals crossed swords in friendly competitions, and improved their techniques.

When the Olympics were resumed in 1920, many great fencers with greatly improved techniques and styles competed internationally. Seventeen countries were represented, and the teams of most countries reflected the great interest in fencing by their armed forces. The United States team was no exception. Its coaches were George Heintz of the U. S. Naval Academy, and Maitre F. H. Darrieulat, a French fencing master. Ten of the eleven members of the United States team were from the armed forces. Ensigns E. G. Fullenweider, R. S. Bowman, F. J. Cunningham, C. J. Walker, and George Calnan represented the Navy, and the Army was represented by Colonel Henry Breckenridge, Lt. Colonel Robert Sears, Major Harold Rayner, Major F. W. Honeycutt, and Sgt. John Dimond. The American team surprised everyone by coming up with some real fencing, in a sport in which theretofore the United States had not been much of a contestant. The foil team placed third, the épée team sixth, and the saber team seventh. George Calnan, one of the greatest fencers developed in the United States, began to show his great talent in these Olympics. First honors went to Italy, which won the individual foil with Nedo Nadi—who repeated the victory he had won eight years before at the 1912 Olympics. Italy also won the team foil. André Massard of France won the individual épée, but Italy won the team event in this weapon. Nedo Nadi surprised everyone by overcoming the Hungarians at their own game and winning the individual saber, and helped the Italian team upset the Hungarians in the team saber. Nadi established himself as the all-time greatest fencer of the world and of the modern Olympics. He was, however, to be seriously challenged by a man whose career was just beginning and who may be properly considered the second greatest swordsman of modern times—Lucien Gaudin of France, who first appeared in the 1920 Olympics. Fonst, had he been in his prime in this period of top competition, might be more highly rated in any evaluation of all-time greatness, but he was handicapped by the limited nature of his competition at the 1904 Olympics.

United States fencing, like Hungarian fencing, owes its real start to imported teaching. An Italian master is the founder of Hungarian fencing, while a French coach, Louis Vauthier, was responsible for America's earliest interest and later improved performance. Vauthier was an honor graduate of Joinville-le-Pont, the great French physical training school for fencing masters. He came to the United States in 1893 and coached at the New York Fencers Club and then went to West Point, where he remained over thirty years, twenty as fencing coach. Vauthier's West Point teams dominated the intercollegiates in the United States, winning the all-around championship for ten years and placing second for four years out of fourteen years of competition. West Point discontinued fencing during the remaining years, as a result of World War I. Vauthier developed or coached many United States national champions, including the Olympic fencers Breckenridge, Sears, F. W. Honeycutt, H. M. Rayner, W. Castner, and Jack Dimond. Dimond succeeded him as West Point coach and developed United States national champions and Olympic fencers R. W. Mayo, T. G. Sands, F. R. Weber, and G. M. Heiss, between world wars.

In the years between 1920 and 1924, many international games were held, bringing to all sports great technical development, so that by the time the 1924 Olympics came along, not only were there more contestants and more countries entered in fencing (19), but also the quality of the competition was greatly improved.

The 1924 Olympic fencing was won by France, with the help of Lucien Gaudin in the team competitions. Roger Ducret of France won the individual foil, and France won the team foil. H. Delporte of Belgium won the individual épée, and France won the team épée. Alexandre Posta of Hungary won the individual saber, with Italy nosing out Hungary for the team saber title. Women began to compete in fencing in the individual foil in these Olympics, with Mrs. E. O. Osiier of Denmark winning the first women's Olympic title.

The American team was coached by F. M. Costello and Darrieulat, both Europeans. As in 1920, the armed services contributed most of the team—Breckenridge, Castner, Jeter, Allison, and Walker from the Army, and Fullenweider and George Calnan of the Navy. Calnan, in foil, was the first American ever to reach a semifinal round in fencing. Two American women did quite well in the women's foil—Mrs. Irma Hopper and Adeline Gehrig, sister of Lou Gehrig. In the team épée, Portugal and the United States tied in bouts, and when it came time to count touches, mistakes were discovered in the running of the match, so it was agreed to run the entire match off again from scratch. In this exciting contest, Portugal finally eliminated the United States by 10 to 6.

Further progress was made in international fencing competition between the 1924 and 1928 Olympics. Twenty-two nations competed for Olympic medals in 1928 in one of the most hard-fought Olympic competitions of all time. Lucien Gaudin of France established himself as, probably next to Nadi, one of the three greatest swordsmen in modern times. He won the individual foil, although Italy won the team foil, and he also doubled up, a rare accomplishment, by winning the individual épée, although here also Italy nosed out France for the team title. The Hungarians took over in saber and have never been beaten since. E. Tercztyansky won the individual saber, and Hungary won the team.

Helene Mayer of Germany won the women's foil. She was one of the greatest women fencers of modern times and probably could have beaten all but a very few male contestants in her specialty. She later came to the United States and became an American citizen, winning the United States National women's foil championship in 1934, 1935, 1937, 1938, 1939, 1941, 1942, and 1946. She was second in the 1936 Olympics, and won the world's title in 1937—both for Germany, and before she became an American citizen. She could never represent the United States, however, for a rule makes it impossible for anyone who has represented one nation in the Olympics to represent another later. On a Hollywood set, Helene Mayer, introduced as an unknown extra, was asked to fence against Cornel Wilde, a motion picture star with fencing experience and ability, by a fencing coach directing some fencing scenes in a movie. She beat Wilde with great ease. He felt better after finding out her true identity. (Incidentally, whenever you see a duel or sword combat in a Hollywood movie today, you can be fairly certain the scene was directed and supervised by Ralph Faulkner, a member of the 1928 United States team.)

The United States team in 1928 was coached by Georgio Santelli, son of the great Italo Santelli of Hungary, and René Pinchart, a Belgian master. Neither of these great instructors was afraid to compete against his pupils. Pinchart won, after a tie with the author, the first Masters or Open Championship (amateurs and professionals) ever held in the United States in épée or in any fencing event. Georgio Santelli was third and George Calnan fourth. Open competitions in fencing did not become annual affairs in the United States, however, until the épée Masters in 1950 (won by the author). In all countries competitions between top amateurs and professionals have helped many sports.

The United States fencing team of 1928 was up with the leaders for the first time. Joe Levis, of M.I.T., the Boston A.A., and the New York Fencers Club, was the first American ever to make the finals in any weapon in Olympic fencing, placing 11th in foil. Calnan was great in both foil and épée, and became the second American to make the finals in Olympic fencing and the first United States Olympic medalist, placing third in the world in épée. Calnan later went on to win 21 out of 28 bouts in team épée.

With regular official World Fencing Championships in 1929, 1930, and 1931 and Open Championships between amateurs and professionals, in addition to National Championships in most countries, fencing made great strides. Interest in the sport increased throughout the world.

The 1932 Olympics were held at Los Angeles, in a country where fencing is not considered even an important minor sport. Nevertheless the occasion produced many records. As if inspired by being the host nation and by the unexpectedly large crowds of Americans who turned out to see the fencing, the United States team made its greatest record in the modern Olympics. Levis won the silver medal in the individual foil, with the United States winning third in the foil team. Calnan was seventh in the épée, with the United States winning third in épée team. In saber, Santelli's coaching began to show, as the United States qualified its first two sabermen to the finals in that weapon—Dr. John R. Huffman of Yale and the N.Y.A.C. and Norman Armitage of Columbia and the New York Fencers Club. Huffman placed sixth, and the United States placed fourth in the saber team. Marion Lloyd also made the finals, scoring ninth place in the women's foil. These Olympics were the high-water mark of United States fencing. Thereafter the efforts of Italy, France, and Hungary to retain their leadership proved too much for the United States, and the United States has never again scored as well—three medals, one fourth, and finalists in six of seven events—as in 1932.

Another European who made an important contribution to American fencing was Leo Nunes, a great sportsman and amateur fencer who came to New York City from Italy and later became a United States citizen. Nunes won a second at the 1919 Inter-Allied games against the best amateurs and professionals in the world and was appointed a member of the 1924 Italian Olympic team. In the United States he won fifteen foil, épée, saber, and three-weapon national championships between 1917 and 1932.

A great loss to United States fencing came with the death of George Calnan, who took the opening Olympic Oath at the Los Angeles 1932 Olympics as a fourth-time member of a United States Olympic team. He and another Navy Olympic fencer, Lt. Calloway, lost their lives in the catastrophe of the dirigible *Akron*. An indication of the friendships that grow out of competitive athletics and the Olympics is the fact that condolences from the governments, athletes, and athletic officials of twenty-two countries were received by Calnan's widow.

At the 1936 Olympics in Berlin many fencing records were broken; there were more contestants, longer fencing sessions and competitions (contestants fenced in morning, afternoon, and evening sessions), and more spectators than ever before. Two large gymnasiums, as well as hard clay tennis courts, on which épée competitions were held, were crowded day and night with spectators. Stamina and youth became very important, for the long fencing sessions wore down even the greatest among the older veterans.

The 1936 Olympics mark a new era in fencing, for electrical judging equipment, officially adopted by the *Fédéra-*

tion Internationale d'Escrime (F.I.E.), was used for the first time at any Olympics. An electrical machine, developed in Geneva by L. Pagan, was capable of measuring a difference of 1/25 of a second between touches in the épée (where the fencer to hit the other first scores). From the 1936 Olympics on, very little was left to chance or to the officials' eyesight or judgment of time in épée competition, as the machine positively identified the winner.

Italy almost made a clean sweep, with first in both épée and foil teams and a very close second in saber team. In ten individual events, Italy placed first, second, and third in individual épée, first and third in individual foil, and second in individual saber. Andre Kabos of Hungary, World Saber Champion in 1933 and 1934, won the World or Olympic title; Franco Riccardi of Italy won the épée, and Giulio Gaudini the foil. The 1932 winner of the women's foil is probably the greatest woman fencer of modern times. Ilona Elek of Hungary won the World Championship in 1934 and 1935, repeated in the 1936 Olympics, defeating Helene Mayer, and then, just to prove her class, came back after World War II to win in the Olympics again in 1948 and win another World Championship in 1951. In 1936 not a single United States individual or team reached the finals.

West Point's swan song as a contributor to Olympic fencing in the United States was sung in the 1936 Olympics, when it contributed John Dimond as épée coach and the three top men in épée—Weber, Heiss, and Sands. Heiss and Sands were both United States national épée champions —Heiss for four years, Sands for two. After 1940, with Vauthier and Dimond gone, West Point lost interest in fencing, but intercollegiate fencing in the United States rose to an all-time high in 1955, when 39 colleges participated in a national tournament won by Illinois, with Columbia and Navy second and third. All three of these colleges have contributed many fencers to United States Olympic teams.

An unpleasant incident marred the 1936 games, but showed how new nations were learning the game and threatening the leaders although some of these leaders sometimes used unsportsmanlike tactics to try to maintain their leadership. Major Haro Oliva, Mexican army officer, like Ramon Fonst of Cuba years before, lived in Paris for many years and became interested in fencing. As Mexico's Junior Military Attaché, as a student at the French War College, and as Mexico's Military Attaché, he learned fencing from French masters and gained experience in European international competitions. He became the Western Hemisphere's greatest fencer since Fonst. In fact, in one World's Championship he made the finals in both épée and saber, finishing sixth in épée and eighth in saber in the world. Making the finals in a World Championship in two weapons is unusual. The 1936 Olympics was the time he had pointed for and had trained for during all his adult life. His target was the world's épée title, which only one man from the Western Hemisphere had ever won before—Fonst, in 1900 and 1904. In fact, no one from the Western Hemisphere but Fonst has even won any regular fencing title in 60 years.

Oliva qualified through the preliminary strips (equivalent to heats), the quarter-finals, the semifinals, and reached the finals. Oliva won his first bouts in the finals and seemed headed for the championship, to the obvious concern and annoyance of some Europeans. There was a lot of whispering and finally a group of European officials came over and began examining, testing, and measuring Oliva's weapons—his electrical épées. These had been tested and measured as normally provided for before the opening of the fencing competitions by official technical personnel. The Italian and French officials now found that one of his épées, the one they maintained he had been using, was about one-fifth inch too long. The directors of the competition ruled that Oliva would have to fence all his bouts over again, from the first preliminary round, with other épées of regulation length, to be checked before each bout. Oliva started to fence his bouts over again, although there was insufficient time to complete them before the final started. Mexican officials appealed that Oliva be permitted to fence in the final, subject to some later ruling, but the German officials supported the Italians to exclude him completely.

At the 1948 Olympic games, twenty-two countries competed in the fencing tournament. The coaches of the 1948 United States team were again René Pinchart and Georgio Santelli, who had been with United States fencing since 1928. Levis placed seventh in foil, Lewis ninth in épée, Worth fifth and Dr. Nyilas seventh in saber, with the United States coming in third in saber team. Maria Cerra was fourth in women's foil. The French won the individual foil (Jean Buhan) and the foil team. Italy, with Luigi Cantone, won the individual épée but was edged out by France in the épée team, and Hungary performed as usual, winning the saber team and the individual saber with Aladar Gerevich.

The progress of fencing between 1952 and 1956 was great. With the war over, World Championships were held and were well attended in 1949, 1950, and 1951. For the first time fencers from the United States and other Western Hemisphere nations began to participate in these competitions. Interest increased throughout the world, and thirty-two nations sent fencers to the 1952 Olympics in Helsinki. The countries where fencing is a major national sport—Italy, Hungary, and France—won all the firsts, all but one of the seconds, and all but three of the thirds. Switzerland won the all-around fourth place. The winners are listed in the appendix. The Russians returned to Olympic fencing for the first time since 1912, when the Czar and his Imperial Guard officers had been interested in the sport. A Russian team and a United States team met in the first preliminary round in épée. The result was eight wins for Russia and eight wins for the United States; but the United States won by having been hit only 29 times, as against 32 hits scored against the Russians.

The United States team, coached again by Georgio Santelli and René Pinchart, obtained some new coaching blood in Stanley Sieja, a phenomenal developer of new national and international épée talent at Princeton University. Norman C. Armitage, saber member of five Olympic fencing teams from 1928 through 1952 and ten times national champion, was chosen to carry the United States flag at the opening ceremonies in Helsinki. Janice Lee York won fourth place in the women's foil, and the United States saber team placed fourth.

Much to the surprise of many Americans, the quality of the teams and the tremendous popular appeal in the U.S.S.R., Poland, Rumania, Czechoslovakia, Yugoslavia, as well as in Hungary, would indicate that fencing is considered a sport for the people in these countries, and not for the privileged. Perhaps competitive athletics not only overcome differences of nationality, race, and religion, but also of classes and ideologies. Fencing and riding behind the Iron Curtain, as on this side of it, are sports like any others, and victory in these sports, as in others, goes to the best man.

The 1956 Olympics should display better fencing and more competitors from more countries than any other Olympics and the sport is sure to attract wider public interest. For the first time, foil will be electrically judged with machines somewhat similar to those used in épée. These machines have already proved their merit—in the 1955 World Championships in Rome. More countries, contestants, and spectators have attended these World Championships each year since 1952, and the United States has improved by experience gained in them. The United States Navy sent a full American team to the 1955 World Championships, and the United States Air Force and Navy officers have distinguished themselves in the new World's Military Fencing Championships, which are now run off annually in Europe in addition to the regular World Championships, between Olympics. Some day we can expect the fencing picture to change. In the near future, perhaps, it may be the turn of Russia or the United States to win in fencing, with perhaps Egypt and Panama in close pursuit.

CHAPTER VIII

GYMNASTICS

ONE OF the world's least publicized sports is gymnastics. Yet gymnasts perform in a single evening acts of greater daring and greater difficulty than most baseball and football players or track and field men are called upon to equal in a whole season. Unfortunately, however, gymnastics has no great crowd appeal and all of the greatest gymnasts in America do not attract in an entire year as many spectators as are attracted to a baseball park or a football stadium in a single afternoon to see a single game. Similarly, gymnastics are an almost unnoticed part of the modern Olympic games.

But gymnastics as a sport has proved itself by having outlived many other sports and is today a feature of the modern Olympics. The sport dates from the ancient Greeks, and the words "gymnastics" and "gymnasium" come from the Greek *gymnazein,* meaning to exercise (naked). Gymnastics, weight lifting, and track and field were, in the days of the ancient Greeks, coupled together as the proper regimen for young men. Students in ancient Greece were required to learn to run, jump, lift and throw weights, wrestle, and perform disciplinary gymnastics. Every city of ancient Greece had a gymnasium or many gymnasiums in which gymnastics was practiced.

In the early years of gymnastics in the United States, the sport was engaged in chiefly by European-Americans from countries where such exercises were extremely popular. In 1897 the Amateur Athletic Union assumed national control of the sport. Shortly thereafter, the colleges began to take an interest in gymnastics, and forty-three years later, in 1940, the University of Illinois, a college team, captured the national championship. In more recent years, high schools and junior high schools have taken an interest in gymnastics and have developed performers who will compete and compare favorably with the greatest in any other country.

In modern gymnastics, the all-around championship is won by the contestant making the best showing in free calisthenics, long horse, side horse, horizontal bar, parallel bar, and flying rings. One compulsory and one optional exercise are required for the horizontal bar, parallel bar, side horse, and long horse. Each contestant must execute the compulsory exercises, and the optional is some exercise of his own choosing in which he feels he will appear at his best. The judges base their decisions on the degree of difficulty in performing the exercise, the execution of the movement, and the form displayed. On the flying ring, one still and one brisk-swinging exercise are demanded. In rope climbing, each contestant receives three chances, and speed alone determines the winner. The rope is twenty feet long. In tumbling, the contestant performs one optional routine. The judging is on the basis of the amount of tumbling performed and the degree of difficulty. In club swinging, the contestant is allowed one trial of four minutes. The club must weigh one pound, and the dropping of a club ends the exercise. In free calisthenics, one optional exercise is performed in one and a half to two minutes, without hand apparatus.

Probably the greatest gymnast ever developed in the United States was Alfred Jochim, and the most famous club was the Swiss Turnverein of Hudson County, New Jersey, of which Jochim was a member. Jochim was the all-around winner in all national AAU championships from 1925 to 1930, and then came back in 1933 to win his seventh crown. The Swiss Turnverein won its first team championship in 1926, then repeated in every year from 1928 to 1934. Another extraordinary performer was Edward A. Hennig of Cleveland, who won the first AAU national championship in Indian club swinging in 1904 and then repeated in 1911, 1933, 1936, 1937, 1939, 1940, 1942, 1945, 1946, 1947, 1950, and 1951, besides winning the 1904 world's championship or Olympic gold medal in that event.

Women's gymnastics first appeared as an AAU championship event in 1931. Probably the greatest American performer among women gymnasts was Clara M. Schroth Lomady of Philadelphia, who won the all-around title in 1945, 1946, 1949, 1950, 1951, and 1952.

At the first modern Olympics at Athens in 1896, eight events were contested by competitors from some half-dozen countries. The unofficial team title in this sport was won by

Germany. There was no all-around competition, either individual or team, but only individual events. If there had been an all-around individual championship, Zutter of Switzerland probably would have won it; he excelled in several different events.

The gymnastics at the 1900 Olympics in Paris was won by the host nation. These were the first Olympic games to hold an all-around gymnastics individual competition, which was won by Sandras of France; there was still no all-around team championship. In 1904, according to the report by the committee running the Olympics in St. Louis, there were official gymnastic events and the all-around championship was won by the United States. According to other sources, there is considerable doubt that the gymnastic events were recognized as official. However, the United States won practically every event except the all-around team, which was won by Germany. The greatest individual stars were Anton Heida of the United States, who won the all-around individual, tied for the long horse, and won the side horse and tied for the horizontal bar, and George Eyser, also of the United States, who tied for first in the long horse and horizontal bar and won the parallel bars and rope climb.

In the 1906 games in Athens, generally counted as one of the modern Olympics, France won the unofficial gymnastic championship, although Denmark and Norway tied in the all-around gymnastic team event. A Frenchman, Payssee, won the all-around gymnastic individual title, and a Greek, G. Aliprantis, won the rope climb in an astonishingly slow time. A prince of the royal family of Greece officiated at this Olympic gymnastic meet.

There is considerable argument about who won the all-around championship at the London games of 1908. Italy, Great Britain, and Sweden claimed the top honors, each basing its claim on its own method of scoring. Sweden won the gymnastic team event. Italy served notice of her future strength in this sport, uncovering a new star, Alberto Braglia, who won the all-around individual event.

The 1912 Olympic games emphasized gymnastics, and the host nation, Sweden, one of the greatest supporters of the gymnastics schedule and winner or co-winner in 1908, contributed to making the gymnastic competitions more interesting than they had been in any previous Olympics. Many new events were added, such as calisthenics, team exercise, both free system and Swedish system, and a special team competition. Italy was a close second to Sweden, and Alberto Braglia repeated his 1908 victory as the best all-around gymnast. Italy also won the team gymnastics event.

When the 1920 Olympics came around, an even larger program of gymnastic events was scheduled. Fourteen countries participated, and Italy made good her earlier promise by taking the gymnastic team championship and winning the unofficial all-around team. Sweden won one and Denmark won two of the calisthenics competitions. The United States sent only four men. The American who finished highest in the rankings was Frank Kriz, who finished tenth. Roy E. Moore was manager of the team and came back to the United States certain that, with proper organization and proper selection and training, Americans could do well in future gymnastic events in the Olympics.

Thanks to the enthusiasm and dedication of Mr. Moore, who also managed the 1924 team, the United States broke into the winning column in the 1924 Paris Olympics, although the Italians won the unofficial all-around championship. The United States Olympic team in 1924 was selected after many tryouts and a very thrilling final tryout held at Madison Square Garden in New York City, on May 27, 1924. Nine nations competed in the all-around event, finishing in the following order: Italy, France, Switzerland, Yugoslavia, the United States, Great Britain, Finland, Luxembourg, Czechoslovakia. In the individual events, Frank J. Kriz was first in the long horse, with Max H. Wandrer of the United States placing fifth in this event. Kriz also placed sixth in the rope climb. For the first time since 1904, the system of giving gold medals and awarding places in the individual events as well as for the all-around scoring was used. Switzerland made the greatest improvement of any country, and came out second from an all-around standpoint. At these Olympics, it was proposed that gymnastic events for women be added to the program, and it was decided that beginning in 1928 there would be a women's gymnastics team event and later, perhaps, an individual all-around competition.

The gymnastic competition at the IX Olympiad in Amsterdam covered a period of three days. Switzerland won, with Czechoslovakia second, Yugoslavia third, France fourth, Finland fifth, Italy sixth, the United States seventh, Holland eighth, Luxembourg ninth, Hungary tenth, and England eleventh. No member of the United States team was able to place in any event. Alfred Jochim, who had also been a member of the 1924 team, was high man of the United States entries. Roy E. Moore was again manager and coach of the team.

Switzerland made almost a clean sweep, winning the gymnastic team, the gymnastic all-around individual, the long horse, the side horse, the horizontal bar, and the side horse vaults, the last an event held only in 1924 and 1928. The remaining two titles went to Czechoslovakia and Yugoslavia. The women's gymnastic team event, held for the first time, was won by the host nation, Holland. The addition of individual events for women was postponed.

Only seven countries brought gymnastic teams to the X Olympiad at Los Angeles in 1932, but there were more competitors than at any gymnastic meet of the Olympics up until that time and the level of performance was high. There were eleven events, extending over a period of five days, and attendance at the Olympic stadium ranged from 3,000 to 27,000. The United States won the unofficial championship, with Italy second, Hungary third, and Finland fourth. The United States took the first three places in the rope climb; the first three places in tumbling; a third and fourth in the tumble horse; first, second, and fourth in flying rings; sixth in the parallel bars; first in the horizontal bars; first, second, and third in the Indian clubs; second and third in the long horse vaulting; second in the team all-around; and sixth in the individual all-around. It was the high-water mark of American effort in gymnastics. Alfred Jochim was an important member of the 1932 team, as he had been in the 1924 and 1928. Roy E. Moore, the manager and coach of the team, played a major role in the United States' climb from last to first place.

The 1936 Olympic gymnastic championships in Berlin brought back one of Germany's oldest traditions in competitive athletics. In 1896, at the first gymnastic championship of the first modern Olympics, Germany had been the winner. Germany was also the winner at Berlin, winning five Olympic titles, including the individual men's all-around and the men's team all-around. The United States finished tenth among the fourteen countries competing, each of which was represented by a team of eight men. The gymnastic competition took place at the Reichssportfeld in the Dietrich Eckart Stadium. Crowds of 25,000 to 30,000 enthusiastic spectators attested to the great popular interest in this sport in Germany.

After Germany, the thirteen other countries finished in the following order: Switzerland, Finland, Czechoslovakia, Italy, Yugoslavia, Hungary, France, Japan, the United States, Austria, Luxembourg, Bulgaria, and Rumania. There were some complaints about the judging, based on the fact that the Germans, after agreeing to name three judges from every country, allowed only one judge from the United States.

Whatever the validity of these complaints, the United States fared very badly in the individual competition, our highest-ranked contestant coming in 38th. Alfred Jochim was for the fourth time a member of the United States team.

There had been no women's gymnastic events in 1932, but the 1936 Olympics in Germany featured a regular schedule of gymnastic events for women and the United States was represented by a women's gymnastic team for the first time. Eight nations entered teams of eight women each. They finished in the following order: Germany, Czechoslovakia, Hungary, Yugoslavia, the United States, Poland, Italy, Great Britain. Miss Conseppa Caruccio was the United States' high scorer.

The 1948 Olympiad saw outstanding competitions in both the men's and women's gymnastic championships. Sixteen countries entered teams in the men's competition, eleven in the women's. The outcome of the men's championships was so close that different methods of scoring give different winners—Finland according to one and Switzerland according to another, although Finland did take the men's all-around gymnastic team championship and a Finn won the all-around men's individual. The Swiss, however, won three individual gold medals, as against two for Finland, and scored many points in the individual events. The team events for the men were: free exercises, pommeled horse, rings, parallel bars, horizontal bars, and vaults. The final standing in the men's team was: Finland, Switzerland, Hungary, France, Italy, Czechoslovakia, the United States, Denmark, Austria, Yugoslavia, Luxembourg, Great Britain, Egypt, Cuba, Argentina, and Mexico, in that order. In the all-around men's individual, Finns placed first and third and the Swiss captured second, fourth fifth, and sixth places.

In the women's team championship, consisting of free exercises, beam, vault, rings, and hand apparatus, the results were as follows: Czechoslovakia, Hungary, the United States, Sweden, the Netherlands, Austria, Yugoslavia, Italy, Great Britain, France, and Belgium.

The United States men's team was coached by Eugene Wettstone and George Miele, with the women's coached by Joseph Salzman. The women's team showed to great advantage and, according to many, did not get the breaks in judging. The United States officials and experts in gymnastics were surprised by the showing of their women's team, but very disappointed in the men's team. On the other hand, they pointed out that the United States, by adopting better training policies and stimulating competition, could achieve prominence in

69

gymnastics, and gave as an example the experience of the Finns, who had first entered a team at Amsterdam in 1928, where they placed a poor fifth. At Los Angeles in 1932 and at Berlin in 1936, the Finns placed third, and at London in 1948 they came into their own and were first or tied for first—depending on whose scoring you accept.

The XV Olympiad at Helsinki in 1952 attracted an even greater number of competitors than any earlier modern Olympics had. These games also featured the arrival of a nation new to Olympic gymnastic competition—Russia. The Russians, who won with ease, were impressive because of their superb condition, their consistency, and their strength. Their optionals on horizontal bar and parallel bar were very short and may not have been the fluent longer combination work expected at international tournaments, but their exactitude and perfection on the compulsory routines showed the effect of long and excellent training. The United States, coached by Thomas E. Maloney, finished eighth in the 29-nation competition. The 1952 games produced a new world star, E. V. Tchoukarine, of Russia, who won the all-around men's individual competition of twelve events, and also won gold medals in the tumble horse and long horse, and a silver medal in the parallel bars.

The men's team championship placed the nations in the following order: Russia, Switzerland, Finland, Germany, Japan, Hungary and Czechoslovakia (tied), the United States, Bulgaria, France, Italy, Austria, Poland, Denmark, Norway, Egypt, Sweden, Luxembourg, Rumania, Yugoslavia, Great Britain, the Saar, Portugal, Belgium, Cuba, South Africa, Argentina, Spain, and India.

In the women's gymnastics, eighteen nations participated, and finished in the following order: Russia, Hungary, Czechoslovakia, Sweden, Bulgaria, Germany, Italy, Poland, Rumania, France, Yugoslavia, Austria, Finland, the Netherlands, the United States, Great Britain, Norway, and Portugal.

The women's gymnastics enjoyed great popularity at Helsinki; the spectators saw some very glamorous performers. The program of women's events was greatly expanded because of the great popular interest, and it now includes not only an all-around individual competition of eight events, but also beam, parallel bars, long horse, free standing exercise, and—a new event—team calisthenics.

If the past history of this sport can be taken as a suggestion of its future, then it seems likely that before the first century of modern Olympiads has been completed at least fifty nations will be regularly sending gymnastic teams to compete in friendly contests of skill, strength, and discipline, in the ancient Greek tradition.

CHAPTER IX

THE MODERN PENTATHLON

AFTER THE 17th Olympic games in ancient Greece, the warlike Spartans complained that the Olympics did not have an all-around athletic competition for warriors, and as a result the pentathlon, a contest consisting of five events, was initiated in the 18th Olympics (708 B.C.). The pentathlon was designed purely for the soldier athlete. It was an elimination contest in which all entrants first took part in a broad-jumping contest. Those who cleared a certain distance qualified for a second event, a spear- or javelin-throwing contest. At this time the spear or javelin was the major equipment of the Greek soldier, from private to general. Only the four best in this military event were qualified to participate in the third event, a sprint of one length of the stadium, or approximately 200 yards. One more athlete was eliminated here. The fourth challenge for the remaining contestants was the discus throw, and in this event one more contestant was eliminated. Then the two surviving athletes, in the grand finale of this grueling competition, wrestled each other to a finish. The winner was the Olympic pentathlon winner. Later the pentathlon, and perhaps the decathlon (ten events), were restricted to competitions testing track and field prowess only, and wrestling became a separate event.

When the modern Olympic games were inaugurated in 1896 there was too much confusion, and too much scrambling by partisans of various sports, for the sponsors to worry about a pentathlon or decathlon. Efforts were made, after the modern Olympics began, to add a pentathlon and, later, a decathlon, but both were all-around tests involving track and field events only. These efforts led to the inclusion of a pentathlon, which was discontinued after 1924, and the regular decathlon, which is still contested in the track and field program of the modern Olympics.

Before the 1912 Olympics, the organizers of the Olympic games felt that there was room for a dramatic event with a military background that would appeal to the armed forces of the various nations of the world. It is even said that the idea was first suggested in a conversation between Latour and de Coubertin. Some even claim that de Coubertin said that to stimulate better international relations and to insure peace, the armies of the world should be made to meet in friendly competition in some event that would particularly attract army personnel. In any case, the modern pentathlon, personally sponsored by Baron de Coubertin, was added to the Olympic program in 1912.

The modern pentathlon, which should have been called the "military pentathlon," was based on the function of the dramatic military courier or aide-de-camp who in the glorious Napoleonic days or even as late as 1912 was often called upon to deliver on the battlefield a message or an order that might mean victory for his country. The aide-de-camp or courier, before the advent of radio, had to be able to ride a strange horse over hill and dale and over obstacles of every kind and, when his horse became exhausted or was shot from under him, had to proceed on foot by running cross-country; and when he came to a stream or river he had to cross it by swimming, and if he encountered an enemy he had to shoot his way through with his pistol; and then, at close quarters, he had to fight any remaining enemy with his sword, if he was finally to deliver the message. This might well be called the swashbuckling or motion-picture event, if it were considered literally; as a sports competition it was an excellent test of athletic versatility.

The modern pentathlon requires each contestant to run 4,000 meters cross-country, to ride a strange horse over a 5,000-meter steeplechase course with some 30 jumps, to compete in rapid-fire pistol shooting at a silhouette target, to fence with a dueling sword, and to swim 300 meters free style. With the exception of the fencing bouts or tests, contestants do not compete against each other but against time, just as a courier would in riding, running, or swimming to deliver his message. There are many people who believe that this is the most interesting event in the entire Olympic program. Certainly it is the greatest test of all-around athletic ability. There is, fortunately or unfortunately, one big element of luck in this event: the drawing of horses by lot. A contestant can draw a good, average, or bad horse, and the horse's performance will definitely affect his placement in the riding event.

The 1912 Olympics were the first in which the modern pentathlon was an official event. It was considered an individual event and only unofficially a team event of three contestants per nation until 1952, when it became a team event with an official team scoring system. Olympic medals, however, are still awarded to the first three individuals to finish, as well as to the first three teams.

Americans have traditionally excelled in riding, shooting, swimming, and running, yet no American has ever placed first in the individual standings, and the United States has never won the unofficial or official team championship in the 44-year history of this event. The military forces of many countries throughout the world became so enthusiastic about the event that an International Modern Pentathlon Association was formed, and for some twenty years, except during the last war, there have been annual world championships in the modern pentathlon. This has improved training techniques and performance. The last world championship was held in Switzerland in October of 1955; seventeen nations participated, with Hungary, Russia, Switzerland, Sweden, the United States, and Finland winning places, in that order. The writer helped coach the 1955 United States team and the 1924, 1936, and 1952 teams.

In the 1912 Olympics a slim young American cavalry lieutenant named George Patton, the first United States entrant in this event—who was to be known later, when he was a combat general in World War II, as "Old Blood and Guts"— finished fifth. Although Patton was a great shot, his use of a United States Army revolver while the Swedes used target pistols was too great a handicap in the competition. The Swedes practically monopolized the first modern pentathlon competition in Stockholm, winning first, second, third, and fourth places. Patton was twenty-first in shooting, seventh in swimming, fourth in fencing, sixth in riding, and third in running, for a general standing of fifth.

In 1920 the Swedes again won both the individual and the team titles, again taking the first four places. A Dane was fifth; and the American to finish best, Harold Rayner, was sixth. The other American competing, Robert Sears, placed eighth. By 1920 the pentathlon pistol shooting had been standardized and consisted of 20 rapid-fire shots, in four series of five, fired at turning silhouette targets at 25 meters with any type of .22-caliber pistol. As far back as the 1920 Olympics the United States entrants were falling behind, mainly because of their poor showing in riding. Major Rayner, for instance, who placed sixth in 1920, was fourth in running, fifth in shooting, twelfth in swimming, thirteenth in fencing— but fourteenth in riding.

73

The 1924 modern pentathlon was again won by the Swedes, who took the first three places. The first American entrant to finish, Lt. George Bare of the United States Army, was tenth. The French sent one of the most improved modern pentathlon teams to these Olympics, placing three men in the first twelve. Every one of the contestants representing the United States later became a combat general in World War II, and Major William C. Rose, the manager of the 1924 modern pentathlon team, became a major general and is today the chairman of the Modern Pentathlon Committee of the American Olympic Committee. The experiences of the American team in riding in this modern pentathlon demonstrated the great element of luck in the drawing for horses. Captain Harmon of the United States Cavalry, who was without doubt the best rider of the four American competitors, drew such a balky and unruly horse—an outlaw—that this horse should never have been permitted in the competition. Captain Harmon, a good enough rider to have won a place on the American Olympic equestrian team, took several minutes to break the horse before starting and by fighting him over every jump managed to finish the course, but with such poor time that he was 26th in a field of 40. Lt. Bare, on the other hand, probably the most inexperienced horseman or rider of the four Americans—an infantryman and a football player who weighed close to 190 pounds—drew one of the finest horses and rode a beautiful race to place sixth in riding. The equestrian event or course was rather unusual in the fact that wings at hurdles and jumps were used, although they were never used at any Olympics before or since.

Next to riding, fencing was the greatest obstacle to most American contestants in these Olympics, as was demonstrated by the fact that Lt. Bare, who placed first of the United States entrants and tenth in the competition, was fourteenth in shooting, fifteenth in swimming, sixth in riding, thirteenth in running, but twenty-seventh in fencing. All of the contestants were either officers or noncommissioned officers in the various armies of the countries participating.

In the 1928 Olympics the modern pentathlon was again won by the Swedes, with a first, second, and fourth; but Germany showed tremendous improvement with a third, fifth, and eighth. There were entries from many countries that had not competed before. Sweden, Germany, Great Britain, Holland, Denmark, Italy, Poland, Finland, the United States, Hungary, Belgium, France, Czechoslovakia, and Portugal were represented by teams. Again the United States did poorly, finishing fifteenth, nineteenth, and twentieth. The winner was Sven

Thofelt, now a colonel in the Swedish Army and Secretary-General of the International Modern Pentathlon Association. Major Harold Rayner, a pentathlon contestant and fencer in previous Olympics, was the manager of the United States team, and the team members were Richard W. Mayo, Peter C. Haines, and Audrey S. Newman—now all generals in the United States Army.

The 1932 Olympic games brought together contestants from ten nations and, as if by habit, Sweden again captured the team honors with a first, second, and fourth. The fourth, incidentally, was Sven Thofelt, Sweden's winner in 1928. Richard Mayo was the first American ever to win a medal in the modern pentathlon, placing third. Mayo's background combined perfectly the elements of the modern pentathlon: He was a field artilleryman, an expert horseman, and had been an intercollegiate fencing champion and an Olympic fencer; he was also a crack shot and winner of many shooting competitions. His weakness lay in the two events in which most of the Americans had been good in the past. Although he placed second in riding, fourth in fencing, and first in shooting, he was fourteenth in swimming and seventeenth in running. General Guy V. Henry of the United States Army was in charge of the team.

In 1936 the army and the United States Military Academy made an all-out effort to break the grip of the Swedes on this event. Twelve officers and fifteen cadets trained for months at the United States Military Academy. Several civilians had competed in the tryouts in 1932 and one competed in 1936— C. B. Smith of Los Angeles. Warrant Officer Jack Dimond of West Point was selected as coach, and Captain Mayo was manager. All three of the representatives of the United States placed in the first ten. According to the unofficial scoring system used in all Olympic sports at that time, the Germans properly laid claim to the team championship, since they had a first and a sixth. Sixteen nations participated. According to the point system later adopted as one of the methods of scoring this event as a team competition, the Germans won by 160 to 186. By using another method of arriving at a team score, based on the relative placings of all three team members, the United States could claim a win by 18 to 19 (low score indicating the winner). Lt. Charles Leonard, who scored an unprecedented 200 out of a possible 200 in the shooting event, won the silver medal for second place. Leonard got his second place by coming in first in shooting, sixth in swimming, seventh in running, tenth in fencing, but—as so often Americans do in this event—fell down to fifteenth in riding.

75

Lt. Gotthardt Handrick of the German Army finished some eight points ahead of Leonard and won first place. Captain Silvano Abba of the Italian Army was third and our old friend Sven Thofelt was fourth. This was his third Olympiad. Lt. Alfred Starbird was seventh and Lt. Frederick Weber was ninth. Weber was considered the iron man of the United States team, participating in the five events of the modern pentathlon and also in both épée individual and épée team in the fencing events at the same Olympics. He was first in fencing in this modern pentathlon competition and second in shooting; but twenty-second in riding, thirty-fourth in swimming, and twentieth in running.

The 1948 competition was won by a Swede, as usual. Finland, however, won the unofficial team title, although the Finns were given a close race by Sweden, which scored a first and a third. The third member of the Swedish team, however, was seventeenth, whereas the Finns placed fourth, fifth, and tenth. The individual championship was won by Capt. W. O. Grut of the Swedish cavalry. Second was Major George Moore of the United States, third Lt. Gardin of Sweden, fourth Lt. Vilkko of Finland, fifth Major Larkas of Finland, sixth Lt. Reim of Switzerland. The other American contestants, Lts. R. L. Gruenther and H. Baugh, finished eighth and thirteenth respectively. This pentathlon competition included, for the first time, a great many teams from Latin America—Argentina (first in the team riding), Brazil, Chile, Mexico, Cuba, and Uruguay. Lt. Col. Weber was the manager-coach of the United States team.

Competitors from Sweden, Hungary, Russia, Finland, the United States, Brazil, Great Britain, Argentina, Chile, Switzerland, France, Uruguay, Italy, Germany, Portugal, Belgium, and South Africa entered the modern pentathlon event in 1952. Hungary won the team championship—the first official team championship awarded on the basis of an official Olympic scoring system. Lt. L. Hall of Sweden won first in the individual; second was G. Benedek of Hungary, third I. Szondi of Hungary, and fourth I. K. Novikov of Russia. In fifth place was O. A. Mannonen, an unusually old contestant who improved so much in the succeeding three years that he was a very close second in the 1955 World Championship in Switzerland. The Russians served notice in the 1952 Olympics and in the annual World Championships in 1955 that they were going to go all-out and some day win this event. Constatin Szalnikov, of Kasachstan, Russia, a former riding instructor in the Soviet Army, won the world's individual championship in 1955, although Novikov, his compatriot, dropped to seventeenth.

The highest-ranking American in the 1952 Olympics was Capt. F. L. Denman, who placed sixth. The other entries, Pvt. W. T. McArthur and Capt. Guy Troy, placed eighth and fourteenth respectively. The first ten teams were Hungary, Sweden, Finland, the United States, Russia, Brazil, Chile, Argentina, Switzerland, and Great Britain, in that order.

It is expected that more nations will enter the modern pentathlon in 1956 than ever before. At least three pre-Olympic international meets in the modern pentathlon will improve the competition and performance in Melbourne. One, already run off in San Antonio, Texas, brought together teams from Latin America and the United States, with Mexico winning; one was held in Stockholm in August, and another in Switzerland in September. Poland, Czechoslovakia, Russia, Hungary and Yugoslavia have served notice that they will be at Melbourne in force in this event. It is interesting to note that this event was created by a Frenchman, that it was dominated for a long time by the Swedes—who brought it to Hungary and to Finland—and that today the Hungarians, Finns, and Russians believe they will win in 1956. It is also interesting to note that from the United States and from Mexico, which won this event in the Pan-American games of 1955, the modern pentathlon has spread to practically every country in Latin America. Just as other events make for friendly understanding between the peoples of the world, this particular competition has helped to establish friendly relations between the armies of the world; although civilians are, of course, not excluded from it.

Annual World Championships run by the International Modern Pentathlon Association now bring together teams from the United States, Latin America, Europe, and other continents. Cities vie for the opportunity to be hosts to these competitions, such as Rome, Rio de Janeiro, and Houston for 1957. Major General Gustaf Dyrssen of Sweden, Olympic winner in 1920, is President of the International Association.

CHAPTER X

ROWING AND SCULLING

EDGAR THE PEACEFUL, King of England from 944 to 975 A.D., wrote an unusual page in the history of rowing when in 973 he launched an eight-man crew consisting of eight kings—including the King of Scotland—all of whom had sworn submission and allegiance to him. Edgar, as coxswain, sat at the stern, while the crew of kings rowed him down the Dee River from his palace in Chester to the nearby church of St. John. Because he was racing to his own coronation, the river banks were crowded with spectators.

The story of rowing, however, goes much further back, and to another corner of the world. The Chinese were the first to engage in the sport of longboat racing on rivers and tidal waters and to this day Chinese festivals include races of dragon boats, great shallow-draft boats seventy-three feet long propelled by twenty-seven oarsmen. Paddle and oar racing in Siam and Burma go back to the dawn of history, and there are records of races between state barges in Egypt in 6000 B.C.

The ancient Greek author Thucydides refers to a sculling boat, as do the Romans Cicero and Livy, and although crew racing and sculling were not recorded events in the ancient Olympics, boat races probably did constitute part of the Panathenaic and Isthmian festivals. Vergil describes a boat race in vivid detail.

However, 2000 years later racing in oared craft had yet to be organized. Then, on August 1, 1715, a well-known comedian of the day, Thomas Doggett, posted a notice at London Bridge. This notice proposed a six-crew boat race from London Bridge to Chelsea for a prize and announced that the race would be held annually.

Since there were about ten thousand watermen on the reaches of the Thames River, it was more of a problem to select than to solicit contestants. The race was held, and has continued to the present day, supported by the proceeds of a sum which Thomas Doggett left in trust at his death to be administered by the Fishmongers' Company.

Thereafter river races were organized all over England—mostly on an informal basis. In America interest in crew racing resulted in the formation of several rowing clubs, and in 1834 the various clubs combined to form the Castle Garden Boat Club Association in New York, which sponsored the first organized boat races for six-oared shells on the Hudson River at Poughkeepsie in 1837. From this beginning crew races spread to the colleges, and the first intercollegiate Poughkeepsie Regatta was held in 1875.

However, it was not until rowing appeared in the Olympic games that the sport began to become popular all over the world. But if there was to be successful international competition, many obstacles had to be surmounted. In rowing there was not only the problem of standardizing the events to be contested—pairs, fours, sixes, eights—but also the problem of standardizing the equipment. Probably in no other sport has there been greater progress in equipment, and it has been extremely difficult to keep competition athletic rather than technological.

First came Clasper, an Oxford inventor who, in 1845, designed an oarlock which was suspended out over the water from light iron brackets. This changed the position of the fulcrum; and the oar, being essentially a lever of the second class, could be more effectively stroked by the rower. This principle was immediately seized on by all crews in England and America and, later, throughout the world. Then came Matt Taylor, in 1856, with the first keel-less boat in England, an innovation that changed rowing style to its present form. In 1856 smooth sides to boats were introduced, and in 1869 the greatest improvement of all, that of Walter Brown—the sliding seat. It was used for the first time in 1872, at Henley in England, the center of modern oared-craft racing. The sliding seat was almost immediately credited with taking half-minutes to minutes off the time records of various courses.

The history of sculling, which goes hand in hand with rowing, took a different turn in the United States, Canada, England, and Australia, where sculling first attained popularity in the latter part of the nineteenth century. The sport took an almost exclusively professional direction. Professional scullers raced locally for purses ranging from fifty to a hundred dollars, with side bets many times higher, and some international match purses are said to have been more than $60,000. However, due to excesses and corruption growing out of its tremendous popularity, professional sculling disappeared after 1900, except for a mild revival in the 1920's.

The Olympics revived interest in amateur sculling and rowing, and spread the sport to countries in which it had not been known before. Not counting the regatta involving only boats of the Greek Navy and Greek rowing and sculling clubs at the 1896 Olympics, by the time the first Olympic crew races were held in 1900, all the improvements and features of to-day's shells had been generally adopted. After a period of experimentation with varying lengths, oarsmen of eight-man boats had settled on a length of about 60 feet and a width of about two feet or a little less. Sliding seats with a slide of fif-teen to seventeen inches are the only kind ever used in modern competition.

The effect of the sliding seat in increasing efficiency cannot be minimized. Before the introduction of the slide, the oars-man's legs were used only to provide him with a means of bracing his feet for the application of the back and arm pull. Now, however, by sliding his seat nearer to the foot brace, the oarsman is in a position to gain a greater amount of leverage on the oar and also shift the burden of the pull to his great-est source of power, the legs. In all other respects the tech-nique of the stroke remains the same.

The first modern Olympics, the Athens games of 1896, presented rowing and sculling exhibitions, but no contests; but in 1900 the sport was represented by four competitive events on the program, including single sculls and pair oars, and fours and eights with coxswain. In the twenty years pre-ceding this Olympic competition, rowing had caught the fancy of many European nations, and, in fact, it was the newcomers to the sport who took three of the first places. Nine nations participated. In the race for fours with coxswain, Germany triumphed, while Holland, represented by Brandt and Klein, won the pair-oar championship. Barrelet of France won the single sculls. The venerable United States Vespers Club won the eight-oar title. France won the unofficial all-around title.

The roster of victors in the 1904 Olympics was not very international, with the United States winning three events. The Atlanta Boat Club of New York rowed a double sculls dem-onstration, while the Sewanhaka Boat Club captured the pair oar without coxswain title against competition. In the eights, the powerful and consistent Vespers crew was without compe-tition, and rowed a demonstration event. In the fours without coxswain, the Century Boat Club was victorious. The single sculls championship was won by Frank Greer, also of the United States.

At the 1906 Olympiad at Athens, the rowing was won by Italy, with Greece second, France third, and Belgium fourth. There were five events.

In 1908 Great Britain won the eight-oar race, the double

sculls, the four-oar shell with coxswain, the pair oar shell without coxswain, and the single sculls—won, in fact, all of the four events included in that year's Olympics. Few points were made by anyone except the all-winning British, but the United States and Belgium tied for second and Canada and Holland tied for fourth in all-around rowing and sculling. H. T. Blackstaffe of Britain won the most popular event of the time—the single sculls.

In 1912 there were twelve nations in the rowing and sculling events. The all-around point scoring shows Great Britain as the world's champion in rowing and sculling, followed by Germany, Denmark, Norway, Belgium, Sweden, Canada, and Russia. The eight-oared shell event and the single sculls were both won by the British.

Following the World War I hiatus, the Olympics were resumed in 1920 at Antwerp, with competitions for eights, fours with coxswain, pairs with coxswain, double sculls, and single sculls. The Naval Academy crew, because of its outstanding record during the 1920 intercollegiate season, was chosen to represent the United States, and embarked for Belgium with twenty-five men and their boat. On the same ship, the cruiser *Frederick,* were also the members of the Pennsylvania Barge Club, who were to seek the fours-with-coxswain title. John Kelly, the national rowing champion entered in the single sculls, and Paul Costello, also a member of the Vespers Boat Club, were on hand in Antwerp for the double sculls competition.

The races that year were rowed on the main canal between Antwerp and Brussels. In the preliminaries of the eights, the United States defeated Belgium, Norway defeated Czechoslovakia, England beat Switzerland, and France won over Holland. The French team was drawn for the semifinals by the United States, and was defeated by eight lengths. England won her semifinal match with Norway, and so, for the championship, it was once again a contest between the two oldest rivals.

The English crew was the Leander Club crew, and the race started off with a furious pace of 42 for Leander and 40 for Navy. Navy soon dropped the stroke to a long, powerful 38, but England maintained a relentless 40 and soon had her shell three-quarters of a length in front of the United States. After about 1600 meters of the 2000-meter course, Navy picked up some distance on Leander, and at about the 1850-meter mark the United States crew upped its 38 to match England's never-varying 40. The Leander Club had set itself too big a task, and the Americans won the race by a good half-length, shooting ahead of their opponents by about four feet every stroke at the finish. The time—6 minutes, 2 3/5 seconds—was a new world's record for 2000 meters.

In the four-oar with coxswain, the Swiss team navigated the 2000-meter course on the canal in 6 minutes, 54 seconds, establishing a new European record. The Pennsylvania Barge Club from the United States finished second, with Norway third.

There has probably never been a championship sculler more consistent than John B. Kelly was during those years immediately before and after the war, and the combination of Kelly and Paul V. Costello was invincible in the double scull championship. Despite the fact that Kelly had just rowed and won his single sculls championship thirty minutes before the race, he and Costello won over Italy, which was second, and France, which was third. When Kelly, father of Princess Grace of Monaco, won the single sculls, the Englishman in second place was J. Beresford, a popular oarsman who was to go on to make amateur and professional sculling and rowing history. The unofficial scoring on an all-around basis put the United States first, Italy second, Switzerland third, Great Britain fourth. In the finals of the other race, pair oar with coxswain, Italy held on to win after her two opponents had collapsed, after all three had been neck-and-neck 50 yards from the finish line.

Possibly the most romantic river in the world was the site of the 1924 Olympic crew races, for they were held on the Seine at the Argenteuil Basin, only several minutes from the Olympic stadium at Colombes, France. The 2000-meter course was a straight line, and the French went to considerable effort to transmit standings during each race to a master scoreboard at the main stands a hundred meters from the Paris-Rouen railroad bridge.

John B. Kelly and Paul V. Costello of the United States again won the double sculls. The race was close and exciting, as the French combination of Stock and Detton led all the way in the final four-contestant match, yielding only at the very finish. Switzerland was third, Brazil fourth. In the pair oared shell, Holland won by defeating France in the finals by a half yard. England was third. Switzerland and Italy, finishing one-two, showed their mastery of the pair oars with coxswain, with the United States third. Brazil forfeited, and France came in fourth. Belgium was eliminated in the preliminaries. This event had not been held before 1924. Four oars without coxswain was won by Great Britain, with Canada second and Switzerland third. In the fours with coxswain, no less than twelve nations were entered. Switzerland won the final; France was second, the United States third, and Italy fourth. Thirteen nations registered for the eight-oar race, with ten actually showing up. England, Canada, the United States, and Italy qualified for the finals. The United States eight, the Yale university crew undefeated in two years, was a sensation, having won its preliminary heat in the fabulous time of 5 minutes, 51 1/5 seconds. Although, in the final, because of wind and roughness, the time of the winning United States team was slowed to 6 minutes, 33 2/5 seconds, the exceptional class of the crew was obvious. Canada, which came in second, was 16 seconds slower than the United States eight. Italy was third and England a disappointing fourth. Beresford of England won the single sculls, with W. Gilmore of the United States second and J. Schneider of Switzerland third.

The IX Olympiad featured eighteen nations in rowing and sculling. Holland, the site of the 1928 Olympics, provided a course only 105 feet wide. This necessitated many heats and an extended period of tension for the record number of contestants in the various events. Nevertheless, the performances at this Olympiad were outstanding. The University of California crew, representing the United States, won the eight oar championships, but was forced to win five separate races to do so. The English eight was defeated in the finals, and Canada was awarded third place. The single sculls was won by an Australian, Bobby Pearce, whose father and grandfather were rowing champions of Australia, with Kenneth Myers of the United States second. Paul V. Costello raced without his two-time Olympic teammate, John Kelly, in the double sculls. However, Charles McIlvaine, a 24-year-old Philadelphia undertaker, showed himself a superb oarsman in Kelly's stead, and this event also went to the United States, with Canada and Austria second and third in that order. Italy, Switzerland, and Poland came in one-two-three in the four oars with coxswain, while England, the United States, and Italy finished in that order in the fours without coxswain. In the pair without coxswain, Germany beat England and the United States. Switzerland took the pair with coxswain, with France and Belgium next. The over-all unofficial title went to the United States, with Great Britain, Germany, Italy, and Switzerland close behind.

In 1932 Los Angeles brought good luck to the United States team, which scored its most resounding unofficial rowing championship since 1904. There was plenty of competition, with thirteen nations represented. The British were second, with the Germans and Italians tied for third. The site of the competitions was the Long Beach Marine Stadium, about 30 miles from Los Angeles, and the final eight-oared race was like a page straight from a home-town movie script, for it was the University of California crew which represented the United States. Over 130,000 people were on hand for the final in this event, a titanic competition of great crews in superb physical condition. The California crew, accustomed to the California sun, nosed out the Italians by a fraction of a boat length. Canada and Great Britain followed in order. Germany was successful in the four with coxswain, once again bringing despair to the desperate Italian rowers, who were beaten only in the last hundred yards, to lose by a foot. Philadelphia, which has produced many sculling champions, came through again for the United States with the double-scull team of Kenneth Myers and W. E. Garrett Gilmore. They defeated Germany, Canada, and Italy, who finished in that order, in the final heat. For the first time, Japan entered a crew.

Bobby Pearce of Australia won the single sculls again; he had not been defeated in almost six years. W. G. Miller of the United States and G. R. Doublas of Uruguay were second and third.

Another Philadelphia crew—Shauers, Kieffer, and Jennings (coxswain) won first place for the United States in the pair oars with coxswain, Poland, France, and Brazil earning the next places. Jack Beresford (four-time winner of the Diamond sculls, single sculls, Olympic champion in 1924 and four-time Olympic regatta competitor) was one of the crew of the British four without coxswain which won in that event, defeating Germany, Italy, and the United States. Great Britain also won the pair without coxswain.

The XI Olympiad featured twenty-three nations in rowing, with Germany winning in a startling and impressive manner. Writing in the official 1936 United States Olympic Report, United States manager Henry Penn Burke reports: "Our previous opinion of German oarsmen was that the majority were mediocre and inclined to be overweight, but their oarsmen now are trained down like greyhounds. They don't look like the same breed at all." And they weren't. In the double sculls, they were second only to Great Britain, followed by Poland, France, the United States, and Australia. Jack Beresford, one of the greatest oarsmen of modern times, competing in his fifth Olympiad, was one of the gold medalists in Britain's win in double sculls. Germany won the pair-oared shell without coxswain, beating out Denmark, Argentina, Hungary, Switzerland, and Poland. Then they proved they could also win the same race *with* coxswain.

This time, Germany set down Italy (fast becoming the per-
ennial second crew of Olympic matches), France, Denmark,
Switzerland, and Yugoslavia. It was the same story in four-
oar shells, both with and without coxswain. Germany was
almost unbeatable, taking first in both these races. In fact,
with Pearce of Australia no longer an amateur and therefore not competing, Germany even won the single scull
championship. It was the first time in 36 years that this
race was not won by a sculler from the United States, Great
Britain, or Australia.

The finish of the eight-oar race in 1936 at Grünau remains the most exciting in the history of the games. The
United States eight-oared crew was from the University of
Washington, and eager to gain the fifth straight eight-oar
title for the United States. And Italy was eager to avenge
her heartbreaking loss at Long Beach in 1932, where she lost
by a fraction of a boat length. And Germany was on the
verge of sweeping all the rowing events. When these three
leading crews in the final flashed across the finish line, the
thousands of spectators along the banks could not tell which
of the three had won. Then the order of finish was posted:
the United States first, Italy second, Germany third. Less
than one second separated the first and third crews.

It was 1948 before the world was ready for the XIV
Olympiad. London was the site, and for the crew and rowing events, this meant the most famous rowing course in
the world—Henley. The games drew a record number of
crews, with 27 countries represented. Racing had never
been more international. The Italians overcame their old
second-place jinx in many events, winning the unofficial
over-all championship for the first time since 1906. Italy
won the four without coxswain, defeating Denmark and
the United States in the finals. She came in third in the
pair without coxswain, behind Great Britain and Switzerland, and second in the pair with coxswain, beating Hungary
but losing to Denmark. Indeed, it was Denmark which
showed the greatest improvement in these Olympics, taking
one first place, two seconds, and a third. The University of
Washington crew represented the United States in the four
with coxswain, and beat Switzerland and Denmark. Another
West Coast crew, the University of California, repeated the
United States' win in the eight-oar shell for the sixth time.
Great Britain was second and Norway third. Denmark's other
second place was in the double sculls, won this time by Great
Britain, with Uruguay third. The single-scull title went back
to Australia, with Uruguay second.

The XV Olympiad indicated the general growth of rowing and sculling in many ways. The number of nations entered in the rowing events in 1952 was a record—there were thirty-three nations competing for seven titles. Russia made her first appearance on the water in Olympic competition since 1912 and, although she won only one event, showed great promise in many events. In the eight-oar shells, the United States took its seventh consecutive Olympic championship, with the Naval Academy crew as its representative. However, it was the Russian eight which doggedly hung on to come in second, 5 2/5 seconds behind the winner, a splendid effort in this first year of Olympic competition for the U.S.S.R. Australia was third, with Great Britain and Germany fourth and fifth. In the double sculls, Russia was also second, this time to Argentina. Uruguay placed third. France took first place in the coxed pairs, winning over Germany, Denmark, Italy, and Sweden.

For the first time, the United States won the coxswainless pairs, beating Belgium, Switzerland, Great Britain, and France in the finals. Czechoslovakia took the coxed fours, with Switzerland second, the United States third, and Great Britain and Finland next. The 1952 Olympiad saw Great Britain fall into an uncharacteristic rowing slump, failing to place once, but coming in fourth in four races. Yugoslavia won the coxswainless fours, with J. Tjukalov of Russia, to the great surprise of the rowing world, winning the single sculls crown after two grueling races with Wood of Australia and John B. Kelly, Jr. of the United States. Wood came in second, but Kocerka of Poland was third. Thus Russia and Poland, using the experience and techniques of the British, Americans, and Australians, developed outstanding athletes to win, in their turn, single scull Olympic honors. Denmark was a disappointment in these Olympics, after such a promising showing four years before, gaining only one third place.

The United States won the over-all point score in rowing and sculling in 1952, with Russia second, France third, and Argentina and Czechoslovakia tied for fourth. Although the competition was unusually keen, there was great sportsmanship and unusual friendship shown by the contestants in rowing and sculling at these Olympics, especially between the Russians and the Americans.

With Australia, a country who has produced some of the world's greatest oarsmen, as host, the XVI Olympiad will undoubtedly be a focal point for the interest of rowers and scullers throughout the world. Melbourne expects to see many records broken as old competitors seek to repeat past successes and new ones seek to surprise the world with their first victories. Will the Russians catch up and go from second to first in over-all points? Will Tjukalov repeat, as Pearce of Australia did, for two successive single-scull Olympic wins? Will the United States win its eighth consecutive Olympic victory in the eight-oar crew? Whatever happens, there will be little change from the races described by Vergil:

"Their bent arms churn the waters into foam.
The sea gapes open, by the oars uptorn.
With shouts and cheers of eager partisans
The woodlands ring, the shelter'd beach rolls up
The sound, the hills re-echo with the din."

CHAPTER XI

SHOOTING

SHOOTING IS the sport of marksmanship with small firearms. It includes bulls-eye or silhouette-target shooting with the pistol and rifle and shooting with hunting weapons at trap, skeet, or running-deer targets. The shooting competition in the Olympics has varied a great deal. Marksmanship is the direct descendant and the modern counterpart of archery, an earlier and less lethal form of warfare. Archery played a major part in early human history, from the ancient Pharaohs to the Spanish Armada in 1588. The English, although the greatest bowmen in the world, discarded archery as obsolete in their defense preparations against the Spanish invasion. Archery was once featured in the modern Olympics, but has been discontinued. Shooting, however, remains.

In the United States, competitive shooting dates from a period shortly after the Civil War. The National Rifle Association, which grew out of competitions between various units of the National Guard throughout the states, was organized in 1871. The first act of the organization was to try to standardize the targets and distances. The N.R.A. is still in control of the sport in the United States, governing competition in both rifle and pistol. An indication of the great early interest in the sport can be found in the fact that a championship held in 1872 at Creedmoor, Long Island, in which a team of crack shots from Ireland participated, attracted 100,000 spectators, most of whom were taken from New York to the ranges in special trains. The 1952 schedule called for a free pistol 50-meter contest, a rapid-fire or silhouette-pistol at 25 meters match, a free rifle at 300 meters, a small-bore rifle at 50 meters shoot (the free rifle and small-bore rifle being at the standing, kneeling, and prone positions), the small-bore rifle prone at 50 meters test, and the clay-pigeon and running-deer competitions with hunting weapons. (In the past, there has been a greater variety of events in the shooting competition than there has been in any other sport contested in the Olympic games.)

Eight countries sent contestants to compete in this sport at the 1896 games in Athens, but twenty-eight years later, in 1924, 20 nations sent contestants to compete in the various shooting events at Paris, and fifty-six years later, in 1952, there were contestants from 38 countries—ten from the Western Hemisphere, twenty-two from Europe (including Russia and such smaller powers as Monaco), and six from Asia, Africa, or Oceania. Shooting with hunting weapons is popular in many countries widely separated, and is —partly for that reason—a difficult sport to standardize.

Shooting is one of the most complicated of Olympic sports to follow. When one considers the pistol, one must think of revolvers, pistols, and target pistols, and one must also think of bulls-eye targets and silhouette targets, slow fire and rapid fire, as well as various distances or ranges. When one considers rifle marksmanship, one has to think of a wide variety of "free" rifles, military rifles, and sporting or hunting rifles and shotguns, miniature or small-bore rifles, slow fire or rapid fire (as well as slow-fire or rapid-fire types of targets and moving targets), not to mention distances or ranges. This very wealth of possible tests of skill has caused confusion in the sport for many years.

In the 1896 Olympics there were four shooting events: any-rifle individual, which was won by Orphanidhis of Greece; any target revolver, 30 meters, which was won by S. Paine of the United States; automatic pistol (25 meters) individual, which was won by Phrangoudhis of Greece; and revolver individual (25 meters), which was won by J. Paine, the brother of S. Paine, of the United States. In all-around rankings, the Greeks won the unofficial team championship.

In 1900 increased interest in the sport led to the inclusion of seven events: automatic pistol or revolver individual; pistol or revolver team; any target pistol, 50 meters; clay-bird shooting individual; running-deer shooting, single shot, individual; army rifle individual; and army rifle team. Although the Swiss won more titles, the French scored enough points to win the unofficial championship in shooting. There was no shooting at the 1904 Olympics.

In 1906 pretty much the same events were run off, but one more of them was doubled up as both an individual and team competition, making a total of eight events. The French won again.

By 1908, when Great Britain won the all-around championship, the number of events had been increased to fourteen, with clay-bird shooting individual and team, running-deer shooting individual and team, pistol or revolver individual and team, and rifle individual and team, army rifle individual and team, miniature rifle (or, as it is now called, small-bore rifle) individual and team, free rifle 50 meters, and rifle at odd distances.

The 1912 Olympic shooting events were won by Sweden, and in these competitions at Stockholm the number of events was increased to sixteen, pretty evenly distributed between the non-sporting and the sporting.

In 1920, for the first time, the United States won the all-around championship, although determining the winner was almost a job for an adding machine. There were nineteen events, and contestants from nineteen countries. There were both individual and team matches with rifle, pistol, and shotgun at various ranges.

At the 1924 Olympic games the military events were dropped and there were only ten events. This simplification indicated a tendency to standardize the shooting events. Twenty nations sent competitors, with the United States repeating its 1920 victory. Sergeant Morris Fisher of the United States won the any-rifle individual event in 1920 (and again in 1924) and he was the 1923 international world's champion in shooting. As in other sports, the Olympics had led to international competitions and world's championships between Olympics. A running-deer-shooting expert from Norway, Lilloe-Olsen, won the running-deer-shooting double-shot individual in both 1920 and 1924, and also helped Norway win the team championship in 1920—although the Norwegians were nosed out in 1924 by Great Britain. On the United States team was a 17-year-old named Dinwiddie, from Washington, D. C., who broke the Olympic record in the miniature rifle individual, only to come in second to Charles DeLisle of France, who shot 398 out of a possible 400.

There were no shooting competitions in the 1928 Olympics because there was a conflict in the International Olympic

Committee about the definition of an amateur in shooting. The committee members could not resolve their disagreements in time for the Olympic games and cancelled the shooting event. But at a meeting of the International Olympic Committee at Oslo in February of 1935, it was agreed to admit as eligible for competition any marksman who had not received a money prize for shooting since August 1, 1934.

The matter of amateur status again came up to plague the various committees in the Olympic competition, not only in 1928 but also in 1932 and 1948, the crux of this conflict being that since shooting is not a spectator sport there is no reason for any competitive shot to turn "pro" except as an exhibition shot for arms or ammunition manufacturers. It had been the custom in the United States, and in many other countries, to offer small cash prizes in shooting tournaments, but these prizes were not valuable enough to reimburse the winner for his expenses or his equipment and could scarcely place him in the class of a professional. However, the acceptance of even one dollar is sufficient, under normal Olympic rules, to make any marksman accepting cash prizes a professional. The Olympic rules, it was believed by the United States and certain other countries, should be interpreted to mean that any country could enter its best marksmen if it excluded exhibition shots actually employed by the munitions industry. Certainly most people agreed that the hundreds of competitive sharpshooters who had accepted past cash prizes as amateurs instead of medals, hams, or turkeys should not be banned from future competition. Most people also agreed that cash prizes should be banned in the future.

In 1932 shooting was back on the Olympic schedule, but in a very restricted way. Only small-bore or miniature rifle individual at 50 meters and figure shooting at six targets with a pistol were included. This abbreviated schedule of two events brought complaints from nearly every country, including the United States, that had competed in this sport in earlier Olympics. The influence of the military in the Axis countries was quite evident in the 1932 Olympics —Italy and Germany capturing the first four places in the pistol shoot, although the honors in the rifle competition, which wound up in a number of ties, were fairly well spread. Competitors from Sweden and Hungary tied for first, with the Swede winning the shoot-off; a Hungarian and an Italian tied for second place, actually third, with the Hungarian winning the shoot-off. Italy won the unofficial team championship.

In the 1936 Olympic games a number of events that had been contested in earlier Olympics were reinstated. The unofficial team championship was won by Germany, with Sweden second, Denmark third, and France and Hungary following. The performance of the competitors in these Olympics was exceptionally good. The target pistol event, at 50 meters, was won by Torsten Ullman of Sweden, who broke the Olympic and world record (his record is still the world's record), making a score of 559 out of a possible 600. Erich Krempel of Germany was second and Charles de Jammonnières of France was third. The American who finished highest in the scoring, Elliott Jones, was sixth. The automatic pistol or revolver 25-meter event was won by two Germans; Torsten Ullman of Sweden, who placed first and broke the world's record in the other pistol event, was third. The miniature rifle at 50 meters was won by Willie Rogeberg of Norway, who established an Olympic and world's record by shooting 300 out of a possible 300; in second place was Dr. Ralf Berzsenyi of Hungary; Wladyslaw Karas of Poland was third.

There was general dissatisfaction expressed by many of the countries with the events chosen for championship competition. It was pointed out that, with the greatest shots of the world gathered for competition, it was ridiculous to have only two events in pistol and one in small-bore rifle, and that something like the old schedule should be brought back—so that the test for the Olympic championship would include a variety of events with all types of weapons.

The 1948 Olympic games, after a hiatus of twelve years, brought many nations together in the shooting competitions. Sweden won the unofficial all-around championship, with the United States second, Switzerland third, Finland fourth, Czechoslovakia and Norway tied for fifth, Peru (a newcomer) sixth, and Hungary seventh. Colonel Roy D. Jones was in charge of the United States Olympic pistol team for the third time, and Major General Milton A. Reckord was in charge of the United States rifle team committee, as he had been in 1932 and 1936. Teams from 22 nations participated in the shooting events in the 1948 Olympics. The free pistol was won by a Peruvian, with H. L. Benner of the United States tying for third. In the small-bore rifle competition at 50 meters, the United States placed first and second, A. E. Cook and W. Tomsen being tied with 599 out of 600. In the rapid-fire pistol a Hungarian, K. Takacs, won, with Diaz Valiente of Argentina second and Lundquist of Sweden third. Torsten Ullman of Sweden, who won the 50-meter pistol in the 1936 Olympics, not only came in third in that event in 1948 but also scored fourth in the rapid-fire pistol. The free-rifle 300-meter competition was won by E. Grunig of Switzerland; second was Janhonen of Finland, third Rogeberg of Norway. Swanson, the American who ranked highest, came in tenth.

In the 1952 Olympic games there was a better rounded program that included more events than had been included in many years. As a result of the better rounded program there was more interest, more competitors from more countries, and better performance. The events were: free pistol, 50 meters; silhouette, or rapid-fire pistol, 25 meters; free rifle, 300 meters; small-bore rifle, 50 meters; small-bore rifle, prone, 50 meters; clay pigeons; and running deer. The unofficial team championship was won by Norway, with Russia second, Hungary third, the United States fourth, Rumania fifth, and Canada sixth. Thirty-one nations—more than ever before—entered the Olympic shooting competitions. H. Benner of the United States won the free pistol 50 meters, the first win in pistol shooting for the United States in 32 years. He made a higher score than any other American had ever made. A. Jackson of the United States came in third in the small-bore rifle prone event. A nation new to the shooting competition—the U.S.S.R.—showed great promise and will undoubtedly be a strong challenger at Melbourne. Norway was the only country to have two winners in 1952, the winners of single championships being the United States, Hungary, Russia, Rumania, and Canada. Two Olympic records and one world's record were broken.

It is reported that forty nations have entered teams in the 1956 Melbourne games. The shooting competitions to be held there are designed to appeal to target and sports sharpshooters alike.

CHAPTER XII

SWIMMING AND DIVING

MAN FIRST learned to swim either by instinct or by watching animals go into a swimming motion in the water in order not to drown. Just how far back swimming goes as a recreational or competitive sport is not known. Early mosaics and drawings in the Middle East show men swimming and using the "dog" stroke. The Greeks and Romans were able swimmers and divers. Plato stated that the man who did not know how to swim or dive was uneducated. History tells us that Caesar was a great swimmer, that Charlemagne was noted for his swimming stroke—which might have been the forerunner of the crawl—and Louis XI of France often swam in the Seine. It remained for the English, however, according to the records, to take up swimming as a competitive sport.

In 1837, in London, there were competitive swimming exhibitions and six swimming pools located in the city. In 1844 some North American Indians were brought over to London to swim in competition and they beat everyone, with an Indian named Flying Gull allegedly swimming the length of a 130-foot pool in 30 seconds. These Indians, it was remarked, swam in an "uncivilized" or "different" manner, while the "civilized" British swam the breast stroke. In the late nineteenth century, two great swimmers, Captain Matthew Webb, the first man to swim the English Channel, in 1875, and J. Arthur Trudgen, began to make swimming history. Trudgen, who had gone to South America in 1860, learned a stroke there from the natives which was a double overhand and which he made so famous it was named after him. However, Trudgen had failed to observe that the South American Indians kicked their legs, and therefore taught his pupils the double overhand but had them retain the scissor-like movement of the legs.

Although Trudgen should be credited with a great advance in the technique of swimming, the greatest step forward in the sport was wrought by the remarkable Cavill family, who introduced the Australian Crawl to the world. In 1878, Frederick Cavill, a competitive swimmer, left England for Australia, where he had six sons and built and operated swimming "tanks" and taught swimming. The Cavills studied the natives and finally found that their leg action involved a "kick" generating extra speed. The Cavills introduced this new method of swimming to the English in Australia and it became known as the Australian Crawl. Richard Cavill, the eldest son, went to England and used the crawl to win championships. He coached the British to many wins in international competitions. Another son, Sydney, came to the United States as a swimming coach and taught the crawl to America. He was swimming coach of San Francisco's Olympic Club for 25 years. In the United States, a man named Daniels, of the New York Athletic Club, had been using the Trudgen stroke, but on seeing the style brought to the States by Sydney Cavill, began to experiment with a kick timed to the stroking of the arms, with the result that he developed the American Crawl of today.

This history of the early development of swimming is part of the saga of the earliest swimming competitions of the Olympics. The Olympic games, more than any other factor, accelerated the technical advancement and popularity of swimming as a competitive sport throughout the world.

The same Daniels represented the United States in the 1904 Olympic games, where he was third in the 50-yard dash, second in the 100-meter free style, first in the 220-yard free style, and first in the 440-yard free style. He broke all existing records and won 33 National AAU Championships, from 50 yards to the mile, and won four Olympic titles, reaching his peak in 1910, when he lowered his world's record for 100 yards to 54.8 seconds.

Before Daniels' time, the British had dominated swimming, with a slight interruption by Hungary. The 1896 unofficial swimming team championship of the Olympics went to Hungary, but by 1900 the English were in command again. In 1904, with the assistance of Daniels, English coaching, and the Australian Crawl, the United States won the aquatic title, if diving events are included in the scoring. The 1906 and 1908 unofficial championships were won by Hungary and Great Britain respectively. In 1911 a Hawaiian, Duke Kahanamoku, arrived in San Francisco from Honolulu with a great reputation as a swimmer, and was eligible for membership on the United States Olympic team. It was immediately noticed that he was using the latest crawl stroke, and upon being asked who had taught it to him, he said that he had no teacher but that his people had been using this stroke for many generations, if not centuries.

The 1912 Olympic aquatic events were won by Germany. Many nations competed, and drew capacity crowds. The

Hawaiian, Duke Kahanamoku, was the central attraction and individual star of the meet—breaking the 100-meter record of the famous Daniels, who had won this event in 1906 and 1908. G. R. Hodgson of Canada was the surprise winner of both the 400 meters and the 1500 meters. An American won the backstroke, and Germany won the 200-meter and 400-meter breast stroke and the springboard dive. Australia won the 800 meter. The Swedes won the high dive and Great Britain repeated her 1908 victory in water polo. For the first time, women's swimming events were featured: the 100-meter, which was won by Fanny Durack of Australia; the 400-meter relay team, which was won by Great Britain; and the high dive, which was won by Greta Johansson of Sweden.

In 1920, for the first time, the actual swimming competitions were won by the United States. Our 1904 unofficial team victory had been due to two firsts, one second, and two thirds in diving. In 1920, however, eleven of the sixteen aquatic events were won by the United States, which in addition succeeded in winning seven second, six third, and eight fourth places. In five events the United States won the first three places. The most successful individual competitors were Norman Ross of Chicago and Ethelda Bleibtrey of New York, with three gold medals each, and Duke Kahanamoku of Hawaii, with two. The victory of the United States was overwhelming and unique. Sweden was second, England third, Australia fourth, followed by Belgium and Finland. Despite the terrifically cold water—around 55 degrees—representatives of the United States established four world's records and six Olympic records. The American team included seven Hawaiians. In water polo, the temperature of the water was so low that many of the regular United States team could not play in successive games. Great Britain won, the United States taking fourth place.

The VIII Olympiad, held in Paris in July of 1924, presented to the world the greatest swimming and water polo teams ever formed in the history of American swimming. Duke Kahanamoku was elected captain of the swimming team, which won the team championship, and Hal Vollmer of the New York Athletic Club was chosen as captain of the water polo team. Evidences of the spread of swimming competition were seen at the 1924 Olympics, for a number of countries sent swimming teams for the first time—including Japan. The star of the American team was Johnny Weissmuller of the Illinois A. C. He succeeded in winning the 100-meter and the 400-meter free-style events, breaking the records in both. He also was anchor man on the victorious relay team, which also established a world's record, and played the final game of water polo, in which the Americans finished in third place. Al White of Stanford University won both the springboard and high fancy diving events. Warren Kealoha of Hawaii repeated his victory in the Antwerp games by winning the backstroke event in world's record time. Robert Skelton of the Illinois A. C. broke the world's record in winning the 200-meter breast stroke. The Misses Ethel Lackie of the Illinois A. C., Martha Norelius of New York, Sybil Bauer of the Illinois A. C., Elizabeth Becker of Atlantic City, and Carolyn Smith of Cairo, Illinois, won the 100-meter free style, 400-meter free style, 100-meter backstroke, fancy diving, and high plain diving, respectively. The head swimming coach of this successful aggregation was William Bachrach of the Illinois A. C.

The 1928 swimming competition brought together more nations and more contestants and produced better competition. The American team won. It was again coached by William Bachrach, ably assisted by Robert Kiphuth, who went on to achieve one of the greatest coaching records in America in any sport, leading Yale University to 445 dual swimming meet victories out of 457, from 1918 to 1953. The stars of the American team were Johnny Weissmuller, George Kojac, Buster Crabbe, and Ray Ruddy. Another great diving star was presented by the United States in the person of Peter Des Jardins of Miami Beach, who won both the springboard diving and the high diving. One of the greatest threats to American supremacy in diving was Simaika of Egypt, who placed second in high fancy diving and third in springboard diving. Simaika, although an Egyptian, owed much of his prowess in his sport to American diving experience and coaching; he had received all of his training and acquired all of his competitive experience in the United States. (The winners of the various events can be found in the appendix.)

In 1932 Robert Kiphuth became head coach of the swimming team, and took twenty-seven men swimmers and divers, eleven water polo players, and twenty women swimmers and divers to Los Angeles. The Olympic competition lasted eight days, with contests every morning and every afternoon. The seating capacity of the swimming stadium was 10,000, but there was a sellout for every session every day. The final point score, which was very close until the very last day, was Japan 87, United States 71. Japan won five firsts, four seconds, and two thirds. The outstanding individual performance in swimming was Buster Crabbe's winning of the 400-meter race. Jean Taris of France, the world's record holder at this dis-

96

tance, led by over ten yards at the halfway mark. Crabbe won in the last stroke by 1/10 of a second, in a new Olympic record. Crabbe now ranks with Daniels, Kahanamoku, Ross, and Weissmuller in the history of American swimming. In the diving, the United States asserted its supremacy, with Mickey Riley and Dutch Smith winning first and second in both diving events and contributing 30 of the United States' 71 points.

The United States won the first points in water polo it had scored since 1904, finishing a very close third behind the German team. Hungary was first. One of the outstanding features of the swimming meet in Los Angeles was the extraordinary work of one of the officials. Captain Roy E. Davis of Chicago did not make one false start during the entire competition, an accomplishment believed unequaled in the history of Olympic swimming.

The American women swimmers did better than the men, in winning six of the seven events, losing only the breast stroke (to Australia). The United States women also won first, second, and third places in both dives, and the women's final point total was 96. Australia and Great Britain tied for second place. The individual star of the women's swimming was Miss Helene Madison, who won two events, the only double winner for either men or women. It was a fitting climax to a short but remarkable swimming career in which she established new records for every free-style swimming event from 50 yards to a mile. It would be improper to omit mention of Miss Eleanor Holm, who won the 100-meter backstroke in 1932 but was prevented from representing the United States at Berlin in 1936, even though she was a member of the team, because she engaged in some champagne drinking on the boat en route to Europe. She later became a star in the entertainment world.

Great advances in swimming technique were made during the period 1932-1936 because there was a great deal of international championship competition. The United States accepted Japanese invitations for some of our star swimmers to visit Japan in 1934 and for fourteen American champion swimmers and divers to visit Japan in 1935. Japan, after its swimming victory in 1932, had made swimming a national sport, and the experience gained by the American groups in Japan was of great value.

Kiphuth was again head coach of the United States Olympic team in 1936. The swimming events were held in a magnificent swimming stadium, with a seating capacity of 20,000 and standing room for 5000 more. The popularity of swimming was indicated by the fact that the stadium was sold out for all of the swimming competitions. According to the host nation, over 100,000 persons had to be turned away. There were some difficulties in the officiating, due to the fact that not enough persons could stand in a line facing the finish line, so that there was considerable confusion and the judges' placement rulings were not always in agreement with the photograph of the finish.

At this meet there was tremendous anxiety and nervousness on the part of Japanese and American swimmers, who both expected to win the overall championship. They had raced against each other so often that they watched each other so carefully they did not perform up to their standards. This enabled, for instance, the Hungarian, Csik, who was in the outside lane in the 100-meter final, to swim his own race and win in very slow time, much slower than the record set by Peter Fick, who finished fourth. Jack Medica won the 400-meter race, establishing a new Olympic record and beating two great competitors, Uto and Makino of Japan. Flanagan of Miami, who had beaten Medica several times in the United States, swam a nervous and disappointing race. The Japanese were too much for the Americans in the 1500-meter, and although Medica was able to win second place, the Japanese won first, third, and fourth. The Japanese also won the relay. The 200-meter breast stroke was another disappointment for the United States. Higgins of the United States, the American record holder, was beaten by two Japanese and a German.

In diving the United States again showed world superiority.

The swimming competition in the 1936 Olympics demonstrated a new high in world interest in competitive swimming, with thirty-six countries represented.

In swimming and diving combined, the United States nosed out Japan by a score of 43 to 41, with Hungary third and Germany fourth. However, if, as the Japanese claim, a swimming championship involves only points scored in swimming, with diving and water polo left out, then the Japanese repeated their 1932 win in 1936.

In water polo the United States was again disappointed, although it must be said that the caliber of water polo had been improving by leaps and bounds. The American team just could not compare with the Hungarian teams that had been winning this event. Hungary won again in 1936.

In the women's swimming the United States, by the slimmest of margins, continued its 16-year reign as top nation in this event. Holland was second, only 2½ points behind. The Dutch figured in every final and won all but one—

the 20-meter breast stroke taken by Miss Maehata of Japan. The Dutch claim, quite reasonably, to have won in the women's swimming, for without counting the diving events, in which the United States won five out of six places, the Dutch women's team far outscored the United States. The number of wins scored by Holland's women swimmers was quite unexpected, although four members of the Dutch team held a total of eleven world's records. Willie den Ouden, who held seven world's records, placed only fourth in the 100-meter free style, but was a member of the winning relay team. She did not swim up to her best form at Berlin.

After twelve years without any Olympics, the swimming competition at the 14th Olympics in London in 1948 showed a drop in the number of nations engaged in the sport—only 21. The United States won, with plenty to spare, the over-all aquatic competition, with 145 points for the men and 82 points for the women. The nearest nation in points for men was Hungary, with 30, and on the women's side Denmark, with 46. The men won all six championships, and only three of the eighteen men on the swimming team failed to reach the finals in their events. Of the eighteen swimming medals, the United States won eleven—six firsts, four seconds, and one third. In diving the United States won first, second, and third in the 3-meter springboard, and first and second in the high board. Robert Kiphuth was again coach of the United States team.

Notwithstanding this great showing in both swimming and diving, our showing in water polo was, as usual, disappointing, and we were eliminated. The final placings in water polo were: first, Italy; second, Hungary; third, the Netherlands; fourth, Belgium; fifth, Sweden; sixth, France; seventh, Egypt; and eighth, Spain.

In the women's diving the star was Vicky Draves, who won both diving events. Many people believe, however, that equally deserving of stardom was Ann Curtis, who won the 400-meter free style after losing a very close decision in the 100 meter. Miss Curtis was credited with a great performance when she swam anchor in the 400-meter relay, overcoming a seemingly insurmountable lead and bringing the United States team an Olympic title.

At the 15th Olympic games in 1952 in Helsinki, forty-four countries, a new high, competed in the swimming, with the United States again winning the over-all title. The coach of the United States team was Matt Mann of Michigan. The competition was keen, the number of competitors large, and the attendance a sellout. Every Olympic record was shattered during the meet. The United States men won six out of eight swimming and diving events and lost the other two by a whisker. France, with contestants in every one of the finals, was always a great threat. Japan qualified many men, but failed to win any gold medals for the first time in many years. Hungary, South Africa, Australia, England, Russia, Czechoslovakia, and Brazil—a newcomer—all showed capable performances, with their contestants reaching the finals.

The greatest thrill of the swimming competition at the 1952 Olympics, from the standpoint of the United States, was the 800-meter relay. The United States team—Moore, Woolsey, Konno, and McLane—did a tremendous job in beating a crack Japanese team which used the unusual strategy of swimming its men in reverse order of ability. McLane's anchor leg put the eventual winners, the United States, in the lead for the first time.

The impression of all who witnessed the meet was that swimming technique, coaching, and performance outside of the United States were improving rapidly. The facilities of other nations are consistently getting better and their interest is increasing. It is not just one nation, like Japan, to whom we must look for our keenest competition. We must now take cognizance of tremendously growing strength in all the Scandinavian countries, as well as in France, England, Australia, South Africa, Italy, Russia, and Brazil.

Major Sammy Lee of the U. S. Army broke an all-time Olympic record in diving by repeating with a championship in the highboard diving in 1952, having won the same event in the 1948 Olympics. This is the only double in this event in the history of the modern Olympics. In water polo a number of new nations participated, but Hungary, as usual, won. The order of finish after the winning Hungarians was: Yugoslavia, Italy, the United States, the Netherlands, Belgium, Russia, and Spain. There was an entertaining diversion in the swimming competition: The first act of France's Jean Boiteux after he had won the 400-meter free style was to assist his father out of the pool, into which the old man had impetuously leaped to tender his son prompt and effusive Parisian congratulations.

The women's team starred Pat McCormick, who won two gold medals in the two diving events, but in general the American women did not show up as well as usual. The 100-meter free style was won by K. Szoke of Hungary; second was J. Termeulen of the Netherlands, third J. Temes of Hungary. In the 200-meter breast stroke, E. Szekely of Hungary was first, E. Novak of Hungary second, H. Gordon of Great

Britain third. The winners in the 100-meter backstroke were: first, J. Harrison of South Africa; second, G. Wielema of the Netherlands; third, J. Stewart of New Zealand. In the 400-meter free style, first was V. Gyenge of Hungary, second E. Novak of Hungary, third E. Kawamoto of the United States. In the 400-meter relay, Hungary was first, the Netherlands second, the United States third. In the diving events, as usual, the United States did well, taking five of the six places. Only M. Moreau of France, who took second place in springboard diving, kept the United States from scoring a clean sweep. But—except in diving—this was the worst showing of any United States women's swimming team in many Olympics.

With the impetus of the Olympics, international competition has made for such tremendous strides in technique and performance that the times of the great swimmers of yesterday, whose marks stood for years, seem slow to us now. Robert Kiphuth has made an interesting tabulation to show the march of progress in swimming. It shows that in 1897 the 100-yard free style world's record was 60 seconds, set by J. H. Derbyshire of Manchester, England. Ten years later, in 1907, the world's record was 55.4, set by Charles M. Daniels of the United States. Daniels, in 1910, lowered it to 54.8. In 1917 the world's record was 53.0, made by Duke Kahanamoku of the United States; in 1927 it was 51.0, set by Johnny Weissmuller of the United States; and the world's record today, made in 1952 by Richard Cleveland of the United States, is 49.2 seconds. In 55 years the record has been improved by almost 11 seconds out of 60.

It is safe to predict that contestants of the near future, perhaps from countries still unheard of in swimming, may lower the 100-yard world's record to 47 seconds flat. Perhaps when this happens there will be fifty or more nations competing, with 100,000 people present and millions more witnessing the great event on television.

CHAPTER XIII

TEAM GAMES

1. BASEBALL

ALTHOUGH BASEBALL is known as the "great American game," it had its roots in England and is said to have been played there as early as 1744. This was probably a form of the game of rounders, which was popular in West England at the time. Early British settlers in America brought this pastime with them, and there is evidence that soldiers and Princeton students played a form of the game in New Jersey long before Abner Doubleday first set up teams to play at Cooperstown, New York, in 1839. However, the first formal teams organized were formed by the Knickerbocker Baseball Club of New York. At this time, Alexander Cartwright, Jr., set up standard rules of play and the first game with the new rules was played at Hoboken, New Jersey, in 1846 between the Knickerbockers and the New York Nine. By 1858 there were so many baseball teams in New York that they grouped together into the National Association of Baseball Players, and by 1860 the game had spread all along the Atlantic seaboard. The Civil War then carried it further and by 1869 the first professional team was organized—the Cincinnati Red Stockings—and the game was on its way. It spread to practically every town in the country. Sunday afternoon games between local teams provided recreation for the community and soon became a symbol of the American way of life.

The movement to develop the sport in other countries began when other athletic teams participating in the Olympics were asked to demonstrate this American game which was gaining so much popularity and was being enjoyed by so many people. In 1928, at Amsterdam, the American soccer team played an exhibition game of baseball, which excited the interest of many Europeans, but it was not until the 1936 games that baseball got its real international push. The baseball demonstration that year was no spur-of-the-moment affair. Germany had requested that the United States present a baseball game as a demonstration and the United States Baseball Congress had asked all colleges and baseball commissioners to select the outstanding players in their territories.

More than 125,000 people came to see the Berlin game—the largest attendance of any professional or amateur baseball game. Leslie Mann, the manager of the team, gave a series of lectures on the technique of the game for teachers and athletic coaches of other nations. So much enthusiasm was generated that the lectures were printed overnight in various languages. The Japanese introduced the game on a wide scale in their country so that they could participate in a baseball tournament at the next Olympics. The sport eventually spread so rapidly in Japan that it is now practically the Japanese national sport.

Perhaps the most important result of the Berlin exhibition was the organization of an International Baseball Congress, with no less than twenty-one countries represented. These countries agreed to hold a baseball tournament at the next Olympics, scheduled for 1940. These Olympics were, of course, never held.

During the war years baseball did not have much chance to spread throughout the world—though armed services teams did compete overseas and excited a good deal of interest—but in 1952 the United States was again asked to demonstrate the game at the XV Olympiad. The games that year were held at Helsinki, and the Finns were most enthusiastic. They and other Scandinavians had developed their own version of baseball called "pesapallo," which they also demonstrated, but baseball leagues of the American version were growing and functioning on a wider scale throughout the world. Foreign countries were impressed at hearing about the physical and recreational good resulting from the interest of youth in baseball. In the United States alone four youth leagues enrolled over one million players between the ages of eight and seventeen in one year, and championship games among their teams drew crowds of over 40,000.

The Pan-American games, another outgrowth of the Olympics, held by the nations of the Western Hemisphere every four years between Olympics, featured baseball as its most important team game. In addition, baseball drew more interest and spectators at the first two Pan-American games—the first in Buenos Aires in 1951 and the second in Mexico City in 1955—than any other event. Cuba defeated the United States in the final game to win in 1951, and the Dominican Republic won in 1955.

Baseball will be on exhibition again at Melbourne, and someday it may become the great team game of the Olympics, and arrangements for the use of the main stadium before or after the track and field events will be in order. The future may well bring a fifty-team tournament, on a single-elimination or sudden-death basis, witnessed by over 200,000 fans, with morning, afternoon and night games. Perhaps these Olympic baseball games will be broadcast around the world by television as sports, gaining strength everywhere, will be on the march in the direction of common understanding and world peace.

2. BASKETBALL

Basketball is probably the only game in Olympic competition that has strictly American roots, and differs from most sports in that it was deliberately "invented." Credit for the game is given to Dr. James Naismith, who, as an instructor at the famous Y.M.C.A. College in Springfield, Massachusetts, tried to think of some kind of competitive game that could be played indoors, still be exciting for the players, and afford practice in teamwork. He had some form of soccer in mind and in 1891 brought a group together to try out his new game. When it came to deciding what kind of goal to use, into which the ball could be thrown, he thought of an elevated box and asked the superintendent of buildings for some old crates. Crates not being available, he was given two peach baskets, which were fastened to the gymnasium balcony—and the game of basketball was born. The problem of dislodging the ball when a goal was made from the floor was solved by knocking out the bottom of the basket. The sport caught on immediately. Twelve of the thirteen rules that Naismith laid down are still basic, although the game itself has vastly improved. It was picked up in schools and colleges in the United States, particularly along the Eastern seaboard, and by 1940 was popular in over seventy-five countries of the world.

Although there was a demonstration game of basketball in the 1904 Olympic games in St. Louis, there was no formal Olympic competition until 1936. In the Berlin games, twenty-two nations entered the basketball competition, more than competed in any other team event that year. The American team won, with Canada placing second and Mexico third. Poland was fourth and was the only European country to place among the top six teams. The American team members averaged over 6' 3" in height (two members even towering 6' 8"), which must have had an overpowering psychological effect on the other teams. The United States team was composed mostly of members of teams that had competed in the AAU national championships. Dr. Naismith, the originator of the game, attended the Berlin Olympics.

The next Olympic games were held in 1948 in London, and basketball was again part of the program, with twenty-three nations represented. The sport had spread rapidly throughout the world, and before World War II there were twenty million players and official rule books had been printed in over thirty languages. By 1948, basketball in the United States had achieved such popularity that as a result of a series of exhibition games the Olympic team, after paying all training expenses, was able to contribute $75,000 to the Olympic Committee. In the actual Olympic games in London, the team from the United States was composed of five members from the Phillips 66 team and five from the University of Kentucky. The United States again showed its basketball supremacy.

At Helsinki in 1952 the United States maintained its undefeated record in basketball against the teams of twenty-two other countries. However, it was obvious that the competition was going to become increasingly strong. The international rules were different from the American rules. Even the ball was different. It was not perfectly round, but was made of eighteen pieces of leather put together in a rather lopsided fashion, which made it less suitable for dribbling and long shooting. Because of the undefeated position of the United States in this sport, everyone was out to try to beat the American team. The tournament in 1952 attracted great crowds, with the United States having its first really tough game, against Uruguay. However, Bob Kurland—a 7' 1" player, who had also been on the 1948 team—scored 21 points and the United States won, 57-44.

The United States team played the team from Russia twice, and so many people wanted to see these two games that they had to be moved to a larger hall, and even then thousands of people were turned away. The Russian team had been undefeated in 900 games with various local teams in Russia and Europe prior to the Olympics, and expected to win. The first game was not a close contest, the United States winning by a score of 86-58. In the second game, the Russians imitated Brazil, which had given the United States a tough game by purely defensive playing and held the United States team to a score of 26-24, which was much closer. At half-time the United States' lead was only two points, 17-15, but the Americans finally won, 36-25. The final standing of the teams was: United States first, Russia second, Uruguay third, and then Argentina, Chile, Brazil, Bulgaria, and France.

It is believed that the 1956 Olympics will popularize basketball in Oceania, Asia, and Africa, so that future tournaments in this sport may include every nation throughout the world.

3. FIELD HOCKEY

Field hockey is said to be the oldest game played with a ball and stick in the world, and according to most historians had its roots in Persia around 2000 B.C. It is further known that the ancient Greeks played a game with a ball and a stick which resembled hockey.

Centuries later the game appeared in France under the name of "hoquet" (which was the French word for a shepherd's stick) and was played from time to time during the Middle Ages. Eventually it made its way across the Channel to Great Britain, and the word was Anglicized to "hockey." At one time in England the game was outlawed, along with practically every other sport except archery; archery seemed to the English to be the only practical means of training young men to be soldiers.

The present game of field hockey was developed in England around 1850 from the crude French game. The rules varied from time to time and underwent many changes until 1883, when the Wimbledon Hockey Club of London formulated new rules which made field hockey the fast, exciting game that it is today. Interest spread very quickly throughout England, especially by means of school and college competition. Because it was a game that was not dangerous and could be played only as fast and as rough as the individual teams desired, women took it up, and as early as 1887 it was considered England's national sport for women, and has retained that status ever since.

In fact, the game was introduced in the United States by an English hockey enthusiast for women. Louise Robert, in 1926, was an English teacher at a girls' school in Connecticut, and she interested Henry Greer of Rye, New York, in the sport. Greer, in the years to come, was to coach every American Olympic team, and at that time he tried to arrange hockey matches among men. He wasn't successful at first, but persevered until, in 1928, formal matches were arranged and the sport began to catch on in various schools.

In the meantime, due largely to British enthusiasm for the sport, field hockey received a tremendous spark from Olympic competition. As early as 1900 it was played in the Paris Olympics, but each visiting team was matched against one from the host country and no official champion was determined. It was played at the Olympics in 1908 and again in 1920 on a championship basis, and both times the teams from Great

106

Britain won. During the latter part of the nineteenth century and the first part of the twentieth century British Army officers and British Army teams had introduced the sport in India and it soon became the national sport of that country, with thousands of teams and matches. In 1928, in the next Olympic hockey tournament, India won the field hockey championship and has held the title ever since, consistently producing the greatest hockey teams in the world. Their fast, sure playing is partly due to a development of their own: They shortened the toe of the stick, so the player can turn it over for reverse play without relaxing his grip. This slight refinement in equipment brought greater flexibility to the play, and eventually it was adopted by most European countries in the hope of wresting the championship from India.

In 1932, for the first time, the United States sent a team to compete in Olympic hockey. Although they came in third and actually managed to score a goal against the great Indian team, they were, of course, as green as the grass they played on. The Indian team, on the other hand, was so good that Los Angeles sportswriters voted the showing they made in the Olympics the most outstanding exhibition of skill in any sport.

In the 1936 games at Berlin, although India easily retained her supremacy, the German team put up a very good fight. The Germans had developed a hockey game combining the best features of the English and Indian methods of play. The United States team, with many players back from 1932, showed great improvement. Japan, Hungary, Afghanistan, Denmark, Holland, France, Belgium and Switzerland also participated.

At the Olympic games in 1948, in London, hockey teams of seventeen countries competed for the world's championship. India defeated Great Britain in the final match, 4-0. While the United States team did not fare well, it toured Europe and gained valuable experience.

The United States Olympic Committee turned down the application of the hockey team to participate in the 1952 Olympic games, but it is hoped that the United States will not give up this sport because of our inexperience or inability to win. The way other countries have taken up American basketball should serve as a challenging example to the United States.

4. SOCCER

Soccer is one of the many offshoots of ancient football,

which is as old as history itself; there is evidence that football games were played in both Babylon and early Egypt. In the Sixth Book of Homer's *Odyssey* is a specific allusion to football. The early Greeks referred to the game as "harpaston" and from all indications it was very similar to modern Rugby football. The game of harpaston was the prime means of training the Spartan warriors, and with the growth of Spartan culture the game was widely played in Greece and later spread to the Romans. Many detailed descriptions of the Roman game of football, startlingly like our own game, can be found in the works of Julius Pollux, an Egyptian sophist of the second century.

With the advent of the barbarians and the fall of Rome, football almost disappeared in the confusion and chaos of the troubled Dark Ages. However, the Augustan game was played throughout Italy until the Middle Ages, and was revised in Florence as late as 1898. It was one of the few games which lived through the Middle Ages.

Throughout the Middle Ages, a new Italian form of the game was played, called "calcio." This game was very similar to the Greek harpaston. However, the most fertile field for the development of football was England. The Roman legionnaire brought the game of football with him fairly early, and the Anglo-Saxon took to the game and developed it rapidly. Towns and even countries played against each other.

When Edward II was king, football was popular in London —but unpopular with merchants, whose windows were broken, and with parents of sons who were hurt playing the game. It was a primitive, rough, and almost brutal game, and in 1314 things were so bad that Edward II forbade its being played.

In the next century, its tremendous popularity among the people kept the game alive, and it survived the edicts of a series of kings and queens and remained the favorite sport of both the people and soldiers of England to the beginning of the seventeenth century. Several new types of football games were played, which were not as rough as the original game. These developed into Rugby and, about 1870, association football, which is also known as soccer. Largely through the influence of the military, the standardization and development of the game was accomplished during the Crimean and Colonial wars of the early nineteenth century. Soccer had a small following in the United States as a result of English influence, but it wasn't until Olympic competition drew international attention to the sport that it reached any great height of popularity throughout the world.

In the early years of Olympic soccer, beginning in 1900, the competition was mostly between European countries, with Great Britain usually the winner—with the exception of the 1906 Olympics, when Great Britain did not send a team and the Olympic championship was won by Denmark. In 1912, Denmark still showed great strength, but finished second to Great Britain.

In the 1920 games at Antwerp, two comparative newcomers at the game took over the star role. Belgium defeated Czechoslovakia in the finals.

In 1924, the United States sent its first soccer team to compete in the Paris Olympiad. The United States defeated Estonia, 1-0, in its first match, but was eliminated by Uruguay, 0-3, in the next round. Uruguay went on to win the world's championship, with Switzerland second, Sweden third, and Holland fourth.

George Burford, who trained the United States team in 1924, took over the job of preparing for the 1928 games in Amsterdam. There the United States drew Argentina as its first opponent—an Argentine team which had recently defeated Uruguay in the South American championships. It is to be noted that even in team sports the Olympics inspired international competition and continental and world's championships between the years of the Olympics. The increase in the popularity of soccer is attested to by the fact that there were twenty-one teams from twenty-one nations present to compete for the Olympic title. Uruguay won, with Argentina second and Germany third. After the Olympics, the United States team toured Europe and gained valuable experience, and spread the message of friendly competition and sportsmanship far more than if the United States were parading its superiority in its own specialties.

In 1932 the Olympic games were held at Los Angeles. Unfortunately, soccer was not included in the program. This was not because the United States desired to exclude it, but because most of the countries could not afford to send the large groups necessary to field soccer teams on such a long voyage.

In the 1936 games in Berlin, the Italian soccer team, which had recently won the world's championship, won the Olympic title, defeating Austria in an exciting overtime match, 2-1. Austria was second, Norway third, and Poland fourth. A total of sixteen nations had teams in this championship, including China. The United States, for the first time, showed definite class. It was eliminated by Italy, but in a very close game which ended with the score 1-0. Experts agreed that the

Americans might have been the second or third strongest team but were unlucky in drawing the winner in the first round.

In 1948, American interest in soccer had spread widely and there was considerable competition within the United States. Over 5,000 soccer players participated in the pre-Olympic trials, and it was believed that the United States had a chance to win its first Olympic medal in this sport.

The 1948 Olympiad at London included a soccer tournament of eighteen nations, and for the first time the soccer championship was won by Sweden, with Yugoslavia second, Denmark third, and Great Britain fourth. The United States team, perhaps because of overconfidence, was eliminated by Italy in an early round. The team made a post-Olympic tour of Ireland and Norway and, returning to New York, played the national team of Israel, defeating it twice.

Between the 1948 and 1952 Olympics, soccer seemed to make greater progress throughout the world than ever before, particularly in Latin America. World's championships and international meets, which had grown up as a result of the Olympics, became so important, especially to Latin America, that the world's largest stadium was built in Rio de Janeiro in time for the 1950 world's championship in soccer. This stadium, one-half mile in circumference, held the record-breaking crowd of 199,855 people for the final game of the championships. This showed to what extent the Olympics had spread soccer and an interest in this team game throughout the world. This stadium should be impressive even to Americans, who seem to believe that they have the greatest audiences in the world for sports events. Brazil is bidding for the Olympic games, and this stadium may well be the site of an Olympiad in the future.

The 1952 Olympics at Helsinki featured twenty-five nations in the soccer tournament. Russia entered a team for the first time. Italy, as usual, proved a jinx for the United States team in the early rounds, although in exhibition games after the regular competition the United States scored wins over Finland, India, and Brazil, and the national champions of Finland, the Kotka Workers Club. Experts commented that the individual American players were now very definitely up to the standard of those in other countries, but that team coordination and strategy were still not up to the international level. The results of the 1952 games were as follows: first, Hungary; second, Yugoslavia; third, Sweden; fourth, Germany.

The future of soccer as a team game on the Olympic program is secure and within the next few Olympiads every one of the Latin American countries will send strong soccer teams to the games to compete against teams from the rest of the world. With improved, faster, and cheaper means of transportation, team competitions will be able to spread common understanding and friendship.

CHAPTER XIV

TRACK AND FIELD

SINCE THE ancient Olympics began 3100 years ago with foot racing, to which later were added jumping and throwing, the Greeks gave us the track and field events, which are often thought of as the main course in the Olympic diet, probably because the events in track and field competition involve the first athletic gestures of man. Another reason for the great popularity of track and field is that it is held in great open spaces and, as a result, can be witnessed by a practically unlimited audience. Because certain events in track and field are at various periods specialties of different countries throughout the world, the entire track and field program has great international appeal. It also includes events for women, to further increase its appeal. Track and field, however, has been overemphasized in connection with the Olympic games. While there is no question of its importance, it should not overshadow the other sports within the Olympic competition. Unfortunately, there is a tendency in the United States to regard the Olympics as purely an international track and field meet, with the other sports as side shows. Naturally the United States should be proud of having won men's track and field in every Olympiad, but someday, with American methods, techniques, equipment and contributions, following the Olympic tradition, other countries may well take over for a while.

The events in track and field are the normal athletic motions of any man, woman, or child. They consist primarily of walking, running, jumping, and throwing, or combinations of these actions. To prehistoric man, these basic actions were more important than they are to us. Walking was his only way of going from one place to another. Running and jumping sometimes saved him from becoming a meal for some man-eating prehistoric animal, and throwing enabled him to kill animals for food. It was natural that skill in these vital activities became the basis of the earliest athletic competitions.

Running was the first event in the ancient Olympic games.

Just as in boxing, there is very little today that is completely new in track and field. From the sprint of one length of the stadium (200 yards), a middle-distance race of twice around the stadium (less than one-half mile), and a race of twelve times around the stadium (about two and one half miles), the number of events contested in the ancient Olympics has been increased to include all kinds of distances in walking and running. The original standing broad jump, usually from a marble step into a loose sand pit, has led to the running jump, the triple jump—now called the hop, step, and jump—the high jump, and later, with the help of a pole, to the pole vault. Since primitive man had to hurdle stones and bushes as he ran away from a mammoth, hurdle races were also added. In the throwing, the objects thrown were the javelin, the discus, the "stone" or shot, and the hammer. According to the Irish, the last-named weight throwing event can be traced to the Tailtean games in County Meath, Ireland, in 1829 B.C.

From the earliest days, great stars were developed in track and field. The first victor at the first Olympic games in 776 B.C. was the winner of the 200-yard dash, an Elian—that is, a native of Elis—named Coroebos. A man named Hermogenes of Xanthos won eight crowns in the foot races during three very early Olympiads. As a result, he received the nickname of "Hippos," which was not the Greek word for a hippopotamus but for a race horse. Argeus was a great long-distance runner and when he won his Olympic victory he ran home to Argos from Olympia, a distance of thirty-four miles, to tell his girl friend about it. Two other great runners in the ancient Olympics were Dandes, also of Argos, and Ladas of Lacedaemon. Later the foot races were dominated for some considerable time by contestants from a Greek city in Italy named Crotona, where a great running coach evidently resided.

After the ancient Olympics were broken up, there is a lapse of eight centuries in sports. This absence of competitive athletics, except for horse racing, jousting, and wrestling, is one of the great mysteries of history. However, it is interesting to note that this same period was one of wars, dictators, chaos, and cruel injustices and inhumanities. We do not find the beginnings of track and field competition in England until the thirteenth century, and finally we find track and field gaining a firm grip in England by 1834, when the first amateur athletic organizations began to make formal rules and to organize competitions in running, jumping, and throwing. The first college track and field meet in the world, as far as can be ascertained, took place in 1864, when Oxford competed against Cambridge. The first national meet to determine the champions of England occurred shortly thereafter. In 1868 the New York Athletic Club arranged for the first amateur track and field meet in the history of the United States. All during the nineteenth century there was a great interest in track and field events in many countries throughout the world —in Scandinavia, led by Sweden and Finland; in Russia; in Central Europe, especially in Hungary. In France, too, there was an upsurge of interest in track and field. When the first modern Olympics rolled around in 1896, the flags of France, Russia, the United States, Germany, Sweden, England, Hungary, Australia, Holland, Bohemia, Italy, Belgium, and Spain were waving over the re-created stadium to usher in another golden age of athletics. These flags were those of the original pioneers and originators of the modern Olympics. The participating nations at the first Olympiad were: Great Britain (including Australia), Denmark, France, Germany, Greece, Hungary, Sweden, Switzerland, and the United States.

The silhouette of the Grecian temple had never been lost, but the stadium had disappeared with the athletes and their audiences. A living stadium had not been seen for centuries. And now the restored stadium was alive with people. There was room for 50,000 spectators. Portions of the stadium were of wood; there had not been time to replace all the marble. After the games this work would be completed, thanks to the generous gift of George Averoff. The track was not the sandy track of the ancient Greeks, but had been replaced by a cinder track built by experts brought from England. Such was the scene at the opening of the track and field competition of the first Olympics in April, 1896, as the King and Queen of Greece, the former in full military uniform and the latter in white, officially opened the ceremony. Athletes, officials, and a choir added color to the scene. A chorus of several hundred voices sang the Olympic hymn. The oldest show on earth had reopened. It was to be an American show. In fact, of the twelve official track and field events, nine were won by Americans. Two events were won by E. H. Flack of Australia, and the marathon, which turned out to be the most dramatic race of the show, was won by S. Loues of Greece. Baron de Coubertin, to whom this Olympics owed so much, was all but ignored by the Greeks and the Greek government, but he was there nevertheless, helping in a major way to prepare for the future.

The United States Expeditionary Forces to Greece in the first Olympic games were volunteers. Baron de Coubertin had, at a very early stage in the preparation of the Olympics, enlisted the help of the American professor, William Sloane, to represent the United States in the preliminary Olympic Congress. Unfortunately, few Americans paid much attention to Sloane when he returned, but the Boston Athletic Association finally decided that it should send a team to Athens. The athletes selected were Tom Burke, sprinter; E. H. Clark, Harvard all-around athlete; Thomas P. Curtis, hurdler; Arthur Blake, middle- and long-distance runner; John and Sumner Paine, revolver shots; W. W. Hoyt, pole vaulter; C. B. Williams, swimmer; and John Graham, the coach of the Boston Athletic Association. This team, after various difficulties en route, arrived in Athens in the nick of time, and was joined by other Americans. Robert S. Garrett, captain of the Princeton track and field team, had decided he would like to go to Athens. Although he had never seen a discus, he had heard about the modern discus competition; he dug up the dimensions of a discus somewhere and had a steel one made. He practiced throwing the discus at Princeton for a while and then set forth for Athens. James B. Connelly, later to become a well-known author, was a student at Harvard with an interest in athletics. He became interested in going to Athens and applied to Harvard for a leave of absence, which was refused. He quit school and went to Athens anyway. The Americans, who went to Athens informally on a catch-as-catch-can basis, were just too good and won practically all the events.

By far the most exciting event was the marathon. The contest was run over the exact course that Pheidippides had taken in bringing the news of the Greek victory at Marathon to anxious Athens. There were twenty-five starters.

Spiridion Loues was a Greek shepherd. He had heard on the hills, as he watched over his sheep, that athletes from all over the world were coming to Athens and that his country would have a difficult time upholding the tradition of the past. A tireless runner, although physically a very small, short man, he saw himself as the one hope of Greece to win the marathon. Baron de Coubertin, a great public relations expert, told the world that Loues spent two nights before the race praying and that the day before the race he fasted. In any case, he was one of the starters the next morning. The favorite, Lermusiaux, a Frenchman, led for almost half the race. Then he was passed by Arthur Blake of the Boston Athletic Association, who had never run twenty-six miles before. After nineteen miles, Blake had to quit. Loues, who had kept a steady pace, was the next to take the lead. When three miles remained to go, Loues was still in the lead position. Word was sent ahead to the Royal Box and to the crowd—a Greek crowd—who were waiting in a frenzy of enthusiasm. An uproar burst as Loues trotted into the stadium. To make the day even more glorious for Greece, a Greek was second and a Greek was third.

The second modern Olympic games, in Paris in 1900, listed the track and field championships merely as an international meet at the World's Fair. The United States entered fifty-five athletes as their official track and field team, although actually this team consisted of many groups from various colleges—Yale, Princeton, Pennsylvania, Syracuse, Georgetown, Michigan, and Chicago—and some club representatives. Each college financed its own group. The New York Athletic Club also financed a team. The unattached entrants reached into their own pockets for their expenses.

The site of the track meet was bad, and the facilities almost non-existent. There wasn't even a cinder path for running. The sprint course was on turf and was not level. The discus had to be thrown into trees. There was much confusion in the running off of the meet. Just as at Athens, it was an American show. The star was Alvin Kraenzlein of Pennsylvania, who won four Olympic championships—the 60-meter sprint, the 110-meter hurdles, the 200 meter hurdles, and the running broad jump. One of the most interesting features of the second Olympic games was the fact that, notwithstanding the confusion, bad management, the horrible site, and the lack of proper facilities, every record made at Athens in 1896 was broken. Although all of the events that he was in have been discontinued, Ray Ewry of the United States was in a class by himself in the standing jump events, capturing all three of them. Sheldon of the United States broke the 16-pound shot record by no less than ten feet. Great Britain showed up quite well in this track meet, winning four gold medals, including the relay. Hungary, one of the original sponsors of the Olympic games, won its first track and field victory in the classical discus event. One other Olympic pioneer nation scored a victory in the stadium—France in the classic marathon race, when Teato defeated a great field. The great originator of the Olympics, Baron de Coubertin, was ignored by his own government in the running of the 1900 games, just as he had been by the Greek government in the 1896 games. However, he was not one to be discouraged, and he continued to be present to help in any way he could, and to lay proper plans for the next Olympics and the continuation of his great idea and ideals.

The track and field competition in the III Olympiad at St. Louis, in 1904, was again won by the United States and almost exclusively by college athletes, who broke records in almost every event. The competition included a large number of competitors, although there were comparatively few Europeans. There were a number of athletes who captured more than one first place. Archie Hahn won the 60-, the 100-, and the 200-meter sprints. Ray Ewry took first place in the standing broad jump, the standing high jump, and the standing hop, step, and jump, repeating the victories he had scored at the II Olympiad. Harry Hillman won the 200- and the 400-meter hurdles and the 400-meter flat. J. B. Lightbody took first in the 800-meter and 1500-meter runs and the 2500-meter steeplechase, and Myer Prinstein won the broad jump and the hop, step, and jump. Martin Sheridan, a New York policeman, won his first Olympic discus throw.

Although there were big crowds and a lot of enthusiasm at the St. Louis games, the track and field events were so badly mixed up with the St. Louis Fair and there was so much confusion and so many side-shows that it is doubtful if it could be called any improvement on the very poorly run Paris Olympiad of four years before. Baron de Coubertin, as usual, weaved with the punches and took advantage of every opportunity to keep improving and advancing the Olympic games.

The 1906 Olympic games, usually referred to as the "unofficial" Olympics, were actually the first to which many countries sent large teams. The United States, which had won in St. Louis more or less by default, was determined to demonstrate its strength against real competition, and did win the unofficial all-around honors in the track and field events, paced by stars such as Paul Pilgrim, the New York Athletic Club surprise winner of the 400- and 800-meter run. Pilgrim is now Director of Athletics at the New York Athletic Club, which still contributes many track and field stars to United States Olympic teams. The Greeks received a sad disappointment in having Sherring, a Canadian, win the marathon and Jarvinen, a Finn, win the Greek-style discus. However, as usual, there was something to swell Greek pride, for their representative in the shotput—or, as it was then called, the "stone throw"—George Georgantus, won this event.

One of the outstanding features of the games was the actual, active, and effective participation of the Greek royal family. The Crown Prince presided at the games and the Princes George, Nicholas, and Andrew all actively officiated and did so with skill. The King and Queen of Greece were present at the games every day, and the King of Servia and the Prince of Wales also attended the games as guests of Greece. It was a great show in the finally completed marble stadium. 1906 was a turning point between the experiments, the uncertainties, the petty jealousies, and the grabbing of management of the Olympics by various local organizations, governments, and fairs, and the smooth-running modern Olympics managed and controlled by the International Olympic Committee and the various national Olympic Committees together with the Olympic Organizing Committee of the host nation.

The 1908 or IV Olympiad in London is said, according to many, to have supplied more drama than any other Olympics up until that time. The stadium for the track and field events —the Olympia—was overflowing with 80,000 people. In one tremendous surge, in two years instead of four, Baron de Coubertin's idea had become a world force. The modern Olympics were here—to survive for perhaps longer than the ancient Olympics. For the first time a true organizing committee followed the comprehensive, carefully drawn plans of de Coubertin. The London games were not without controversies, but as a whole they were well run and laid the groundwork for the future. The stadium had a 660-yard concrete cycling track, and inside of that was a five-laps-to-the-mile cinder track. In front of the main stands, within the oval, was a swimming pool 100 meters in length, with a diving tower that could be collapsed and disappear from sight when not in use. King Edward VII and Queen Alexandra of England formally opened the games.

The track and field competition was undoubtedly the greatest in athletic history up to that time. Many unusual happenings added to the excitement. Reggie Walker, a 19-year-old South African not originally picked to represent his country, outsprinted a great field to win the 100 meters. Lt. Halswelle of Great Britain, who had run the fastest 400-meter semifinal, ran against three Americans in the final. As two of the three had been accused of technical fouls—namely, cutting in front of Halswelle—the officials declared the race null and void. Only one of the Americans was officially disqualified, and the officials ordered the race re-run by Halswelle and the other two Americans. However, the United States representatives refused to start again, and as a result the Englishman was allowed to trot alone around the track to win the event. The British fared better than ever, winning most of the long-distance events and most of the places in the steeplechase. Ray Ewry of the United States brought his total of Olympic gold medals to ten, a record which has never been surpassed. Martin Sheridan repeated his Olympic discus win at St. Louis, and John Flanagan won the hammer throw for the third time in succession.

Great Britain had expected to win the track and field. While the British did win the unofficial all-around championship of the IV Olympiad, they were not able to head off the Americans in the unofficial track and field team championship. As in the case of the first three Olympiads, there was great interest in the running of the marathon. At the start of the race, two English distance runners named Lord and Jack ran the first four miles in record time, with J. Price, a third Englishman, following closely behind, trailed by Hefferon of South Africa and Dorando Pietri of Italy. Jack was soon exhausted and eliminated, but the others continued at an unbelievable pace for about 15 miles. Then Price and Lord both dropped back, while Hefferon, followed by Dorando Pietri, kept pushing ahead until they were about three miles from the stadium. Dorando started to gain on Hefferon and, coming in sight of him at the 25th mile, sprinted after the tired South African and passed him within sight of the stadium. Dorando's sprint having worn him down, he had to slow up. When he entered the stadium he was greeted by a mighty roar from the crowd but he became confused and at first started running in the wrong direction and then collapsed on the track. In the meantime, Johnny Hayes, Joe Forshaw, and A. R. Welton, all Americans, were approaching the stadium. Doctors and officials, in the meantime, had rushed to the Italian and, humanely but illegally, dragged him to his feet and pushed him in the proper direction, not knowing that by so doing they had disqualified him. Dorando, with rubber legs, weaved around the track. A roar from the crowd signalled the fact that Hayes had just entered the stadium. Hayes, in very good shape, swung around the track with a sprint finish and finished a bare half-minute after the Italian runner, who fell unconscious after he had been pushed and dragged over the line. Hayes, of course, was declared the winner of the marathon, and Dorando was disqualified. Hefferon, the big South African, was second, while Forshaw and Welton scored third and fourth honors for the United States. Twenty-seven of the original seventy-five starters finished in what is generally considered the most dramatic race in the annals of the modern Olympics.

South Africa, Canada, and Australia began to take a tremendous interest in international athletics in the Olympics and were represented by some very strong, as well as courageous, contestants.

The V Olympiad was awarded to Stockholm, in recognition of the Swedes' enthusiastic support of the Olympic games from the very beginning. The Stockholm games presented a number of new problems in connection with track and field. Finland wished to compete as an independent nation, but was forced to participate as representing Russia. Similarly, Bohemia desired to send a team of its own, but was forced to represent Austria. The organizing committee in Sweden had to build a stadium, swimming pool, and other facilities from scratch.

The opening ceremony on July 6, 1912 was a solemn and colorful event, reminiscent of the religious openings of the ancient Olympics. A large chorus sang the national anthems. Crown Prince Gustav Adolph and King Gustav V opened the games. Silver trumpets heralded the opening of the track and field competition in the new and imposing stadium. For the first time, electrical timing devices were used to assure accuracy in track events. While the United States, as usual, won the unofficial over-all track and field competition, the Stockholm games were replete with unexpected and unusual performances by nations new to the Olympics and by unknown athletes. While the sprints were fairly easy for the United States, the competition in the middle-distance events was rough. As a result of the Halswelle incident in 1908 at London, the Swedes hit upon the idea of using lanes for the final of the 400 meter. Hans Braun, a great German runner; Ted Meredith, an 18-year-old schoolboy from the United States; and Charles Reidpath and E. F. J. Lindberg, also of the United States, were the finalists. Although Ted Meredith led for the first half of the final, it ended practically in a dead heat between Reidpath, Lindberg, and Braun. The officials picked Reidpath as first, Braun as second, and Lindberg as third. The final of the 800 meter was just as exciting, with Braun again representing Germany and running against six Americans and a Canadian. Mel Sheppard, the 1908 winner, was the favorite and he quickly opened quite a gap. But as the runners reached the final straightaway, they became closely bunched. Again it was almost a dead heat. The decision went to Meredith for first, Sheppard second, Davenport third, Braun fourth, and Caldwell fifth, with the official timing of two-fifths of a second difference between the first man and the fifth.

The 1500 meter, or the "metric mile," was, of course, the special target of many. The only trouble was that too many Americans coveted this particular gold medal, with the result that the Americans in the finals—John Paul Jones of Cornell; Mel Sheppard, the 1908 winner; Norman Taber; Abel Kiviat; and three other Americans—became so intent on out-maneuvering each other, having run against each other often, that they not only allowed Arnaud of France to set the pace for more than half the distance but at the finish permitted A. Jackson of England and Oxford to stage a last minute sprint to win the event. A dramatic race was also presented in the 5000 meters, in which two great runners, Hannes Kolehmainen of Finland and Jean Bouin of France, ran neck and neck for almost 5000 meters and hit the tape together, with Kolehmainen winning by a whisper to set a new record. Kolehmainen went on to win the 10,000-meter flat and the 8000-meter cross country, for three long-distance gold medals. However, possibly his greatest performance was in another event which he did not win, although he broke the existing world's record. The explanation of this unusual occurrence is that he was also entered in the 3000-meter team race, which was run in heats, the winning team alone qualifying for the final. Finland was eliminated by the United States and therefore Kolehmainen did not qualify for the final, although he set a new world's record in winning his heat. Kolehmainen and a teammate of his named Stenroos were each to win a future Olympic marathon. As usual, the marathon was looked on by almost everyone as the climax of the track and field events. Two South Africans, K. K. McArthur and C. W. Gitsham, finished first and second, with Gaston Strobino of the United States third.

However, the greatest performance at Stockholm in track and field was one that is not in the record books. Jim Thorpe won both the pentathlon and decathlon, the all-around track and field events, but was later disqualified. Before his disqualification Thorpe's records in fifteen events attracted the attention of the world, and on his return he was greeted as the hero of the V Olympiad. An American Indian and probably the greatest all-around track and field athlete of all time, Jim Thorpe is generally considered also to have been the greatest natural football player of all time, and was a good enough baseball player to make the big leagues. (A town in Pennsylvania, formerly an Indian town and until 1955 known as Mauch Chunk, has been recently named Jim Thorpe in memory of America's greatest athlete.) Yet F. R. Bie of Norway was officially given the pentathlon title and Hugo Wieslander of Sweden the decathlon crown of the V Olympiad after Jim Thorpe had been disqualified.

Because of his prominence, Thorpe was found to have accepted a small amount of money for playing baseball in a semi-pro league preceding the Olympic games. This fact was not discovered until 1913. The officials of the American Olympic Committee decided it was their duty to award to the men who had won second place in the two events the official victories, to have Thorpe's records eliminated, and to reclaim Thorpe's two gold medals.

The Swedes' handling of technical facilities was great at Stockholm. Not only was an electrical timing device used for the first time in any Olympics, but also the first photo-finish camera, and the first public-address system, and in addition there were charts and other means by which the progress of many events was projected to the great crowd all through the games. Baron de Coubertin expressed the admiration of the Olympic world in a letter to the Swedish Olympic Committee. Great progress was being made in the Olympic games, but it was interrupted, of course, by the World War.

The first announcement that the Olympic games were to be revived after the close of hostilities filled the athletic world with delight, but very little time was left for preparation. The choice of Antwerp was almost unbelievable; it was astounding that the brave Belgians should have been able to gather their resources and get organized at all, as they had suffered so cruelly in the war. Before the games began, a religious service was conducted by Cardinal Mercier, in the imposing cathedral at Antwerp, for the athletes killed in World War I. Following the religious services at the cathedral, the regular Olympic ceremony was held at the stadium, with King Albert of Belgium opening the games. The Olympic flag with the five rings made its first official appearance at these Olympics, although it had made its unofficial debut in 1916 at Paris, when the twentieth anniversary of the revival of the games was celebrated. The stadium had been hastily put together, and the track suffered from continuous rains, which influenced performances adversely, but the games were smoothly run.

There were more surprises at Antwerp than usual, for no one knew the relative abilities of the various contestants. A. G. Hill, an Englishman well past the usual age of competitive runners, surprised everyone by winning both the 800 and the 1500 meter. American sprinters, as usual, dominated the short distances. The long-distance races presented to the Olympic games a new star who was to become the greatest runner of modern times. Paavo Nurmi of Finland, then unknown, opposed in the 5000 meters the great Guillemot, who had a world reputation and was beyond doubt the greatest French runner of all time. The Finn stayed with the Frenchman all the way and lost by a stride. However, Nurmi won the 10,000-meter run and the 10,000-meter cross-country. Hannes Kolehmainen, the outstanding distance runner in the 1912 Olympics eight years before, won the classic marathon race in new record time. Finland surprised the United States by winning most of the field events—the shotput, the discus, the javelin throw, and the hop, step, and jump. A Swede won

121

the broad jump. Although the United States won the track and field section of the VII Olympiad, the Finns, considering the size of their country and the number of their entries, scored even more impressively.

Amsterdam was scheduled to be the site of the next Olympic games, as the Dutch had applied for the 1916 games and in 1920 had voluntarily retired in favor of Antwerp. However, the Dutch withdrew again, with great generosity, this time at the request of the founder of the games, Baron de Coubertin, who wished to have the 1924 games held in Paris.

The VIII Olympiad in Paris was distinguished by the all-out effort of the French government, which was determined that the 30th anniversary of the rebirth of the Olympic games would not be the fiasco of 1900. The great hero of the track and field competition was Paavo Nurmi of Finland. While Nurmi had first shown great exhibitions of long-distance running at Antwerp, his appearance in Paris marked him as a finished performer with a veteran's poise. Nurmi's four gold medals in a single Olympiad surpassed the performance of Alvin Kraenzlein at Paris in 1900. The Finnish runner won the 1500 meter, 5000 meter, 3000-meter steeplechase, and 10,000-meter cross-country.

The United States was set back on its haunches by the surprising wins of the British in short-distance events. Great performances were turned in by contestants from countries new to track and field; for instance, a young Swiss named Paul Martin provided a great thrill by taking second in the 800 meter, a second that many observers believed would have been a first if he had had more experience and had properly timed his closing sprint to the tape. Records fell every day. Probably one of the most interesting feats was the world's broad jump record set by Robert Legendre, an American, with a jump of 25 feet 6 inches while he was performing in the pentathlon. Legendre was not even a competitor in the Olympic broad jumping contest, but on hearing that another American, whom he didn't like, had won this event with a record jump, he announced to everyone that he would break the world's record and beat his teammate when he got around to the broad jump event in the pentathlon, and he made good his promise. To complete this human interest story, Robert Legendre, along with Johnny Weismuller, the swimmer, and Nat Pendleton, the wrestler, was tapped by Hollywood for stardom. While Weismuller became Tarzan on the screen and Nat Pendleton became a leading tough guy and a character who wrestled lions, Robert Legendre, the most photogenic and the greatest prospect for Hollywood stardom, was cut down by pneumonia in three days after several years as a United States naval officer and Navy track coach.

Two 18-year-old Americans, Lee Barnes and Glen Graham, tied for the pole vault title, Barnes winning in a jump-off, and Clarence Houser, another American college star, was a double winner in the shot and the discus. United States relay teams broke two world records and helped to establish the 1924 Paris games as the greatest wholesale factory for Olympic and world's records.

The IX Olympiad at Amsterdam produced another great track and field competition, this time handicapped to some degree by cold and rainy weather, but with a very fine track. The track and field program embraced some 760 male competitors and 121 women representing 40 nations. The competition started out with an unknown Canadian sprinter, Percy Williams, winning both the 100- and 200-meters, with Great Britain providing a surprise runner-up. The United States was in for an even greater surprise, for up until the final track event of the 1928 program, none of the American runners or hurdlers had been able to win a single first place. Ray Barbuti therefore won great fame by winning, at the very finish, the 400 meter final from Ball of Canada. The United States didn't do much better in the middle distances, with Douglas Lowe, Great Britain's 1924 winner, repeating in the 800 meter; and Finland's runners and a great French runner, Ladoumegue, dominated the distance events. Nurmi was unable to repeat his past victories and had to be satisfied with two second places in the 5000 meter and 3000-meter steeplechase and a first in the 10,000 meter. Another great surprise was furnished by Lord David Burghley of Great Britain, who scored an upset over the Americans in the 400-meter hurdle event. In track the United States had to be satisfied with Barbuti's 400-meter victory and with wins in the 400- and 1600-meter relay events. In the field events, however, the United States made up for its deficiency in the track events, winning almost all of the events and making up sufficient points to win the unofficial all-around track and field championship. One of the great showings of the track and field meet was that provided by the Germans, who had been turned away from Olympic competition in 1920 and 1924, and had not participated since 1912. These Olympics also marked the beginning of women's track and field competition. Of the five track events for women, Canada won two and the United States, Germany, and Poland one each.

The X Olympiad in Los Angeles in 1932 brought track and field to one of the largest and finest stadiums in the world.

With the selection of the host nation and city years ahead of time, the site and facilities for the games, and particularly for the track and field competition, could be properly prepared. Los Angeles outdid itself in providing facilities that could not be improved upon. Over 100,000 people, with thousands of disappointed latecomers thronging the nearby streets, witnessed the opening of the Olympics on July 30, 1932. Vice President Charles Curtis of the United States, a track enthusiast, arrived to open the games officially. A white-robed chorus sang "The Star Spangled Banner," while a dazzling column of Olympic athletes in bright uniforms paraded around the track. Trumpets blared while Lt. George Calnan of the U.S. Navy, four-time American Olympic fencer, took the Olympic oath. Because of the excellence of the track, the great improvements in technique and performance, the number and quality of competitors, and the enthusiasm of the tremendous crowd, practically every existing record in track and field was broken during the dramatic competition between the greatest athletes from all over the world.

Eddie Tolan of the United States was the only double winner, with record-breaking performances in both the sprints, while the only 1928 champion to defend his title successfully was Dr. Patrick O'Callaghan of Ireland, in the hammer throw. The most sensational and most controversial race of the track events was the 5000-meter run, in which Ralph Hill, a comparatively unknown American, stayed with the world record holder, Finnish runner Lehtenin, to the head of the stretch. Hill attempted to pass the Finn on the outside, but Lehtenin swung out and cut him off. Then Hill tried to pass him on the inside, only to have the Finn close him off again. As a result of these maneuvers, Hill was beaten by a half yard. The audience of 100,000, believing that the Finn had fouled Hill, broke into such booing that it looked as though a serious incident was imminent. However, a fast-thinking announcer silenced the outburst and brought on immediate applause by cautioning the crowd: "Remember, please, these people are our guests." Outstanding records in the hurdles and in the field events followed. The marathon, as usual, was thrilling, with the four leading contestants all finishing within less than 400 yards. An Argentinian, Juan Zabala, won the gold medal. United States relay teams broke all records. In the women's track and field competition, Mildred Didrikson was the star, winning two gold medals and one silver. At the closing ceremony attended by 110,000 people, the great chorus sang the plaintive Hawaiian farewell "Aloha" while the banners of all of the nations participating in the X Olympiad were lowered.

The XI Olympic games in Berlin, although beset with many problems caused by the Nazi government and Nazi control, were nevertheless successful and their technical direction, with German thoroughness, was nearly perfect. Every possible electrical timing and photo-finish device was improved at Berlin. Devices smoothed the announcing systems for the judges, for the officials, and for the public. Press and radio service was excellent and there is no question that technical arrangements were handled in an outstanding fashion. The athletes were housed in very fine style in the Olympic village and were extended every comfort so that they might be at their best for the competition. These Olympics rang up a record at the box office, for the greatest income the games had yet known—over $2,800,000. The opening ceremony was heightened by the arrival in the stadium of the last of a team of more than 3000 relay runners of many nationalities who had carried a torch lighted on the ancient site of Olympia in Greece across Europe to the games. There was an audience of close to 125,000 people (133,000 at eight other arenas and events), and approximately 5000 athletes from 52 nations were drawn up on the field in uniforms of every color. Spiridion Loues, the Greek shepherd who had won the first Olympic marathon in 1896 at Athens, was on hand. Members of the International Olympic Committee, headed by President Baillet Latour, were there. The ceremonies finished, the oath taken, and the huge Olympic torch blazing at the open end of the stadium, thousands of doors were released and the games and the track and field competition had begun.

However, the great star of the 1936 Olympiad was not the crowds or Adolf Hitler, but Jesse Owens. The accomplishments of Jesse Owens are without parallel in modern Olympic history. Owens won three individual events and ran a decisive lap on a winning relay team, thus winning four gold medals and four of the tiny potted German oak trees that the organizing committee had provided the winners as living memorials of their victories. More startling, Owens broke both the Olympic and world record in the 100 meters, although it was disallowed because of a wind behind his back. He set a new Olympic and world record for 200 meters, he broad-jumped over 26 feet for the first time in Olympic history—another record—and the 400-meter relay team, of which he was a member, set a new Olympic and world record. Another spectacular performance was the 1500 meter win of Dr. Jack Lovelock of New Zealand, who smashed both the Olympic and world records with a great sprint of almost a full lap of a 400-meter track as a climax. Glenn Cunningham, one of America's greatest milers, was second. The Finns continued their dominance of long-distance races, and the historic and dramatic marathon was won by a representative of Japan, who was actually a Korean, as was his teammate, who finished in third place. Helen Stephens was the star of the women's track and field competition, winning the 100 meters and anchoring the winning 400-meter relay team. In the twenty-nine events, fifteen of the track and field records set four years before at Los Angeles were surpassed and three were equaled.

Regardless of their impressiveness, the XI Olympics in Berlin brought up the question of whether the individual athlete and his victory were not being overshadowed by the spectacles, the officials, and the host nation. It also brought up the question of whether the nation the athletes represented was trying to seek too much glory or propaganda benefit for itself rather than merely being proud to honor its winners individually. The twelve years between the XI Olympiad in Berlin and the XIV Olympiad at London were the most difficult and the most dangerous to the half century of progress of the Olympic games. During this period the modern Olympics lost their founder and his chief assistant—Pierre de Coubertin and Henri de Baillet Latour. Baron de Coubertin died in Switzerland at the age of 74 in 1936, after the XI Olympiad. Count Latour died in Brussels during the period of the German occupation in World War II. J. Sigfrid Edströmm of Sweden was the next President of the International Olympic Committee.

The track and field part of the XIV Olympiad in London in 1948 was favored in the preparations for the games by the fact that the chairmanship of the London games was in the hands of Lord David Burghley, former Olympic track star. The opening of the London Olympics in 1948 was impressive. Six thousand athletes from 59 countries were present, as was a capacity crowd of over 82,000 people. Trumpeters of the Household Cavalry filed into the stadium and sounded their fanfare. Then came the massed bands and the Scottish Highlanders, and then the King. Out walked King George VI, accompanied by Queen Elizabeth, Princess Margaret, Dowager Queen Mary, the Duke and Duchess of Gloucester, and other members of the British court. They opened the games. The parade of athletes began soon after, with Greece traditionally number one in the order of nations. After that they were in alphabetical order from Afghanistan to Yugoslavia, with Britain as the host nation at the end of the line. The Olympic flame, which had been lighted in the temple of Zeus at Olympia almost a fortnight before, was carried into the stadium on the last leg of a 1600-man relay.

The first dramatic moment of these Olympics was the 10,000-meter run, considered a Finnish property, with Heino, the Finnish world's record holder, running in a field that included several other strong contenders. However, there was a dark horse named Emil Zatopek, of Czechoslovakia. This race had been won at five out of the last six Olympics by Finns, including Hannes Kolehmainen and Paavo Nurmi. Heino led as a slight drizzle of rain fell, while Emil Zatopek, a Czech Army officer, followed. The grimacing Czech, in a faded red jersey, took over the lead from Heino at the tenth lap of the 25-lap race. For six more laps the two men stayed fairly close together, and then Zatopek in a dozen strides pulled away. In less than a lap the margin was getting bigger and then, to the great surprise of everyone, Heino ran off the track and quit. This seemed, however, to be a signal to Zatopek, who actually sprinted for the last two miles. The second Finn was run into the ground and had to be escorted off the track. The third Finn, Konenen, was so worn out that he was even beaten by two Americans, Eddie O'Toole and Fred Wilt. Zatopek won and broke the Olympic record. About 350 yards behind, in second place, was the Algerian Alain Mimoun-o-Kacha, representing France.

One of the most impressive and interesting victories in the London Olympics in 1948 was that of Harrison Dillard in the classic 100-meter flat. Dillard, a world's record hurdler, fell in the finals of the American Olympic tryout in the hurdles, and was therefore eliminated under the ironbound rules of the AAU. Dillard then turned around and entered the 100-meter flat race and qualified for a position on the Olympic team. In winning the 100 meter dash, he certainly gave an example of great ability and great will-power, for his normal event was the hurdles.

The 1500 meter, which has become one of the greatest and one of the most popular races in the Olympics, presented thirty-six starters. The Swedish Strand, Eriksson, and Bergkvist had all run faster than existing Olympic records. Only one United States contestant, Don Gehrmann, reached the finals. There was also the great Dutch runner, Slijkhuis; and Hansenne, the Frenchman, also had never been beaten at the distance. For the first time in thirty-six years in this event, Sweden placed three men in the first six to finish: Eriksson winning, with Strand second and Slijkhuis third, while Bergkvist took fifth. Eriksson's time, however, was slower than Strand's world record. In the 5,000 meters all eyes were on

Emil Zatopek, the Czech who had previously set the new Olympic record in winning the 10,000 meters, but at the finish Zatopek was some 30 yards behind Slijkhuis, who in turn was led by Gaston Reiff of Belgium. Zatopek started a sprint at the finish and although he was able to pass Slijkhuis, he could not catch Reiff, who won and established a new Olympic record.

There was one controversial incident in the meet and that was in the 400-meter relay, in which the United States team of Barney Ewell, Lorenzo Wright, Harrison Dillard, and Mel Patton finished comfortably in front of the second-place British quartet. However, the United States team was disqualified for allegedly passing the baton outside of the limits of the passing zone. Later a formal protest was entered by the United States and the Jury of Appeal, after reviewing the motion pictures, ruled that the hand-over from Ewell to Wright, which had been questioned, was entirely within the prescribed limits and so the United States team was redesignated as the winner.

The marathon provided the usual thrills, with Gailly of Belgium sprinting into the stadium first but staggering and weaving and almost collapsing. Before he could finish he was passed, in the crowded stadium, by D. Cabrera, an Argentinian running smoothly and effortlessly, and by T. Richards of Great Britain. The first American to finish was Theodore Vogel, who finished 14th. One of the greatest individual performances in the 1948 Olympics was that of Robert Mathias, a 17-year-old high-school boy from Tulare, California, who broke a world's record, scored more than 7000 points, and defeated 27 other contestants from all over the world in the all-around or decathlon championship. In men's track and field, the United States won, of course, but Sweden was a good second, with France a poor third, England a poor fourth, and little Jamaica a surprisingly strong fifth.

In the women's track and field the fabulous Dutch girl, Fannie Blankers-Koen, won four Olympic gold medals by running away from the field in the 100-meter dash (at which she was also the world record holder), winning the 200-meter dash (in which she established a new Olympic record), and the 80-meter hurdles (where she was the world's record holder), and running a tremendous anchor leg that made up a big lead to win the 400-meter relay for the Netherlands. The American women's team did not fare well, winning only one gold medal, in the running high jump, although even here the winner's jump did not equal Fannie Blankers-Koen's world's record. Fannie just could not participate in the many events in which she was the best in the world. She could not enter the running broad jump either, although she also held the world's record. The women's unofficial team championship was won by the Netherlands, if not by Fannie alone.

The 1952 Olympic games in Helsinki, Finland—the XV Olympiad—was an imposing spectacle presented in a stadium of pure modern Finnish architecture strangely reminiscent of classical Greek architecture and the ancient Olympic games. The Finns and the Finnish Organizing Committee did everything they could to make this Olympiad a tremendous success, even retaining many foreign specialists to help organize the games, including the author, who made three visits to Helsinki prior to the games. It might be said, even though it is said every four years, that the Olympic flame never burned brighter than in 1952 and that the XV Olympiad presented more nations, more competitors, better competition, and greater world interest than any other. In the United States, the Olympics received greater support and more attention than ever before, from the President of the United States, who proclaimed an Olympic Week, down to the humblest of sports followers. The Olympic Telethon arranged by Bob Hope and Bing Crosby to raise funds by contributions from the television audience was undoubtedly the greatest event of its kind ever staged, and it is estimated that over 50 million people in the United States witnessed it. Over one million dollars was pledged on the Telethon, but unfortunately only $353,000 was actually collected. The Amateur Athletic Union of the United States, with the late Gustavus Kirby as Fund Raising Chairman, raised $291,518.

More than ever before, it was evident to all that the Olympic games are a great idealistic enterprise. Those who participate, being amateurs, contribute to it and do not seek to take from it. It is free from dollar signs or from political intrigue, and the International Committee aims to keep it that way. Sports cannot be used by any individual or nation for selfish or propaganda purposes. That is why the Olympic movement has spread throughout the world without large funds or huge endowments. From an original start of nine nations, in less than sixty years it has spread to every corner of the globe. Today over eighty national Olympic committees are recognized by the International Olympic Committee. History records nothing to compare with this amazing march of amateur sports despite distances, and differences in language, race, color, religion, and ideology. The Olympic movement in the United States is vigorously promoted under the leadership of Avery Brundage (now President of the International Olympic

Committee), Kenneth L. Wilson, Asa S. Bushnell, J. Lyman Bingham, John T. McGovern, and Carl H. Hansen.

Sixty-nine countries were represented—a new record—in the XV Olympic games. The President of Finland, J. K. Paasikivi, opened the games. The parade, as usual, was led by Greece, and Finland, the host nation, was last. The Olympic torch was carried into the stadium and borne around the arena by none other than Paavo Nurmi, Finland's greatest runner, and was later passed to Hannes Kolehmainen, who lit the flame at the top of the tower overlooking the impressive modern stadium.

The track and field competition involved 995 individual entries from 57 countries. Thirty-nine countries entered contestants in the women's track and field events. Even Bermuda and Singapore were represented.

The men's unofficial track and field championship was won by the United States with a total of 31 medalists; second was Russia with 17 medalists. Russia served notice to the track and field world that, with the techniques, form, equipment and the training methods learned from the United States, it would be a candidate for the track and field championship in the very near future.

The United States track and field team won 14 gold medals, two more than ever before, as well as numerous silver and bronze medals. Robert J. King, the team manager, said in his report: "The games were impeccably conducted and all were impressed by the quietly efficient Finnish people, their graciousness and warm hospitality." Arrangements for track and field in particular set a new high in organization, and the track was in extraordinarily good shape. Seven Olympic records were broken, two tied, and one world's record was surpassed.

The 100-meter dash supplied one of the greatest finishes of any Olympics. Several photos at several angles were necessary to establish the winner. Four men finished under the proverbial blanket in a near dead heat, and although Remigino of the United States was declared the winner, there is still some doubt to this day whether McKenley of Jamaica did not deserve a tie. The metric mile of 1500 meters, as usual, provided tremendous thrills for the crowd of some 74,000 people. Bannister of England, who was later to become the first man ever to break the four-minute barrier for the mile, was fourth. The surprise winner was J. Barthel of Luxembourg. This was no fluke, however, because Barthel's time was an Olympic record and only 2.2 seconds off the world's record. It was, incidentally, the first time that little Luxembourg had won an Olympic gold medal. Emil Zatopek, considered by many to be past his prime, nevertheless won the 5000 meter, the 10,000 meter, and the marathon, and may well go down in history as the greatest long-distance runner of modern times. It is interesting to note that Zatopek had never run the marathon distance and yet won with plenty to spare and was quite fresh at the finish. According to many, he looked fresher and more relaxed than he had appeared in any of his other races during the week. The time of all of the first six men to finish was faster than any marathon ever run in the Olympics. R. Gorno, an Argentinian, finished second, then G. Jansson of Sweden, Yoon Chil Choi of Korea, V. Karvonen of Finland, and in sixth place, D. Cabrera of Argentina, the winner of the marathon at the 1948 London Olympiad.

Harrison Dillard, appearing in his regular specialty—the 110-meter high hurdles—won and established a new Olympic record. Parry O'Brien won the shotput with an Olympic record throw and showed the form which was later to enable him to break the world's record many times. The Rev. Robert E. Richards of LaVerne, California, a standout in the pole vault, won that event with the greatest of ease. Brazil's hop-step-and-jumper, Adehamar Ferreira da Silva, was an outstanding star of the show, breaking the Olympic and world's records; in fact, he exceeded the former world's record many times during the competition. Robert Mathias became the first man in history to win an all-around modern Olympic championship, or decathlon, for a second time. This established him as the greatest all-around track and field athlete in the world. He also broke his own world's record. Strangely enough, however, he was pushed by a new sensation, Milton Campbell, an 18-year-old high-school junior from Plainfield, New Jersey, who came in second. The leading European threat and runner-up in 1948, Heinrich of France, was forced to withdraw after the first day when he aggravated an old injury. The versatility of Mathias, like that of Jim Thorpe, might be commented on here, for Mathias was also an all-American football player.

In the women's track and field, the all-around women's unofficial track championship was won by Russia, with Australia second. The most interesting performances were the winning of the relay by the United States team and the winning of the javelin throw by D. Zatopekova of Czechoslovakia, the wife of Emil Zatopek. Mrs. Zatopek, by the way, broke the Olympic record. Czech and double Czech!

The track and field competition in Melbourne, Australia in 1956 will, it is believed, again break all records for the greatest number of countries (there are already 73 nations entered), the greatest number of competitors, the toughest competition, and the most outstanding performances. The host nation in this case will undoubtedly present a strong track and field team, led by a young schoolteacher, John Landy, the world's record holder at one mile and the only man in the history of mankind who has run the mile under four minutes many times.

In conclusion, it would be interesting to show the progress made in track and field from the beginning of the modern Olympics to the present by a comparison of a few records. The pole vault record of 10 feet 9¾ inches in the 1896 games seems unbelievably low compared with the present world's record of 15 feet 7¾ inches; in the "metric mile" 1500 meter, the winning time at the 1896 games was 4 minutes and 33.2 seconds, while the current world's record for 1956 is 3 minutes and 43 seconds. These figures of competitive athletic improvement in the realm of amateur sports show that man should be able to break any barrier and accomplish almost anything for his own progress and betterment.

IMPORTANT FACTS ABOUT TRACK AND FIELD EQUIPMENT AND DISTANCES

Here is a collection of facts and figures relating to some of the many events in the Olympic games.

First, the marathon race. The distance is 26 miles and 385 yards, or 42 kilometers and 195 meters; it takes about two and a half hours to run.

An early Olympic test was the throwing of rocks and weapons. These events have their counterparts today in four throwing events, the discus, hammer, shot, and javelin.

The first discus was of stone. Now it is a circular wooden plate with a smooth metal ring around its edge and brass plates set flush into the sides. It weighs 2 kilograms, or 4 lbs. 6.4 oz.

The shot or weight is spherical, weighs 16 lbs., and is of solid iron, brass, or any metal not softer than brass; or it can be a shell of such metal filled with lead.

The hammer weighs 16 lbs. over-all, including a handle of spring steel wire or No.-36 piano wire looped at one end to provide a grip and connected to the head by a swivel. This head, like the weight, is spherical, and of iron or brass; the whole must not measure more than 4 ft. in length. It is not, of course, a "hammer," though in the old days a blacksmith's hammer was thrown, and is still used in the Highland Games of Scotland.

The javelin is a wooden spear (made of birch) with a sharp iron or steel point. The space between the foremost point and the center of gravity is between 3 and 3½ ft.; at the center is a grip formed of whipcord without thongs or notches in the shaft. It is circular in section throughout. The length of a javelin is not less than 8 ft. 6 in., and the weight is not less than 1 lb. 12 oz. The women's javelin weighs 1 lb. 5 oz.

By contrast, the pole with which the pole vaulter propels himself upward may be of any material, length, or diameter. It is usually made of aluminum, bamboo, or other wood, and may terminate in a single metal spike. Each competitor brings his own to the meeting; only the best are likely to get higher than 15 ft.

Now for the running track. It is the inner edge that counts; cinder tracks are marked by a border of wood 2 inches high, and grass tracks (for hurdles and steeplechase) by a chalk line. Races of 120 yards or less must be run on a straight course, in lanes whose width is not less than 4 feet. In long-distance races, held on an oval track, the distance a runner has to run is calculated from a point measured 12 inches to the outside of this inside edge. In measuring lanes for distances up to and including 440 yards, the inner lane is measured first, and the others 8 inches from their inside borders.

The relay baton is a smooth, hollow, wooden or metal tube circular in section, a little less than 12 inches in length, and weighing 1¾ oz.

Hurdle races are over ten obstacles; for the 110-meter or 120-yard race these are at 10-yard intervals with a 15-yard run-up from the start to the first hurdle. For this distance the hurdles are 3 ft. 6 in. high, with level top rails, 3 ft. 11 in. wide, weight 22 lb. 3½ oz., and designed so that a force of 8 lbs. applied to the center or the top bar is needed to knock one over.

For the 400-meter or 440-yard race, hurdles are 6 inches lower, the first being placed 49¼ yards from the start, and the rest 38¼ yards apart.

In steeplechases a water jump is included, and there must be five jumps in each lap. The hurdles used in this case are 3 feet high; each obstacle must have a total width of 12 feet. Every competitor must go over or through the water.

The finish in track races is not the tape, but a white line on the ground. The tape is stretched 4 feet above it for the purpose only of assisting the judges. The finishing order is judged by the order in which any part of the competitor's body (the torso, as distinct from the head, arms, hands, or feet) reaches the line. In the event a competitor falls, he is held not to have finished until head, body, and feet are all over the line.

So long as certain countries do not use the metric system, there must be some difficulty in comparing times and distances. In the Olympic games all weights and measures must be in accordance with the metric system.

The 100-meter race is, by United States and British equivalent, 109 yards 1 foot 1 inch. The 800 meters is not an exact half-mile (880 yards) but 874 yards 2 feet 8 inches. The nearest event to the mile (1760 yards) is the 1500 meters, equivalent to 1,640 yards 1 foot 2¾ inches.

CHAPTER XV

WEIGHT LIFTING

MAN OUT of necessity has always been a weight lifter, from the days when our cave man ancestors lifted great rocks to block cave entrances for protection, through the days of ancient Egypt, when the greatest collection of weight lifters in the world was assembled to heave mighty stones into pyramids as monuments to dead kings. There is some evidence that weight lifting and weight throwing were practiced by the ancient Greeks in connection with gymnastics and track and field. There is also positive evidence that weight lifting and weight throwing were part of the ancient Irish Tailtean Games almost four thousand years ago.

However, weight lifting as we know the modern sport originated with the Europeans. Most likely some village youth, in an effort to make a show of his superior muscular prowess to some fair lady, bragged to a rival swain that he was the stronger and could lift a greater weight to prove it. The challenge made and accepted, a new sport and means of diversion was born. In its early years the sport was popular in central Europe and then spread to the Scandinavian countries, Egypt, Turkey, and even to Japan, and about a hundred years ago European settlers brought the sport to America. However, it still had limited appeal, and not until weight lifting had been introduced in the Olympic games did interest in it become widespread in America and all over the world.

In the 1896 Olympic games at Athens, there were only two weight lifting events, the dumbbell and the bar bell. A little byplay which delighted the spectators during this competition was that Prince George of Greece, one of the judges, who stood six feet five and had quite a reputation as a strong man himself, when he saw that an attendant ordered to remove the weights was having trouble doing so, couldn't resist picking up the heaviest of the weights and throwing it a good distance out of the way. In these early games, weight lifting was included as part of the track and field program and the events were contested in the stadium. A Dane and an Englishman each won one of the two events.

In the dumbbell contest in 1904, Americans won all three places—O. S. Osthoff first, F. Winters second, and F. Kungler third. In bar bell lifting, Pericles Kakousis of Greece, who later became known as one of the greatest strong men of his time, won, with Osthoff placing second and Kungler third. Two years later, at the Athens games of 1906, there were no entrants from the United States, and Josef Steinbach of Austria won the one-hand lift while D. Tofolas of Greece won the two-hand.

There appear to have been no official weight lifting events in the 1908 or 1912 Olympics. In 1920, however, interest in standardized weight lifting with definite procedures and rules had grown and it held its own place in the Olympics instead of as part of the track and field program. In that year the events were divided into five weight classes ranging from featherweight to heavyweight, and individual honors were divided among Europeans. The all-around unofficial championship was won by Belgium, with France almost even. Estonia and Italy produced individual winners.

In modern weight lifting the three important lifts are: the two-hand or military press, in which the contestants must toe a line, not move away from it, and after lifting the weight from the floor to rest on chest, neck, or shoulders, then lift it to the limit of arms without bending but retaining military position; the clean and jerk, or the jerk, in which, with either hand or both, the contestant lifts the weight from floor to rest against chest, then lifts it as high as possible on call from referee; the snatch, in which, with either hand or both, contestant picks up the weight and in one continuous movement lifts as high as possible. Contestant must hold weight for referee's count of one-two. There are two judges and a referee. Records are figured by adding totals of press, snatch, and clean and jerk. Weight classifications now in use follow approximately the same limits as in wrestling: bantamweight (123½ lbs.), featherweight (132¼ lbs.), lightweight (148¾ lbs.), middleweight (165⅜ lbs.), light heavyweight (181⅞ lbs.), middle heavyweight (198⅜ lbs.), and heavyweight (weight unlimited).

In 1924, when there were only five weight classes, Italy took three gold medals and France the other two. There was no United States team in either 1920 or 1924.

In 1928, the honors were again well distributed, with Germany, Egypt, France, and Austria all getting gold medals; Germany won the unofficial team championship.

The French took over in 1932 and won three of the five weight lifting titles. The Americans, however, going into weight lifting on a major basis, showed great promise, with Dietrich Wortmann as manager and Mark Berry as coach. Anthony Terlazzo and Henry L. Duey were third-place medal winners for the United States. There were eight countries in the competitions. Germany and Czechoslovakia produced the other two champions.

The 1936 Olympic games saw the United States win its first gold medal in weight lifting and also give promise of eventually attaining supremacy in this sport. Although Americans had won a sort of empty victory at St. Louis in 1904, they had not even entered this sport or any weight lifting events in 1906, 1908, 1912, 1920, or 1924. In 1928 the United States first organized and presented a very creditable team, so the results in 1936 were encouraging. The same manager and the same coach were behind the United States team, which met teams of fifteen nations. The unofficial team results were: first, Egypt, followed by Germany, Austria, the United States, and France. Anthony Terlazzo, who had placed third in 1932, won in the featherweight class, breaking the world's record with a total of a fraction under 689 lbs. At these Olympics eight world's records were broken. L. Hostin of France repeated his 1932 win in the light-heavyweight class, a feat never previously accomplished in Olympic weight lifting. The United States took two fifths and one sixth place, in addition to its one win. Mohammed Ahmed Mesbah of Egypt, in the lightweight class, was the star of the entire competition, breaking three world's records—twice in the clean and jerk, and in his total.

During the war years, American interest in weight lifting more than caught up with the head start of other countries, so there were numerous candidates and very tough competitions to select the United States team for the 1948 Olympiad. The London games attracted competitors from 35 nations in the weight lifting championships. The United States, entering a full team for only the third time, won the unofficial all-around championship with four firsts, three seconds, and two thirds. One hundred thirty-five weight lifters puffed and huffed to create eighteen new Olympic and four new world's records. Dietrich Wortmann's dream and ambition had come true—in three Olympics he had, as manager, brought the United States from nowhere to first place. Robert Hoffman was coach of the winners. John Davis, United States Olympic heavyweight champion, broke one world's record, and U. S. I. Fayad of Egypt, in the featherweight class, broke three. Evidence of the growing popularity of this sport is the fact that there were entries from India and Pakistan, Peru and Argentina, Korea and South Africa, as well as the European nations.

An example of the good sportsmanship shown during these games is the conduct of Stanczyk of the United States. On the third trial he snatched 292 lbs. for a new world record and received the approval of the two judges. However, he reported to the referee that his knee had accidently grazed the platform, and disqualified himself.

In 1952 the late and honored Dietrich Wortmann was again the manager of the United States weight lifting team, and again saw his team win. At his death, the sport suffered a great loss.

The Helsinki 1952 Olympiad surpassed all previous Olympics in the number of contestants and the quality of the performances in weight lifting. Russia was a newcomer to the games but showed great promise, winning three titles to four for the United States (a bantamweight class having been added in 1948 and a middle heavyweight class in these Olympics). Twenty-one Olympic and six world's records were broken. R. Chimishkyan of the U.S.S.R. broke one world's record; N. Schemansky, United States middle heavyweight (199 lbs.), broke three; and T. Kono, United States lightweight (148 lbs.), broke two. Of the 28 world's records (press, snatch, jerk, and total in each of seven weight classifications), American weight lifters now hold 13. To demonstrate the awesome accomplishments of weight lifters, T. Kono, weighing under 148 lbs., can press, snatch, and jerk over 798 lbs.

A great weight lifting meet is expected at the 1956 Olympic games. As in all other sports, improvements and new records are expected at Melbourne.

CHAPTER XVI

WINTER SPORTS

1. SKIING

IT IS not known whether the ski or the snowshoe came first, but both were originally fashioned from animal bones and were used as a means of travel in snow-covered countries thousands of years ago. In fact, a pair of skis said to be 5,000 years old is displayed at a museum in Stockholm. Primarily skiing was a means of transportation and still is, because of climatic conditions in many countries. Human nature, however, naturally seeks diversion and people began to see that skiing could be converted into a sport of many forms. Today skiing seems to have no bounds of climate, for there are ski enthusiasts performing even on sand in warm desert areas and on water.

The old bone skis, naturally, could not be turned up at the ends, and after the beginning of the Christian Era, wood was used which made this innovation possible. The development of the ski is attributed to the Scandinavian countries and even played a part in their history when a more maneuverable, shorter, and better type of ski could mean victory for their soldiers. About 1590 skiing was introduced into central Europe through Austria, famous today for its ideal skiing areas, and has spread to all parts of the world where there is snow.

In the early nineteenth century people began to take notice of little impromptu races held between travelers in Scandinavia. Soon a little jumping was added to the play and by the 1850's, in Norway, carnivals were held for actual competition. Ten years later, the Norwegian royal family took notice of the jumping competitions and the King of Norway became so enthusiastic that he donated a special trophy for the winner. This soon grew to be the greatest sporting event in the country, "The Norwegian Ski Derby."

From Scandinavia, skiing ranged to continental Europe about the middle of the nineteenth century. The first mid-European ski club was formed in Munich in 1890. The Swiss organized their first ski club in 1893. Chamonix, in France, was established as a winter resort in 1898-99.

The facts about the introduction of skis into North America are uncertain. The Canadian Indians used snowshoes and in all probability constructed skis, or snowshoes with long runners for use down steep mountain sides. There are those who contend that early settlers or visitors from Sweden, Denmark, and Norway brought them to Canada. In predominantly Scandinavian settlements in the United States, particularly in the north Midwest, various local clubs were formed. By 1904, these local clubs drew enough attention and support to band together into the National Ski Association, but it wasn't until formal international competition was begun in the modern Olympic games that skiing was brought into the limelight.

Skiing was demonstrated at some of the early Olympic games, but it was not until 1924 that winter sports finally won international recognition and became part of the formal Olympic program. In the games at Chamonix, France, winter sports were an outstanding success. The Norwegians, real masters at skiing, won all four events and in two of them took all of the top four places. Thorleif Haug was a triple gold medal winner, taking first place in the Nordic combined, the 18-kilometer and the 50-kilometer race. In the jumping, the most spectacular of all skiing events, Jacob Thams of Norway won, with Anders Haugen, the only American to place in skiing, in fourth place, which was a good showing considering the limited appeal the sport had in the States in 1924. Norway easily won the all-around winter sports championships, which attracted contestants from sixteen countries. Finland was second, the United States a poor but surprising third, then England, Austria, Sweden, Switzerland, Germany, Canada, Belgium, Czechoslovakia, and Italy, in that order.

The 1924 games at Chamonix were so successful that winter sports were firmly established as part of the Olympic program, and the second Winter Olympics in 1928 were held at St. Moritz, Switzerland. Twenty-five nations sent representatives. During the preceding years, the United States had developed a strong winter sports team, and in the unofficial overall score they placed second to Norway. However, skiing was their weakest point, and again the Scandinavians proved their complete mastery of the sport. The United States made 1 point in skiing, 10 in speed skating, 10 in figure skating, and 24 in bobsledding. Sweden was the over-all third, Finland fourth, and Austria and Canada fifth and sixth.

According to competition rules, forty entries or twenty actual competitors were allowed, but the United States had only three men: Rolf Monsen, Charles Proctor, and Anders

Haugen. In spite of an injured knee, Monsen placed sixth in the main jumping event to earn the only point won by the American ski team. In the combined ski-jumping event a championship performance almost cost Jacob Thams, 1924 Olympic gold medal winner from Norway, his life. It must be explained that the ski jump at St. Moritz is geared for jumps of about 60 meters and is safe only for jumps measuring up to 65 meters, but the object of ski jumping is to see how far you can go and still maintain perfect form, and Thams jumped an unprecedented 73 meters and suffered a terrible fall—this was impossible to prevent because of the physical conditions of the hill—but he miraculously escaped death. A fellow Norwegian, Johann Grottumsbraaten, won this event and also the 18-kilometer race. Andersen of Norway won the gold medal in the special jumping and Pete Hedlund of Sweden the 50-kilometer race.

In the 1932 games at Lake Placid, New York, though the Americans did well in the over-all winter sports competition, they were still green, though game, in skiing. The United States won the over-all games but with just 2 points in skiing as against Norway's 47. In skiing Finland was second with 19 points and Sweden third with 18. The Americans had hoped to gain points in jumping. However, the most hopeful prospect, Casper Oimen, captain of the ski team, had hurt himself during tryouts in the United States before leaving for the games, although he insisted upon participating and took fifth place. Birger Ruud gave Norway the jumping championship and Grottumsbraaten won another medal for Norway in the combined racing and jumping. The 50-kilometer race, won by Saarinen of Finland, was extraordinary in that it was run at all. The weather conditions were almost impossible. In fact, the snow was fast disappearing and part of the race was run on bare ground, with rocks and stumps sticking up. The hardy Finn persevered, however, to win this marathon, and as evidence of the grueling run, when he came across the finish line his face was streaked with blood and his clothes were in shreds.

The coach of the American team, Julius Blegen, after these games reported that, "The 3rd Winter Olympic Games, as far as skiing is concerned, was the biggest boost the sport has ever had in the United States and should in years to come open the eyes of the American boys and girls to the possibilities in this wonderful health-bringing, clean outdoor pastime." This proved to be true and the Lake Placid winter games proved a stimulant to millions of potential enthusiasts, for skiing was seen by people who had never seen it before.

It caught on immediately, with its fascinating combination of danger and grace, and ski groups began mushrooming all over the country. Instructors were brought over from the Scandinavian countries and Austria, France, and Switzerland, and now there are said to be over four million ski enthusiasts in the United States alone.

The 1936 games at Garmisch-Partenkirchen, Germany, opened in a raging blizzard. The greatest number of contestants so far—almost one thousand, representing twenty-eight nations—participated. Skiing was gaining widespread appeal and was attracting more and more contestants from more countries. The Norwegians again maintained their consistently high standard of performance in skiing and also won the over-all winter games championship, with Germany, Sweden, Finland, the United States, and Austria completing the top six. A welcome newcomer to the Olympics was the first of the events for women, the Alpine combined, which Christel Cranz of Germany won. Germany also edged in on the combined downhill and slalom race for men, a combination of the most dangerous and the most graceful of skiing routines. Norway and Sweden took all the other events, and in the 18-kilometer race, in which there were 115 entries, they took the first nine places.

In 1948 there were 942 participants in the winter events, with contestants from twenty-nine nations. Sweden, for the first time, won both the over-all skiing events and the unofficial all-around winter games championship. In all winter sports combined, for both men and women, Switzerland was second, the United States third, Norway fourth, Austria fifth, Finland sixth, and France seventh. The United States entered a ski team with thirty members (in contrast to the earlier three-member team), including women. The inclusion of women in winter events was to bring the United States its first gold medal in skiing. The outstanding success of Mrs. Gretchen Fraser of Vancouver, Washington, in the slalom brought applause from all countries. She also placed second in the Alpine combined. The Norwegians upheld their fine jumping tradition, winning the top three places. Birger Ruud, who had previously won two Olympic championships, took second place and made room for Petter Hugsted in first place. In the jumping, Gorden Wren of the United States came in fifth, the only American to place. The French also gave top performances and Henri Oreiller won two gold medals in the downhill and Alpine combination and a bronze medal in the men's slalom. In the slalom, Edi Reinalter of Switzerland won first place and James Couttet of France second place.

141

Couttet also came in third in the Alpine combination. Karl Molitor of Switzerland was second in the Alpine combination and tied for third with Rolf Olinger, also Swiss, in the downhill. In this last event, Franz Gabl of Austria was second.

Thirty nations with almost 1200 contestants participated in the 1952 games at Oslo. Skiing events drew enormous crowds of spectators and the ranks of competitors were filling up with contestants from as far away as Japan, and in one event there were over eighty contestants. The Nordic events were won mostly by Finland and Norway. An Italian, Zeno Colo, gave a magnificent performance and won the gold medal in the downhill race, and Ol Schneider of Austria won the special slalom for men. The only Americans to place in the men's events were two boys from Dartmouth—William Beck, who came in fifth in the downhill (out of seventy-two contestants), and Joseph Brooks Dodge, sixth in the giant slalom and ninth in the special slalom. However, while the American men gained mostly experience, the women made up for it in honors. Mrs. Andrea Mead Lawrence, a young housewife from Vermont, won two gold medals in skiing—the slalom and the giant slalom. Katy Rodolph and Imogene Upton tied for fifth in the slalom and Catherine Wegeman placed fifth in the giant slalom.

The four-year wait for the 1956 Winter Olympics was worthwhile to the skiing world, for there was unprecedented skiing at Cortina that year. A young, handsome Austrian boy, Toni Sailer, with a fast-gained reputation, won not only both slalom events but the downhill race as well, earning three gold medals, a feat never before accomplished in thirty-two years of Olympic skiing. Besides his flawless skiing form, his good looks must have won over more than one woman to the sport. His boyish shyness won him the American nickname of "Li'l Abner of the Tyrol." Stenersen of Norway won the Nordic combined, with Ericsson of Sweden coming in second and Gasienca of Poland placing third. This was the first time Poland had won a medal in a skiing event. The Japanese had been sending skiers to the Olympics for some time and this year Chiharu Igaya won a silver medal in the men's slalom. Hyvarinen and Kallakorpi of Finland took the first two places in the special jump. The Russians made a grand showing, although it was the first time they had ever been represented in skiing, winning the gold medal in the cross-country relay and third place in the other three cross-country events. With points made in the other winter sports, the U.S.S.R. won the all-around winter sports championship. In the women's events, Kozyreva and Erochina won the first two places in the women's cross-country, the first time this event was held in the Olympics. Ossi Reichert of Germany won the women's giant slalom, and Andrea Mead Lawrence of the United States tied for fourth place in this event. The wide geographical distribution of participants, including Russia, Japan, and Great Britain, in addition to the usual strong central European and Scandinavian representation, is an outstanding example of what the Olympics have done to bring people from all corners of the earth together in common interest and proves that skiing is no longer an exclusively Scandinavian sport but one of worldwide importance and interest.

2. FIGURE SKATING

Skating is a natural means of transportation in icy countries, and ice skates were probably an offshoot of skis and snowshoes. When it was necessary to move faster over icy surfaces, man was forced to use smaller and thinner bone runners. Later, by experimental smoothing and working of the bones, he learned that a flat bottom on the runner would permit a swift, gliding motion, and in this way, ice skates were developed.

As far as the development of skating as a sport is concerned, it is known that Scotland showed an early interest in it. In fact, in 1642 there was a well-established Skating Club of Edinburgh. When the Scots migrated to Canada, skating flourished and regular tournaments were held before the turn of the nineteenth century. The first American to win in any of these tournaments was Benjamin West, the artist, who spent a lot of time in Europe sometime in the 1770's.

In the United States, although skates were in use in the northeastern states for transportation, the practical New Englanders did not use them, as far as is known, for sport's sake until prompted by Canadian enthusiasm, and it was not until a technical improvement was made in the skates themselves that figure skating became really popular. Around 1850 E. W. Bushnell of Philadelphia revolutionized the skating world when he came out with a pair of skates with steel blades. These could be bought for thirty dollars, which represented quite an amount at that time. Despite the price, he was overwhelmed with orders and was able to produce them at a lower price, and they were soon in use all over the world. Steel blades were especially important in fancy figure skating, for they enabled performers to do artistic twists and turns on blades which did not have to be constantly resharpened.

Later it was an American who popularized figure skating

143

throughout the world. This American was Jackson Haines, a ballet master who, in the slump following the Civil War in America, was not getting the business he had before the war. Not wishing to give up his profession, he packed up and went to Vienna where dancing seemed more likely to furnish him a livelihood. When he got there he found that in addition to their love for dancing, the Austrians also liked to skate—so, why not combine the two and skate to music? He transferred first the waltz and later other dance steps to the ice, and the idea and routines were copied throughout Europe, Canada, and the United States. He made a name for himself with this innovation and in Europe he was known as the "American Skating King." With his reputation made, he was able to establish schools, and his pupils improvised even further. One pupil in particular, Louis Rubinstein, a Canadian, came back to North America in 1878 and formed the Amateur Skating Association of Canada. Interest spread to America, and in 1887, the Skating Club of the United States was formed in Philadelphia. Beyond this small group, however, comparatively little interest was evinced until 1908, when figure skating was first included in the Olympic games.

The 1908 events in the first Olympic skating competitions held in England were the same as we have today, individual or singles for men and women and pairs, although there was an extra event in these Olympics probably comparable to our present free style part of the skating program. Generally, skating is judged 60 per cent on prescribed classical school figures or patterns and 40 per cent on free skating, where it is up to the individual to add all the dash and dazzle he can. The 1908 men's singles championship was won by Ulrich Salchow of Sweden, for whom a special figure that he performed is named. Mrs. E. Syers of Great Britain won the same title for the women, and the special figure winner was N. Panin of Russia. Despite the wonderful showing of Panin, Russia did not enter any skating events again until 1956. The honors in pairs went to Miss Hubler and Mr. Burger of Germany.

One of the participants in the 1908 skating events was Irving Brokaw of New York, who had gone to Europe to study. Although Brokaw didn't win any medals, his participation in the games and subsequent discovery of the enthusiastic following the sport was gaining prompted him, upon his return to the United States, to lecture on the sport and to organize American competitions.

In the war years that followed, the sport was eclipsed, but was resumed again in 1920. In the 1920 Olympics in Belgium,

American representation was doubled; we had two members, and therefore, a figure skating team—Miss Theresa Weld and Nathaniel Niles. Ulrich Salchow, who had won the last Olympic men's title and was eleven times world's champion, came in fourth, which should prove the quality of the competition. Grafstrom, another Swede, came in first and Niles placed sixth, surpassing both the English and Swiss national champions in performance. In the pair event, the Jakobssons of Finland, world's amateur champions for some time, won the gold medal, and Miss Weld and Mr. Niles came in fourth. Here also, it is to be noted that the Olympics had brought on annual world's championships between Olympiads. In the ladies singles, Theresa Weld did very well again, placing third to two Swedish skating stars.

Four years later, in 1924, the winter games, including figure and speed skating, were officially recognized as part of the Olympic program and the French arranged a complete series of winter sports at Chamonix which were a great success.

The contestants in figure skating included the best in the world—almost all amateur champions of their countries. In men's figures, Grafstrom again placed first, although because of temporary illness he did not show the absolute perfection displayed at the Antwerp games in 1920. Nathaniel Niles of the United States came in sixth, just as he had in 1920, with Bocklof of Austria and Gautschi of Switzerland moving into second and third places formerly held by Scandinavians. Mrs. Herma von Szabo Plank, world's champion for two years, won the women's singles. Second to Mrs. Plank was America's Beatrix Loughran. Theresa (Weld) Blanchard, the former 1920 team member, was fourth. In the pair skating, two newcomers to the Olympics, Miss Engelman and Mr. Berger of Austria, came in first and Mrs. Blanchard and Mr. Niles placed sixth.

The interest aroused by the elaborate series of winter games staged at the Olympics at Chamonix enabled the United States to send a strong team to the second winter games in 1928. At these games, held in St. Moritz, was a gathering of the world's greatest amateur skaters, and Salchow, 1908 Swedish Olympic gold medal winner and now president of the International Skating Federation, observed that the amateurs present outperformed the professionals of the time. In the women's event, the unanimous choice for first place was a young Norwegian girl who was going to have a great influence on the growth of figure skating. This new Olympic winner was Sonja Henie, who in addition to her top skating performances added glamor to an already exciting sport. In the same event, Beatrix Loughran and Maribel Vinson of the United States placed third and fourth respectively. Miss Loughran and Sherwin Badger placed fourth in the pair event. In the men's singles Grafstrom of Sweden won his third Olympic gold medal.

In 1932 the winter games were held at Lake Placid, New York, and Sonja Henie, the "girl in white," won top honors for women again and was seen by large crowds of Americans for the first time. Maribel Vinson moved up to third place in women's figures at Lake Placid. In the men's figures, Grafstrom of Sweden, three times Olympic champion, placed second to Karl Schafer of Austria. The American Roger Turner, who had placed tenth in the last Olympic games, placed sixth in this event. In pairs, Mr. and Mrs. Brunet of France won the gold medal for the second time and the American pair, Beatrix Loughran and Sherwin Badger, came in a close second.

The 1936 events were held at Garmisch-Partenkirchen, Germany. In the men's competition Karl Schafer of Austria won first place for the second consecutive time, with Ernst Baier of Germany winning second place. George Hill, a 17-year-old newcomer and American champion, placed twelfth out of twenty-five competitors.

Sonja Henie retained her Olympic championship and won for the third successive time first place in the competition for women. Cecilia Colledge of Great Britain gave a brilliant performance in the standard school figures but fell down in the free skating figures, placing second to Miss Henie. Maribel Vinson of New York, medal winner in 1932, took fifth place. A speedy pair from Germany, Maxie Herber and Ernst Baier gave a fascinating gold medal performance in the pair event consisting mostly of "shadow skating"—that is, skating side by side and executing the same steps in perfect unison without touching one another. In the same event, Maribel Vinson and George Hill placed fifth.

It was not until after the 1936 Olympics, however, that skating became truly widespread in the United States. Sonja Henie had now abandoned the ranks of the amateurs and was brought to New York, where her ice show had a booming success. Immediately other ice revues imitated her show, and ice carnivals became gigantic spectacles which attracted enormous audiences throughout the country—which, in turn, popularized skating.

At St. Moritz in 1948, after a twelve-year interim, the winter games were resumed. The proof of the growing popularity of the sport in the United States, with the consequent increase in competition and experience and the improvement of performance was the fact that an American won a first-place gold medal in figure skating for the first time: 18-year-old Dick Button of Englewood, New Jersey, became the new men's champion. In addition to his winning top honors, two other Americans, John Lettengarver and James Grogan, placed fourth and sixth. The second and third places in men's figures were taken by Hans Gerschwiler of Switzerland and Edi Rada of Austria. Another new champion came into the limelight in the women's competition, and the tradition of glamor in the sport was maintained by the blonde and beautiful Barbara Ann Scott of Canada, who won the gold medal for women's figures. Yvonne Sherman of the United States came in sixth.

In the event for pairs, the Belgian duo of Micheline Lannay and Pierre Baugniel managed to outperform other very strong contenders. The American pair of Yvonne Sherman and Robert Swenning came in fourth, while the brother and sister team of Karol and Peter Kennedy placed sixth.

In 1952, the American team's hard work and the ever-increasing popularity of skating in the United States really paid off, and the Americans won more places than any previous figure skating team had. Dick Button won his second Olympic championship and everyone on the team finished in the top six. In the men's competition James Grogan placed third, with Hayes Jenkins fourth. Jeanette Altwegg of Great Britain, who was third in 1948, came in for top honors in 1952, with Tenley Albright a close second. In this same event, Sonya Klopfer and Virginia Baxter placed fourth and fifth respectively. In pairs, a German couple, Ria and Paul Falk, skated through for top honors, with the United States pair, Karol and Peter Kennedy, holding second place and Janet Gerhausen and John Nightingale taking fifth place.

After these games, Button turned professional and so stepped aside to let someone else have a try in the 1956 Olympics. Button, all-time great in the art of skating, won not only two Olympic titles but five straight world championships, seven consecutive United States titles, and three successive North American crowns, an all-time record.

In 1956, the Olympic figure skating championships were very closely contested among the Americans. Tenley Albright of Boston, silver medal winner in 1952, won first place in the women's event despite a deep cut in her right ankle suffered during pre-Olympic practice. Carol Heiss came in for second place, missing first place by only 1.5 points. Ingrid Wendl of Austria was third. In the men's competition, the judging was even closer. Hayes Jenkins won the gold medal, and Ronnie Robertson, in second place, was only one point behind. Hayes' younger brother, Dave Jenkins, won third place.

3. SPEED SKATING

Speed skating grew along with figure skating and also gained most of its impertus from the Olympic games. Even though speed skating came before the introduction of complicated figures, it did not have the wide appeal of the latter, and it wasn't until the 1924 Olympics that speed skating contests were held.

Traditionally the Europeans, especially the Scandinavians, have been great skaters. In speed skating, particularly in the longer races, the north Europeans have surpassed other countries because of their stamina and their conditioning in cold climates.

In the 1924 Olympics, this tradition was upheld and the Finns gained the three top places in the 1500-, 5000-, and 10,000-meter races. However, in the shorter 500-meter race, Charles Jewtraw of the United States won a gold medal.

Before the winter games of 1928, it looked as though the United States had a real winner in the 10,000-meter race in Irving Jaffee. Unfortunately, because of improper ice conditions, the event had to be officially canceled, although Jaffee won the informal contest which was run off. He also came in fourth in the 5000-meter race. Other Americans who did well were O'Neil Farrell, who tied for third in the short race; E. L. Murphy, fifth in the 1500 meter; and Valentine Bialas, who was sixth in both the 1500 and 5000 meter. Clas Thunberg of Finland and Bernt Evensen of Norway tied for first place in the 500 meter. Thunberg also came in to win his second gold medal in the 1500 meter but failed to repeat his 1924 victory in the 5000-meter event, which was won by Ivar Ballangrud of Norway.

The Lake Placid games of 1932 were won by the United States. However, there was not as much competition as there might have been because of the traveling time and expense involved. Jack Shea won the 500-meter and 1500-meter races, and Irving Jaffee came in first for the 5000- and 10,000-meter gold medals. In the latter, Ballangrud, the 1928 Olympic champion, came in second. Americans also scoring points were Edward Murphy, O'Neil Farrell, Ray Murray, Herbert Taylor, Edwin Wedge, and Valentine Bialas.

In the games of 1936, the Americans seemed to be resting on their 1932 laurels, for no United States skater placed in speed skating. The great Norwegian ace, Ivar Ballangrud, won three events—the 500-, 5000-, and 10,000-meter races—and placed second in the 1500 meter, which was won by a fellow countryman of his, Charles Mathisen.

During the years between 1936 and 1948, the Americans started to pick up again in speed skating. In the 1948 Olympic winter games the Scandinavians were all-powerful: The Norwegians won three races, and Seyffarth of Sweden won the 10,000 meter. Kenneth Bartholomew and Robert Fitzgerald of the United States tied for second place in the 500-meter race, with Kenneth Henry and Delbert Lamb taking fifth and sixth places. John Werket was sixth in the 1500 meter.

At Oslo in 1952 a Norwegian truck driver, Hjalmar Andersen, gave a real show and won the first triple championships in speed skating since Ivar Ballangrud, also of Norway, had performed the same feat in 1936. For Andersen to accomplish this, he had to break a world record and two Olympic records. The only title he missed was the 500 meter, which Kenneth Henry of the United States won; Donald McDermott, also of the United States, was second.

In 1956 Russia returned to Olympic skating after an absence of forty-eight years and won three out of four gold medals: Evgeny Grishin won the 500 meter, E. Grishin and Y. Mikhailov tied for first in the 1500 meter, and Boris Shilkov won the 5000 meter. In accomplishing this feat, they also set two world records and three Olympic records. But the 10,000 meter race was won by Sigge Ericsson of Sweden, who also set an Olympic record. The only American to place was Carow, who came in sixth in the 500 meter.

4. BOBSLEDDING

Man probably made his first attempt at sledding when he discovered that he could get down a steep, snow-covered hill faster by just sitting down than by trying to make it on foot. This must have proved chilly, however, so some bright soul stretched animal skins to sit on between two bone runners. This invention may also have grown out of the necessity to transport large animals home for food. The Algonquin Indians of North America had something similar to this in their toboggan (Canadian French adaptation of the Indian word), which was made of wood.

The toboggan is really the forerunner of the modern bobsled, and the use of it in sport can be attributed to a group of Americans and Englishmen who vacationed in the Swiss Alps around the year 1890. This group of vacationers, bored by the peaceful activities offered them, were looking for something to do that would be a little more thrilling than padding over the Alps on snowshoes. They fashioned a long adaptation of the toboggan, proceeded to lay out a course on the mountain, and were soon rocketing down dangerous mountain slopes in suicidal fashion. Other thrill seekers joined them, and even though most people at the time looked upon the devotees of this sport as outright maniacs, the real fans eventually found tobogganing too safe and tame and began to search for something even more adventurous to do. They discovered that if the toboggan were mounted on wooden runners, a far greater speed could be attained, but also the danger was greater because the higher center of gravity made the vehicle trickier to control on turns.

About 1885, new recruits began to appear who developed a heavier sled with added ballast to help keep it on the course —a speedier sled but a safer one. These new sleds were called bobsleighs (bob, because riders would "bob" to increase speed on a straightaway; that is, at command from the brakeman they would bob into a forward position after leaning backward as far as possible; this action, which must be performed in perfect unison by the whole team, can make the sled actually jump forward and thus cut seconds from the time in racing). Enthusiasts of racing with these new sleds joined a toboggan club which had many members, but they eventually found the tobogganers' rules too tame for them and branched off on their own. They laid out their own course in the Swiss Alps, the famous and dangerous Cresta Run. In the original rules for bobsled racing, it was required that two of the passengers be women—whether to add decoration or weight was never explained by the original rule makers—but women willing to rocket down the Alps at breakneck speeds were few and far between, so "two stout men" were substituted on the original five-man crew. The sport drew a larger number of fans each year while new features on the sleds were being developed to increase the speed even more; consequently, the Cresta Run became too dangerous, and an artificial run was built in St. Moritz in 1904. By the outbreak of World War I, there were some hundred bobsled courses in Europe.

National championships were soon held, and by 1924, when the winter games were first included officially as part of the Olympic program, the bobsledders made the most of the occasion and had their first international race, which was won by the four-man Swiss sled driven by E. Scherra.

Enthusiastic Americans vacationing in Switzerland entered into the thrilling sport wholeheartedly and obtained permission to represent their country in the 1928 Olympics. They carried off the Olympic competition that year, with Billy Fiske driving the 5-man team to victory and John Heaton piloting the other 5-man team for second-place honors. John Heaton also won first place in skeleton sled, with his brother Jennison winning second place. This victory was the beginning of many United States victories in this sport.

By the time of the 1932 Olympics, iron runners had been developed, and the Americans, with typical Yankee ingenuity, had inserted these runners in the bottoms of wooden shoes, and experimented with a v-shaped runner. This shape increased speed but cut up the track considerably, and after this competition only runners in the shape of arcs of true circles were allowed, with specific diameters. The Americans really clobbered their opponents in the bobsledding events at Lake Placid. They won first and second places in the four-man event, and in an unexpected upset, Hubert and Curtis Stevens came in first in the two-man, in which another American pair placed third. The National Amateur Athletic Union and the United States Olympic Committee were a little upset before the Lake Placid games because some bobsledders had protested that the teams had not been selected by competition, as demanded by the rules; but the results achieved silenced most of the complaints.

By 1936 the Americans had again added to the development of the sled by substituting steel planks for wooden ones, which made the sleds more flexible and cut down the friction between the runners and the ice. This was done by Bob and Bill Linney of New York, who also are credited with the first use of push handles to insure a fast start. On a running start, all four men could now push and then jump on as soon as they crossed the starting line. These refinements made for faster time.

At Garmisch, the Americans came through again to claim top two-man honors, with Ivan Brown and Bob Washbond winning the gold medal. This was quite an accomplishment, as several team members were injured in the trials because of the soft foundation of the course.

In 1948—with Fox of the 1936 team as coach and Curtis Stevens, the winning brakeman in 1932 and team member in 1936, as manager—things seemed to look promising. F. Fortune and S. Carron of the United States came in third to win a bronze medal in the two-man event. In the four-man event, the United States came through with flying colors and the team of F. Tyler, P. Martin, E. Rimkus, and W. D'Amico captured first place.

Before the games at Oslo in 1952 an amusing incident took place which illustrates the importance of the weight of the team members in bobsledding. The team was supposed to fly to London non-stop before going on to Oslo, but the airline transporting them had not taken into account the fact that many of the passengers represented Olympic bobsled beef, and a special stop had to be made at Gander because of the unexpected weight load.

In the actual games, it was time for another country to prove its strength, and the astute strategy of the Germans brought them a win. In the trial runs, the Germans observed that both the American and Swiss teams were making better time than they were, and decided to sacrifice one team by removing all the heavy men from their number-two team and transferring them to their number-one team. This tactic paid off, for the added weight gave them superior pickup power and they plummeted to victory in both the two- and four-man events. The United States placed second in both events—Stan Benham and Pat Martin in the two-man, and Benham piloting the four-man run.

The fact that the 1956 games were held at Cortina, Italy, seemed to give impetus to the host nation and for the first time an Italian team won first place in bobsledding. Lamberto Dalla Costa drove the gold-medal pair in the two-man event, and Eugenio Monti piloted for second place in both the two- and the four-man event. Switzerland won top honors in the four-man, and the United States came in third, with Art Tyler driving. The following countries entered at least one bobsled crew in the Olympics: Russia, Germany, the United States, Switzerland, France, Belgium, Sweden, Austria, Italy, Norway, Finland, and Argentina. Needless to say, each team entered in this event usually brings its own team physician and nurse to apply treatment to contusions and abrasions.

The modern bobsled, with streamlined cowl and wheel-type steering, able to reach speeds as high as 89 miles per hour, is a far cry from the animal-skin and -bone combination used by primitive man. To ride in this ice rocket on treacherous mountain slopes, where a single slip can cause death, is to participate in a sport for only the most daring—a sport rightly called "the champagne of thrills."

5. ICE HOCKEY

Ice hockey is an icy offshoot of field hockey, which was played by the Persians, Greeks, and Romans in ancient times and is played widely in France, England, and India in modern times. The sport spread throughout Europe, and the Irish and Scotch have always had the reputation of being great hockey players. There are stories of really wild and fierce slamming around between players in the "good old days." The legend of typical Irish temper can be substantiated by the story told about Lalrad Loingsech before he became King of Ireland some time before the Christian Era. The legend goes that he was born dumb, but one day, while he was playing hockey, an opponent gave him such a whack on the shins that he screamed for the first time in his life and thereafter regained his speech. Migrants from Europe brought the sport to Canada, where orginally broom handles and even tree branches were used for hockey sticks.

When methods of making artificial ice were developed and indoor rinks came into use, enthusiasm for the sport spread to America, and the Canadians, who had been holding official hockey matches since the middle of the nineteenth century, really developed the sport and taught the Americans the art of playing it. Canadians have proved their prowess in ice hockey for many years. Even with international competition, Canada has upheld its high standard of performance and has won all Olympic ice hockey competitions since 1920, except in 1936 and 1956, when Great Britain and Russia won top honors.

Americans have usually done well in this event, and came in second to the Canadians in 1920 and 1924. In 1928, for the first time, the United States was not represented, but took second-place honors again in 1932. In 1936 the American team was dropped to third by the British, with Canada again the winner.

American ice hockey representation in the 1948 winter games in St. Moritz caused quite a controversy. Two American teams were sent to the games, one chosen by the Amateur Hockey Association and the other the choice of the United States Olympic Committee. The Swiss favored the Association's team, but then the United States Olympic Committee threatened to withdraw American participation in all winter events. The International Olympic Committee settled the situation by barring both teams from competition. However, the Swiss went ahead and scheduled the Amateur Hockey Association team, and the International Olympic Committee, in turn, struck out hockey from the program. Then the Swiss threatened to call off the winter games. The matter was finally settled by letting the team play but not giving it official rating.

Fortunately, things went more smoothly in 1952. The Americans tied with the Canadians in the final game, but Canada, with an unbeaten record, won first place.

At the Cortina games in 1956 Russia moved in to win the gold medal, with the United States second and Canada third. Sweden, Czechoslovakia, and Germany took fourth, fifth, and sixth places respectively.

CHAPTER XVII

WRESTLING

WRESTLING AS an athletic posture of man goes back, along with boxing, to prehistoric days. Prehistoric man had to wrestle wild beasts in close encounter, and, realizing he had to school himself in the struggle for survival, he may have practiced holds and grips in friendly demonstrations or contests with members of his family or with his neighbors.

Wrestling as a sport undoubtedly goes further back than any existing records. Wall paintings found in the tombs of Beni Hasan, a village in Middle Egypt, show that Egyptians 5000 years ago knew nearly every wrestling hold we know today. There is definite historical evidence that wrestling was an important part of sports programs and festivities in ancient Greece and we find actual records of wrestling as the final event in the pentathlon after the 18th Olympic games, *circa* 708 B.C. Later wrestling became a separate event in the Olympics.

Any consideration of wrestling and the ancient Olympics cannot ignore one of the greatest names in both; Milo of Crotona, the greatest wrestler of antiquity. Although he was mainly a wrestler, he showed great abilities in boxing and in the pancratium. As a boy Milo won the boys' wrestling championship at the Olympic, Pythian, and other games. Later, he won many wrestling and pancratium championships, including six Olympic wrestling championships—which would make him the world's wrestling champion for twenty-four consecutive years.

Milo's strength was fabulous. When he was a small boy, he began carrying a young calf on his shoulder and continued to carry the calf every day thereafter until the calf had become a full-grown bull. Milo could, therefore, be called a star in the sport of weight lifting. He performed all manner of tricks to confuse his enemies, amuse his friends, and attract publicity. One of these was to grasp a pomegranate and challenge anyone to take it away from him. Not only was it impossible to do so, but his powerful grip was so controlled that the fruit was never crushed or damaged in any way. He could stand on a greased discus and make a fool of anyone who tried to push him off it. Another popular feat of Milo's consisted of having a cord tied tight around his head, then holding his breath and making the veins on his head swell until the cord broke, but Milo's tricks and own confidence in his strength proved his undoing in the end. No human being ever threw him in wrestling, but when he tried to replace a wedge in a tree trunk with his hand it became hopelessly entrapped in the aperture and poor Milo was eaten by wild animals. Milo of Crotona was not only never downed in twenty-four years—he never even fell to his knees. He was also known as a great eater. According to records that have come down to us, at one meal he ate seventeen pounds of meat and bread washed down by five quarts of wine. Wrestling in ancient Greece seems to have promoted good health, and wrestlers went on competing for twelve to twenty-four years.

In Japan, a most popular form of wrestling is Sumo, which started over two thousand years ago and is still popular. The champion Sumo wrestlers weigh 300 pounds or more and wear nothing but an ornamental loincloth. Their matches are held in a small, soft, sanded ring marked off with rice straw, and unfair play is scrupulously avoided. The object in Sumo is to push an opponent out of the ring or throw him to the floor. The slightest touch of knee or finger to the ground is a fall. Nearly all countries had similar ancient forms of wrestling, such as the Glima of the Icelanders, the Schwingen of the Swiss, the Cumberland of the Irish, and the Lancashire of the Scotch. In Greco-Roman wrestling, still popular in many countries and still on the Olympic program, the rules stipulate that legs cannot be used for attack or defense and that every hold must be above the belt. This is the type of wrestling that was practiced in ancient Greece and in the early Olympics. Wrestling is centuries old in the civilizations of India and China and has also been popular in Germany for centuries.

Catch-as-catch-can wrestling is the product of America. All American wrestling was amateur at first, and friendly wrestling was held outdoors at picnics and fairs—witness the bouts of Abraham Lincoln. However, after a while, the best wrestlers went on tour, meeting all comers outdoors, and the sport began to achieve a wide popularity.

Wrestling in the early days was developed and improved by the Olympic games, where the greatest wrestlers from the known world vied for world's championships, not only in wrestling but in the pancratium. The competition was tough. In one contest an ancient Greek wrestler named Archacian was awarded the Olympic championship when a toe hold he finally put on his opponent made the latter give up. However, during the contest, Archacian had been under the pressure of such terrific headlocks and strangle holds that when his opponent quit, Archacian rolled over, was proclaimed champion, and then died. In the pancratium we have really the beginning of the catch-as-catch-can, which would permit a toe hold or any other type of hold; in the Greco-Roman or normal wrestling as practiced by the Greeks, such holds would have been ruled illegal.

The ancient Greek wrestlers generally overcame the ancient Greek boxers in the pancratium. We find that the boxers were often being subdued by flying mares, leg holds, toe holds, strangle holds, headlocks, kicking, and above all else by the bending back of the fingers. This last trick not only made many a boxer quit, but ruined many a Greek fist for all time. The most famous exponent, if not the originator, of the technique of bending a man's fingers backward until he yelled "Uncle" or until his fingers and hands were broken is believed to be the great Greek wrestler Sostratos, who won the 104th, 105th, and 106th Olympic wrestling championships (364-356 B.C.), and also took on all boxers at one of these Olympics, winning both the wrestling and pancratium titles.

During the Middle Ages, when most competitive athletics disappeared, international tournaments in wrestling and wrestling matches at great parties given by kings were very popular—particularly in France and England. Francis I of France (1515-1547), the builder of Fontainebleau, became annoyed because French wrestlers were losing consistently to English wrestlers.

When the Spanish and the English, the Dutch and the French began colonizing North America, they found that wrestling was very popular among the Indians and that there was considerable wrestling in the early Americas. The early

156

wrestlers in the United States, such as Ernest Roeber and William Muldoon, followed Greco-Roman rules, but the average neighborhood wrestler, not caring much about rules, adopted catch-as-catch-can methods. Hence the term "catch-as-catch-can wrestling."

Naturally, the first modern Olympics in 1896 included wrestling matches as an important part of the program. In the contest at Athens, five champions (listed as such)—two of them Greeks—took part. The only type of wrestling at the first Olympics was in the Greco-Roman style, and according to the records only one championship was contested, which was won by Schumann of Germany.

There is no record of any wrestling in the 1900 Olympic games, but in 1904, at St. Louis, there was competition for seven wrestling championships in seven classes; all the championships were won by Americans, and the entire competition was on a catch-as-catch-can basis.

After the 1904 Olympics, there was a split-up between the Greco-Roman wrestling, based upon the ancient Olympic style, and the "new" wrestling. In the Greco-Roman, holds were only allowed above the waist. Generally speaking, catch-as-catch-can is of American origin, but various types of catch-as-catch-can had appeared in the first part of the twentieth century in other countries. The Swiss had developed a sort of national sport of "catch" wrestling; the Japanese, with jujitsu, had departed from Greco-Roman. Sumo wrestling was a combination of Greco-Roman and catch-as-catch-can. The Turks had also developed a very tough—and cruel—version of catch-as-catch-can. England had developed its catch-as-catch-can from the Cumberland and Westmoreland styles, which had originally approximated the Greco-Roman. France stuck pretty closely to Greco-Roman until about 1913, when catch-as-catch-can began to appear there for the first time.

In the 1906 Olympics at Athens there were wrestling competitions, with Germany winning the unofficial team title, although the Germans did not win a single individual championship. At the Athens games—unlike the St. Louis games—only Greco-Roman rules were used, and the two Americans who were contestants were at a great disadvantage. J. Jensen of Denmark won the heavyweight championship; W. Weckman of Finland won in the middleweight class and Watzl of Austria in the lightweight class.

The IV Olympiad at London in 1908 was the first to recognize the two schools or classifications and there were separate competitions in catch-as-catch-can and Greco-Roman wrestling. The Americans showed to advantage in the catch-as-catch-can wrestling, although the British won three titles to the United States' two. In Greco-Roman, the Swedes, the Finns, the Italians, and the Hungarians won titles.

The 5th Olympic games in Stockholm in 1912 demonstrated the fact that wrestling as a universal and ancient sport was going to be handicapped—for a while, at least—by the fact that there was great variance between the styles and rules of the several countries. The Swedes did not even recognize catch-as-catch-can wrestling, so Olympic competition was limited to Greco-Roman rules; as a result, Finland and Sweden dominated the Olympic wrestling competition, with three championships being won by Finland and two by Sweden. In the light heavyweight class, A. O. Ahlgren of Sweden and J. Boling of Finland drew, after over nine hours of continuous wrestling.

During World War I wrestling, like boxing and fencing, progressed greatly, particularly catch-as-catch-can. The 1920 Olympics at Antwerp presented really outstanding contestants from a great many countries in both catch-as-catch-can and Greco-Roman. At the 1920 or VII Olympiad, in the catch-as-catch-can class the United States found very worthy competition from English, South African, and Indian teams as well as from the Finns. However, the surprise at the meet was the ability of the Swiss, who up to that time had had no reputation for either ability or knowledge of the game. However, the Swiss had wrestled catch-as-catch-can for many decades. They won one championship and would probably have taken another but for the injury of one of their athletes, who was forced to forfeit his final bout. The rules covering the meet were very unsatisfactory to the American team in that leg scissors were barred. The American form of catch-as-catch-can had used leg and scissor holds on the head and various parts of the body to great advantage.

The final score was the United States 9 1/2, Finland 8, Sweden 5 1/3, Switzerland 5, and England 2. C. E. Ackerly of Cornell University was the only American to win an individual championship. In the middleweight division, Charles F. Johnson of Quincy, Massachusetts, won third place, and in the light heavyweight class, Walter Maurer of the Chicago Hebrew Institute won third place. Nat Pendleton of Columbia University and the New York Athletic Club won second place in the heavyweight division, and Fred Meyer was tied for third place in the same class. The decision which took the final match from Pendleton, a great amateur wrestling star, who later became a tough guy in Hollywood pictures, was probably one of the most unpopular of many unsatisfactory and unfair decisions. It is interesting to note that one of the toughest members of the United States wrestling team at the 1920 Olympics was Paul Berlenbach, who later turned to boxing and became the professional light heavyweight world's champion.

In the Greco-Roman wrestling, the belief of the Americans that American versatility and aggressiveness would give some men with practically no training a chance was proved incorrect—no points were won by American entries. Greco-Roman team honors were won by Finland.

These Olympics showed that, while the popularity of wrestling extended throughout the world, there was no standardization of rules and methods, and that a standardization of the rules in both types of wrestling would be necessary before free and effective competition could be achieved.

The VIII Olympiad at Paris in 1924 presented the best wrestling competition there had been in any modern Olympics. In the Greco-Roman there were 250 competitors, representing twenty-four countries. As in 1912 and 1920, the Finns and the Swedes dominated the competition, Finland winning the unofficial team championship, with Sweden second, Estonia third, and France fourth—Hungary being a close fifth. The American wrestlers decided that until they learned how to wrestle the Greco-Roman style they would not try to compete.

In the catch-as-catch-can, however, the United States won its first overwhelming victory in wrestling, scoring 49 points to win the unofficial team championship, Finland and Switzerland tying for second with 33. There were 187 contestants entered, representing sixteen nations. The United States won four individual world's championships. Robin Reed of Oregon Agricultural College won in the featherweight class and was considered by many to be the best wrestler of this Olympiad. In fact, many experts consider him, pound for pound, one of the greatest amateur and Olympic wrestlers of modern times. Russell Vis of the Los Angeles Athletic Club won in the lightweight class, John P. Spellman of Brown University in the light heavyweight class, and Harry Steele of Ohio State University in the heavyweight class. In addition, second place in the featherweight class was won by Chester Newton of the United States, and third place in the bantamweight was won by Bryant Hines. The wrestling started on the 11th of July and ran morning, afternoon, and night through the 15th of July. Due to the fact that many of the officials were inexperienced, and the fact that the rules had still not been properly standardized, there were some very bad decisions. However, after a meeting of the International Wrestling Federation there was hope that the various countries would standardize their rules and afford wrestling the same opportunity for progress as other sports. W. E. Cann was the United States wrestling coach. The wrestling took place in the Velodrome d'Hiver, the Madison Square Garden of Paris, and was very well attended.

International competitions in the years between Olympics, in both catch-as-catch-can and Greco-Roman wrestling, contributed greatly to the advance of the sport between 1924 and 1928. However, there still was great variation in interpretation of the rules. The development of catch-as-catch-can was undeniably American, but—with the exception of the Swiss—European countries preferred the Greco-Roman style. Other countries differed with the United States, even in the catch-as-catch-can style, with respect to holds, especially leg holds and particularly the body and head scissors. These holds, perfectly legitimate from the United States standpoint, were barred in the Olympic games. Also, from the beginning of the modern form of wrestling one element of the sport had been perennially debated—the rolling fall. In Greco-Roman wrestling, where only the arms are employed, athletes may remain in position, and fast falls are allowed since the lower body and limbs are always free. As a result of the freedom of the limbs, wrestlers can usually prevent a roll, and, if they can't, can very easily bridge. When the legs are tied up in catch-as-catch-can, as they are much of the time on the offensive, the high bridge is impossible and rolling falls must work a great unfairness. The Greco-Roman influence has also made ruling on the flying fall difficult. While the contestants are on their feet, one can pick his opponent up bodily, throw him squarely on his shoulders, and—even though the touch may be only momentary—score a fall. However, when the men are on the mat in catch-as-catch-can, with one man on the offensive or behind his man, as it is called, then the pin fall should be required, with the shoulders held to the mat for a perceptible length of time (two seconds). In 1928 the complaint was that United States wrestlers were eliminated on the basis that any roll, however fast, meant a fall.

George Pinneo was the United States coach in 1928. The Greco-Roman wrestling unofficial team title was won by Germany, while Finland won the catch-as-catch-can unofficial team title. Allie Morrison won the featherweight world's title for the United States. Lloyd Appleton of the United States, now wrestling coach at West Point, was second in the welterweight class. Among the heavyweights who were also-rans in these Olympics were Earl MacCready of Canada and Ed Don George of the United States. Both of these men, although they were unsuccessful in the Olympics, went on to great prominence in professional wrestling. MacCready, a Canadian, learned his wrestling in the United States, at Oklahoma A. and M. He was national intercollegiate heavyweight champion of the United States in 1928, 1929, and 1930, and national AAU title holder in 1930. He later became one of the best wrestlers in the world. G. W. Streit, Jr., of Birmingham, Alabama, manager of the 1924, 1928, and 1932 United States wrestling teams, deserves great credit for his firm but sportsmanlike complaints and arguments on the differences in rules.

The 1932 Olympic games again presented fine competition in wrestling. The American team was considered the best-balanced wrestling team ever to represent the United States. Its coach was Hugo Otapalik. The United States team won three first places and two seconds in the catch-as-catch-can division. R. E. Pearce of the United States won the bantam-weight championship; Edgar Nemir of the United States was second in the featherweight class; Jack Van Bebber, another United States all-time great, won the welterweight title. Peter J. Mehringer of the United States won the light heavyweight title, and John Riley was second in the heavyweight class to Johan Richtoff of Sweden, who won the heavyweight Olympic title in 1928, besting both George and MacCready. In the Greco-Roman wrestling the United States had no entries, but many countries were represented from Scandinavia, continental Europe, and Asia, with Sweden winning the unofficial team title.

Just as in other sports, the interest engendered by the Olympic games and by international amateur wrestling competition and intercollegiate and amateur competition within various countries—particularly the United States—developed great coaching, which in turn improved performance. Prominent among the coaches was the one who created the greatest college wrestling teams in the United States—those of Oklahoma A. and M. College. For decades a mild little man named Ed Gallagher held forth there as coach and annually developed smart, clean, aggressive, splendidly conditioned teams that won many intercollegiate championships. He also trained many Olympic wrestlers.

As a result of the standardization of wrestling all over the world and of greater interest in this sport inspired by the Olympics, a larger number of entrants and better competition and performance marked the XI Olympiad at Berlin in 1936.

The American Olympic team was managed again by G. W. Streit, Jr. The coach of the United States team was William H. Thom of Indiana, ably assisted by honorary coach and advisor Ed Gallagher of Oklahoma A. and M. The unofficial catch-as-catch-can wrestling team championship went to the United States, which won one first place and three seconds. The wrestling competition attracted twenty-eight countries. Ross Flood of Blackwell, Oklahoma; Francis E. Millard of North Adams, Massachusetts; and Richard L. Voliva of Bloomington, Indiana, finished second in the bantamweight, featherweight, and middleweight classes respectively. Sweden was second in the unofficial team championship, with one first, one second, and two third places. The Greco-Roman team championship went to Sweden.

For the first time in Olympic competition the same man won both the catch-as-catch-can and the Greco-Roman titles. Kristjan Palusalu of Estonia won the heavyweight championship in free style wrestling and the heavyweight championship in Greco-Roman style. The wrestling at these Olympics was held at Deutschland Hall, and a capacity crowd attended every session. There was some trouble with officiating, but sportsmanship, as usual, won out. The officiating in wrestling has now improved, as the rules have become more and more standardized over the years.

The XIV Olympiad in London in 1948 brought out tremendous competitions in both catch-as-catch-can and Greco-Roman wrestling. The unofficial team championship in catch-as-catch-can was won by Turkey and in Greco-Roman by Sweden. The United States team was managed by Clifford Keen of Michigan and coached by Art Griffith of Oklahoma A. and M. The team was helped by a number of ex-coaches and Olympic wrestlers, among whom was Ed Don George. The United States team won two championships, one second place, one third, one fifth, and one sixth. Behind Turkey in unofficial first place in the team scoring was Sweden, with the United States third. It is interesting to note that the Turkish team that won and the four Turkish champions who took individual titles were all men in their thirties. From the days of the ancient Olympics to the present good wrestlers have had far longer competitive lives than top competitors in any other sport, except fencing. In Europe and the United States many men wrestle competitively for as much as twenty years. G. Leeman took second in the bantamweight class, R. Hutton of the United States sixth in the heavyweight. W. Koll was fifth in the lightweight, L. Merrill third in the welterweight. G. Brand of the United States was first in the middleweight class, and H. Wittenberg of the United States was first in the light heavyweight class.

Wittenberg, incidentally, was considered by many the most outstanding wrestler in the 1948 Olympic games and is considered by most experts to be one of the best amateur wrestlers ever developed in the United States. He won the national light heavyweight championship in the United States in 1943 and 1944, and again in 1947 and 1948, representing the New York Police Sports Association. Wittenberg won almost 500 matches in succession between 1938 and 1952 before he was beaten by Dale Thomas of East Lansing, Michigan, in the light heavyweight class final for the 1952 Olympic games. He had then been wrestling for almost twenty years. Later he defeated Thomas several times, and again wrestled for the United States in 1952.

In 1948 the catch-as-catch-can wrestling was dominated by the Turks. The Greco-Roman wrestling unofficial team championship was won by Sweden. As usual, the United States did not participate, although interest in Greco-Roman wrestling was beginning in the United States.

In 1948 one thing was certain—that interest in both styles of wrestling was increasing all over the world, with the result that the United States appeared to be falling behind even in the catch-as-catch-can style which it had developed.

The 1952 Olympiad at Helsinki marked the return of Russia into Olympic competition, and they dominated both catch-as-catch-can and Greco-Roman styles. Competitors from thirty-five nations entered the free style or catch-as-catch-can at this Olympiad. Some rather unusual occurrences on the United States Olympic team prior to the final Olympic meet are worthy of notice. One was that light heavyweight Dale Thomas of Michigan State College defeated heavyweight Kerslake twice, but was not allowed by the Olympic officials to wrestle in that class, because he had previously been entered as a light heavyweight. So Kerslake represented the United States in the heavyweight class. Wittenberg had won over Thomas in the light heavyweight class, although Thomas had broken Wittenberg's extraordinary string of victories in the tryout. Raymond Schwartz was the United States coach and B. R. Patterson the manager. Advance reports were that Iran, Turkey, Sweden, and Russia had terrific teams. The Russians did, and won practically everything. Russia was the unofficial team champion of Greco-Roman and catch-as-catch-can. In Greco-Roman, Hungary was second. In catch-as-catch-can, Sweden was a very close second and Turkey a close third.

In catch-as-catch-can, J. Henson of the United States was

third in the featherweight class and T. Evans of the United States was second in the lightweight class. W. Smith of the United States won the title in the welterweight class in an interesting manner. He lost a split decision to Berlin of Sweden, then defeated Modjtabavi of Iran by a fall. Then the Iranian soundly beat the Swede, thus giving Smith the world's title. In the light heavyweight class, Henry Wittenberg, one of the greatest American wrestlers of all time but certainly not at his best after twenty years of competition, lost a hairline decision to Palm of Sweden for the Olympic crown—which Wittenberg had won in 1948. Wittenberg was a great sportsman, and therefore was proud to take second place. W. Kerslake was fifth in the heavyweight class and increased his experience, which enabled him to win, in 1953, not only the heavyweight national championship in the United States in the catch-as-catch-can but also the heavyweight championship in the first Greco-Roman tournament ever held in the United States. In wrestling, the popularity of a European specialty inspired through the Olympics sufficient interest to lead to national tournaments and championships in the United States.

The future of wrestling is bright. It has been developed and improved, and standardized throughout the world, by the Olympic games. Many people believe that wrestling in the future will be dominated someday by Japan, which would mean that the modern sport of wrestling in both the catch-as-catch-can and Greco-Roman styles had circled the globe. Certainly the 1952 victory of Russia as a newcomer to Olympic wrestling shows that supremacy in sports moves around.

The United States, for the first time in the history of the modern Olympics, will send two complete wrestling teams to Melbourne, one catch-as-catch-can and one Greco-Roman. Several years ago the United States AAU, in order to help standardize international wrestling, adopted the international rules, even in catch-as-catch-can, although they deviated from former AAU regulations and handicapped United States wrestlers for a short time. In 1956, for the first time, wrestlers from all over the world will be able to compete, in both schools of wrestling, under rules that will be familiar to all competitors, from Argentina to Zanzibar and from Australia to Yugoslavia.

CHAPTER XVIII

YACHTING

THE OLYMPIC sport of yachting covers sailing races of smaller craft generally referred to throughout the world as yachts. Yacht racing dates from the beginning of the nineteenth century. Long before that, however, Queen Elizabeth had a pleasure ship called a yacht—in 1588. Charles II of England was given a yacht by the Dutch in 1660. He later designed his own 25-ton yacht, called *Jamie*. This yacht was built at Lambeth in 1662. Shortly thereafter *Jamie* raced a small Dutch yacht with the Duke of York at the helm, from Greenwich to Gravesend and back, and won. The King was steering *Jamie*. The winner collected a 100-pound wager. This is considered the first yachting race between two amateurs. The first sailing club was founded in 1720. It was called the Royal Cork Yacht Club, and it was established in Ireland.

The oldest surviving (though it was not the first established) yacht club in the United States is the New York Yacht Club, founded in 1844. However, records indicate that even in colonial times there were privately-owned yachts used principally for pleasure and that some of them actually raced. International yacht racing began in 1851, when a syndicate of New York Yacht Club members built a 101-foot schooner, the *America,* and sailed her to England, where she proved much faster than the British yachts. Thus were started the famous international sailing matches, continued through 1937, in which numerous British, Canadian, and American yachtsmen attempted to take the so-called championship cup from the New York Yacht Club. Ocean-racing yachts range in size from approximately 53 feet down to 35 feet in length, and the races are won or lost on corrected time, each yacht receiving an allowance from the largest, or scratch boat, in proportion to its size and potential speed.

Many changes in the designs of yachts and in the rules and regulations of yacht racing have taken place through the years, but one of the most significant contributions to the sport was made by J. Scott Russell, who, in 1848, argued against the wisdom of building sailing vessels on a cod-head and mackerel-tail plan and enunciated the wave-line theory.

The first international rules were laid down in 1904, with

the Germans, French, and British agreeing to them; the United States did not send an official representative to the conference. The second series of international rules was agreed to during 1919 and 1920.

The class, or closed-course, racing in the Olympics of today is based on the one-design racing sloop. This type of racing was intended as the poor man's racing, for the boats involved cost as little as $250—that is, they did back in 1911, when this branch of the sport was organized. The poor man's racing boat at this time was the Star Class, a 23-foot, thin-keeled sloop. The main sponsor for this type of boat was an American, George A. Corry, and as proof of his vision this class today numbers over 5,000 boats belonging to over 200 fleets scattered around the world in every continent. Racing associations have grown up everywhere there is water, and in addition to the Olympics there are world, continental, and national championships annually. Yachting as a sport gains most of its publicity from racing, but racing is a very small part of the sport of sailing.

In the wake of the Stars, hundreds of other one-design classes became popular—most of them under 40 feet in length, many under 20—many of them holding annual or biennial world's championships. Some of the best known of these are Snipes, Comets, Lightnings, and Thistles. Yachting has become a completely amateur sport, and there are no longer any professional racing-yacht skippers. In yacht racing there are hundreds of championships, but there is no one over-all champion. All classes have their own champions, but they rarely meet each other and there is no final way of deciding that one skipper or one group of sailors or one type of boat is at the top of the entire sport.

In 1896, at the first Olympiad in Athens, plans had originally been made to have an exhibition regatta, including some sailing ships, but a storm came up on the days it was to be held and it was canceled. In 1900, at the second Olympic games in Paris, sailing competitions were held, with France winning the all-around championship in yachting. Switzerland was second, which reminded everyone that there really was a Swiss Navy, even though it might sail or steam on lakes. The competition was restriced to a 6-meter class, 8-meter class, two-ton boat, and ten-ton boat. There was no yachting in 1904, obviously because there were no lakes or oceans suitable for sailing near St. Louis, Missouri. There is also no record of any official sailing or yachting in the 1906 Olympics, but naturally there were official yachting competitions in the 1908 Olympics at London, which Great Britain won on an over-all basis. The competitions were in 6-meter, 7-meter, 8-meter, and 12-meter, and for the first and only time in the Olympics the British introduced motorboat racing with three classes.

In the 1912 Olympic games in Sweden there was great interest in the sailing competitions, which were won by Sweden. There were a 6-meter class, an 8-meter class, a 10-meter class, and a 12-meter class. In the 1912 Olympics, Russia was one of the participants, placing third in the 10-meter class.

At the VII Olympiad, the yachting competitions were held at Ostend, with Norway winning the all-around competition; Sweden was second, Holland third, Great Britain fourth, Belgium fifth, and France sixth. There were tremendous winds and a very rough sea, and the competition tested the courage of the contestants as well as the seaworthiness of their craft. After the games a very big step was made for the future of yachting competitions in the Olympics, for the Olympic Congress decided that standardization was essential, and therefore yachting programs for Olympic games were put under the control of the International Yachting Federation. This organization was charged with the preparation of the program for future Olympics and with notifying the various countries of the program a considerable time ahead of each Olympiad. It was ruled that the events would consist of yachts of 6 meters and 9 meters and probably one of 5 meters or less, that the yachts could be built anywhere but that they had to be manned by citizens of the competing countries and that yachts of 5 meters should have but one man on board, of 6 meters three, of 8 meters five, and, of course, that all crews had to be amateurs. The unfortunate part about this excellent arrangement was that the International Yachting Federation did not include the membership of the United States. However, the Olympic Congress stated that they would press the United States to join the organization.

The VIII Olympiad in 1924 in Paris brought together entries from 19 nations in yachting. These nations finished on an all-around basis in yachting in the following order: first, Norway; second, Belgium; third, Holland; fourth, France; fifth, Denmark and Great Britain, tied; seventh, Finland and Sweden, tied; ninth, Spain and Argentina, tied; eleventh, Cuba; twelfth, Italy; thirteenth, Switzerland; fourteenth, Czechoslovakia; fifteenth, Poland; sixteenth, Monaco; seventeenth, South Africa; eighteenth, Canada; and nineteenth, Portugal. The events were the monotype or dinghy class, the 6-meter, and the 8-meter. The races were staged at Meulan-les-Mureaux and also in the harbor at Le Havre. There was more than passing interest in the yachting events, for there were actually over 9000 spectators on hand.

International competitions involving Americans between the 1924 and 1928 Olympic games finally got the United States into Olympic yachting. The United States also joined the International Yacht Racing Union and submitted entries in the monotype class, the 6-meter, and the 8-meter for the next Olympics.

In the IX Olympiad yachting championships in 1928 the final standing in the 8-meter class was as follows: first, France; second, Holland; third, Sweden; fourth, Italy; and fifth, Norway. Argentina, Great Britain, and the United States were eliminated or withdrew. In the 6-meter class: first, Norway; second, Denmark; third, Estonia; fourth, Holland; fifth, Belgium; sixth, the United States; and seventh, Sweden. Germany, Hungary, France, Italy, Spain, and Portugal were eliminated. In the monotype, or 12-foot class: first, Sweden; second, Finland; third, Italy; fourth, Norway; fifth, Holland; sixth, Germany; seventh, Lithuania; eighth, Great Britain; ninth, Denmark; and tenth, the United States, with Sweden winning the unofficial all-around championship.

The X Olympiad at Los Angeles featured great competition in the yachting events. There were four classes—6-meter, 8-meter, the famous Star class, and the monotype. According to the rules, the monotype was to be manned by one man, the Star by two, the 6-meter by five, and the 8-meter by a crew of seven. The United States, for the first time, won the all-around yachting championship. The events were run in Los Angeles harbor with the assistance of the United States Navy and Coast Guard. There was tremendous competition in the preliminaries, semifinals, and final tryouts to represent the United States. Owen Churchill was manager of the United States Olympic champions in yachting, and was again manager in 1936.

At the 1936 Olympics in Berlin the yachting competitions were held at Kiel and run by the German Navy. Owen Churchill's *Angelita* was the United States entry in the 8-meter class, William A. Bartholomae, Jr.'s *Mystery* was the United States entry in the 6-meter class, and Frank B. Jewett, Jr. was the United States entry in the monotype class. *Three Star Too*, with W. Glen Waterhouse, as captain, and Woodbridge Metcalf, was the American entry in the Star class. The all-around yachting was won by Germany, with Great Britain second, Italy third, Sweden fourth, and Norway next. The United States did not fare so well, coming in tenth in the 8-meter class, ninth in the 6-meter class, fifth in the Star class, and ninth in the monotype. There were 26 nations competing, with Chile, Uruguay, Turkey, and Brazil as newcomers. The monotype boat of each team was supplied by the Olympic Organizing Committee of the host country.

The XIV Olympiad at London brought together entries from 21 countries in the yachting competitions, which consisted of five events—6-meter class, Dragon class, Star class, Swallow class, and Firefly class. They were held at Torquay, Devon, England, with an impressive ceremony at historic Torre Abbey. The competition, held in Tor Bay, was run with the assistance of the British Navy, and anchored at the scene of the competition were the British battleships *Anson* and *King George V*, the aircraft carrier *Victorious*, and a score of American, French, British, and Belgian ships, two Swedish training ships, and the Norwegian royal yacht, with the Crown Prince of Norway aboard. The countries scored in the following order on an all-around basis: United States, Norway, Denmark, and Sweden. The manager of this United States Olympic championship team was Lee Loomis.

The XV Olympiad in Helsinki in 1952 brought out more competitors and greater performance than ever before in the yachting events. The events, held in the beautiful harbor of Helsinki, were run in impeccable style by the Finnish Olympic Sailing Committee, assisted by a distinguished jury headed by Crown Prince Olaf of Norway and Sir Jeffrey Lowles of the United Kingdom. The members of the visiting yachting teams were housed in the private residences of the yachtsmen of Helsinki.

The captain of the United States team was again Owen P. Churchill, and for the first time there was a woman manager, Mrs. Millie Horton, whose husband, William Horton, was the skipper of the United States boat in the Dragon class—his crew being William, Jr., and Joyce Horton. Twenty-eight nations participated. There were five events—the 6-meter class, the 5.5-meter class, the Dragon, Star and Finn class (the Finn class being the equivalent of the old monotype). An interesting feature of this competition was the entry and excellent showing of the U.S.S.R., a nation returning to the yachting competition after a long absence. The entry of Russia suggested to some that yachting, like riding or fencing, is not restricted to any one class.

The unofficial 1952 all-around yachting championship wound up with the United States first, Norway second, Italy third, Denmark fourth, Sweden fifth, and Portugal sixth. The Finn class, which to many is the greatest test in the yachting competition and was the one in which there were representatives from every country, wound up with the countries finishing in the following order: Denmark, Great Britain, Sweden, the Netherlands, Austria, Norway, Italy, Canada, Brazil, Spain, France, Russia, Switzerland, the Bahamas, Germany, South Africa, Portugal, Belgium, Finland, Uruguay, Ireland, Australia, Yugoslavia, Cuba, Argentina, Greece, Japan, and the United States.

Yachting, like other sports, has grown and spread throughout the world. The Olympics have inspired international competition of all kinds, as well as national competition, and all yachtsmen throughout the world are looking forward to the 1956 Olympics in Australia, where once again they will have a chance for friendly competition and an opportunity to further demonstrate and popularize the sport of yachting throughout the world.

MODERN OLYMPIC GAMES

Number	Year	Site	Nations Entered	Number Contestants	Winner (Unofficial)
I	1896	Athens	13	484	Greece
II	1900	Paris	16	1505	France
III	1904	St. Louis	7	1609	United States
#	1906	Athens	21	901	France
IV	1908	London	22	2666	Great Britain
V	1912	Stockholm	27	4742	Sweden
VI	1916	Berlin	—	——	Canceled (World War I)
VII	1920	Antwerp	26	2741	United States
VIII	1924	Paris	45	3385	United States
IX	1928	Amsterdam	46	3905	United States
X	1932	Los Angeles	39	2403	United States
XI	1936	Berlin	51	4069	Germany
XII	1940	(Tokyo) Helsinki	—	——	Canceled (World War II)
XIII	1944	Unawarded	—	——	Canceled (World War II)
XIV	1948	London	59	6005	United States
XV	1952	Helsinki	69	5867	United States
XVI	1956	Melbourne	73*	5050*	United States

\# Unofficial or extra Olympics.

* Estimated from entries May 1, 1956.

OLYMPIC WINTER SPORTS

Number	Year	Site	Nations Entered	Number Contestants	Winner (Unofficial)
I	1924	Chamonix	16	306	Norway
II	1928	St. Moritz	25	518	Norway
III	1932	Lake Placid	17	307	United States
IV	1936	Garmisch-Partenkirchen	28	756	Norway
V	1948	St Moritz	29	932	Sweden
VI	1952	Oslo	30	1178	Norway
VII	1956	Cortina D'Ampezzo	32	1282	Russia

Recapitulation

Number of Modern Olympics held: 13

UNOFFICIAL OVERALL WINNERS:

United States	7	Greece	1
France	2	Germany	1
Great Britain	1	Sweden	1

CHAMPIONSHIPS (WON) BY NATION

I. MODERN OLYMPICS 1896

	CYCLING	FENCING	GYMNASTICS	SHOOTING	SWIMMING	TENNIS	TRACK & FIELD	WRESTLING	TOTAL
United States	—	—	—	2	—	—	9	—	11
Greece	1	1	2	3	—	—	1	—	8
Germany	—	—	5	—	—	½	—	1	6½
France	4	1	—	—	—	—	—	—	5
Great Britain	—	—	—	—	—	1½	1	—	2½
Australia	—	—	—	—	—	—	2	—	2
Austria	1	—	—	—	1	—	—	—	2
Hungary	—	—	—	—	2	—	—	—	2
Denmark	—	—	—	—	—	—	1	—	1
Switzerland	—	—	1	—	—	—	—	—	1

172

CHAMPIONSHIPS (WON) BY NATION

II. MODERN OLYMPICS 1900

	ARCHERY	BOWLING	CROQUET	CYCLING	FENCING	GOLF	GYMNASTICS	POLO	ROWING	SHOOTING	SWIMMING	TENNIS	TRACK & FIELD	WATER POLO	YACHTING	TOTAL
France	2	2	3	1	2	—	1	—	1	8	1	—	1	—	6	28
United States	—	—	—	—	—	2	—	—	1	1	—	—	18	—	—	22
Great Britain	—	—	—	—	—	—	—	1	—	—	2	4	4	1	2	14
Switzerland	—	—	—	—	—	—	—	—	—	6	—	—	—	—	1	7
Germany	—	—	—	—	—	—	—	—	1	—	2	—	—	—	2	5
Belgium	—	—	—	—	—	—	—	—	—	3	—	—	—	—	—	3
Australia	—	—	—	—	—	—	—	—	—	1	2	—	—	—	—	3
Holland	—	—	—	—	—	—	—	—	1	1	—	—	—	—	—	2
Denmark	—	—	—	—	—	—	—	—	—	2	—	—	—	—	—	2
Canada	—	—	—	—	—	—	—	—	—	1	—	—	—	—	—	1
Cuba	—	—	—	—	1	—	—	—	—	—	—	—	—	—	—	1
Hungary	—	—	—	—	—	—	—	—	—	—	—	—	1	—	—	1

CHAMPIONSHIPS (WON) BY NATION

III. MODERN OLYMPICS 1904

	ALL AROUND	ARCHERY	BOXING	CYCLING	FENCING	GOLF	GYMNASTICS	LACROSSE	ROQUE	ROWING	SOCCER	SWIMMING	TENNIS	TRACK & FIELD	TURNING	WATER POLO	WRESTLING	TOTAL
United States	—	6	7	7	1	1	8	—	1	5	—	5	2	24	3	1	7	78
Cuba	—	—	—	—	5	—	—	—	—	—	—	—	—	—	—	—	—	5
Germany	—	—	—	—	—	—	—	—	—	—	—	4	—	—	1	—	—	5
Canada.	—	—	—	—	—	1	—	1	—	—	1	—	—	1	—	—	—	4
Hungary	—	—	—	—	—	—	—	—	—	—	—	2	—	—	—	—	—	2
Greece	—	—	—	—	—	—	—	—	—	—	—	—	—	1	—	—	—	1
Ireland	1	—	—	—	—	—	—	—	—	—	—	—	—	—	—	—	—	1

CHAMPIONSHIPS (WON) BY NATION

UNOFFICIAL OLYMPIC GAMES 1906

	CYCLING	FENCING	GYMNASTICS	ROWING	SHOOTING	SOCCER	SWIMMING	TENNIS	TRACK & FIELD	WRESTLING	TOTAL
France	1	3	1	1	4			3	1		14
United States							1		11		12
Greece	2	1		1				1	3		8
Great Britain	3				2				3		8
Italy		2		4					1		7
Germany			1		2		1		1	1	6
Switzerland					5						5
Norway					3		1				4
Austria			1				1			1	3
Denmark						1				1	2
Finland									1	1	2
Sweden									2		2
Canada									1		1
Hungary							1				1

CHAMPIONSHIPS (WON) BY NATION

IV. MODERN OLYMPICS 1908

	ARCHERY	BOXING	CYCLING	FENCING	FIELD HOCKEY	GYMNASTICS	LACROSSE	MOTOR BOATING	POLO	RACQUETS	ROWING	RUGBY	SHOOTING	SKATING	SOCCER	SWIMMING	TENNIS	TRACK & FIELD	WATER POLO	WRESTLING catch-as-catch-can	WRESTLING greco-roman	YACHTING	TOTAL
United Kingdom	2	5	5		1			2	1	2	4		6	1	1	4	6	8	1	3		4	56
United States													3			1	1	15		2			22
Sweden						1							2	1		1		2			1		8
France	1		1	2				1															5
Canada							1						1					1					3
Germany														1		2							3
Hungary				2																	1		3
Italy						1															1		2
Norway													2										2
Australia												1											1
Belgium													1										1
Finland																					1		1
Russia														1									1
South Africa																		1					1

176

CHAMPIONSHIPS (WON) BY NATION

V. MODERN OLYMPICS 1912

	CYCLING	EQUESTRIAN	FENCING	GYMNASTICS	MODERN PENTATHLON	ROWING	SHOOTING	SOCCER	SWIMMING (men)	SWIMMING (women)	TENNIS	TRACK & FIELD	WATER POLO	WRESTLING	YACHTING	TOTAL
Sweden	1	4		1	1		7		2	1		5		1½	1	24½
United States							7		2			14				23
Great Britain						2	1	1		1	2	2	1			10
Finland												6		3½		9½
France		1					2				3				1	7
Germany						1			3		1					5
Norway				1			1					1			2	5
South Africa	1										2	1				4
Canada									2							4
Hungary			2													3
Italy			1	2												3
Australia									1	1						3
Belgium			2													2
Denmark						1										2
Greece												1				1

CHAMPIONSHIPS (WON) BY NATION

VII. MODERN OLYMPICS 1920

Nation	ARCHERY	BOXING	CYCLING	EQUESTRIAN	FENCING	FIELD HOCKEY	GYMNASTICS	ICE HOCKEY	MODERN PENTATHLON	POLO	ROWING	RUGBY	SHOOTING	SKATING	SOCCER	SWIMMING (men)	SWIMMING (women)	TENNIS	TRACK & FIELD	WATER POLO	WEIGHT LIFTING	WRESTLING catch-as-catch-can	WRESTLING greco-roman	YACHTING	TOTAL
United States		3									3	1	13			7	4		9			1			41
Sweden			1	4			1		1				1	2		3			1			1	2	2	19
Finland														1					9			2	3		15
Great Britain		2	1			1				1								2	5	1				1	14
Norway											1		5						1					7	14
Italy			2	1	5		2												2		1				13
Belgium	4		1	1	1		1								1						1				10
France		1	1		1		1											2			2				8
Canada		1						1					1												3
Denmark							1				1		1												3
Holland											1						1		1						3
South Africa		1														1		1							3
Switzerland			1										1												2
Brazil													1												1
Estonia																					1				1

CHAMPIONSHIPS (WON) BY NATION

VIII. MODERN OLYMPICS 1924

	WINTER GAMES																										
	BOBSLEDDING	ICE HOCKEY	FIGURE SKATING	SPEED SKATING	SKIING	MODERN PENTATHLON	TRACK & FIELD	BOXING	CYCLING	EQUESTRIAN	FENCING	GYMNASTICS	MARKMANSHIP (hunting)	MARKMANSHIP (target)	POLO	ROWING	RUGBY	SOCCER	SWIMMING (men)	SWIMMING (women)	WATER POLO	TENNIS	WEIGHT LIFTING	WRESTLING catch-as-catch-can	WRESTLING greco-roman	YACHTING	TOTAL
United States				1			12	2				1	2	3		2	1		7	6		5		4			46
Finland				3			10																	1	3		17
France									4		3			1							1		2		1		13
Great Britain							3	2					1	1		2				1							10
Italy									1		1	2											3			2	9
Norway					4			1					2													1	8
Switzerland	1									1		2				2								2			5
Sweden			1			1				2															1		5
Belgium								1			1															1	4
Holland									1	2						1											4
Austria			2																								3
Australia																			2								2
Denmark								1			1																2
Hungary											1		1														2
Yugoslavia												2															2
Argentina															1												1
Canada		1																									1
Czechoslovakia												1															1
Estonia																									1		1
South Africa								1																			1
Uruguay																		1									1

179

	WINTER GAMES																							
	Bobsledding	Ice Hockey	Figure Skating	Speed Skating	Skiing	Modern Pentathlon	Track & Field (men)	Track & Field (women)	Boxing	Cycling	Equestrian	Fencing	Field Hockey	Gymnastics	Rowing	Soccer	Swimming (men)	Swimming (women)	Water Polo	Weight Lifting	Wrestling catch-as-catch-can	Wrestling greco-roman	Yachting	TOTAL
United States	2						8	1							2		5	5			1			24
Finland				1½			5														2	1		9½
Germany			1					1			2				1			1	1	1½		1		9½
Sweden			1		1	1															2	1	1	7
France			1							2		2								1			1	7
Italy									3	1		2			1									7
Switzerland														5	1						1			6½
Norway			1	1½	3																		1	6
Holland									1	1	2							1						5
Canada		1					2	2																4
Hungary									1			2												3
Argentina									2								1							3
Denmark										3														3
Great Britain							1								1									2
Czechoslovakia											1			1										2
Egypt																				1		1		2
Estonia																					1	1		2
Japan							1										½							1½
Austria																				1½				1
Australia															1									1
India													1											1
Ireland							1																	1
New Zealand									1															1
Poland								1																1
South Africa							1																	1
Spain											1													1
Uruguay																1								1
Yugoslavia														1										1

CHAMPIONSHIPS (WON) BY NATION

X. MODERN OLYMPICS 1932

	WINTER GAMES					MODERN PENTATHLON	TRACK & FIELD (men)	TRACK & FIELD (women)	BOXING	CYCLING	EQUESTRIAN	FENCING	FIELD HOCKEY	GYMNASTICS	ROWING	SHOOTING	SWIMMING (men)	SWIMMING (women)	WATER POLO	WEIGHT LIFTING	WRESTLING catch-as-catch-can	WRESTLING greco-roman	YACHTING	TOTAL
	ICE HOCKEY	FIGURE SKATING	SPEED SKATING	SKIING	SLEDDING																			
United States			4		2		11	5	2		1			5	3		3	6			3		2	47
Italy							1			3		2		4		1						1		12
France		1								1	2	2								3	1		1	11
Sweden				1		1										1					2	4	1	10
Japan							1				1						5							7
Finland				1			3														1	1		6
Hungary									1			2		2					1					6
Great Britain							2								2									4
Argentina							1		2															3
Australia										1					1			1						3
Canada	1						1		1															3
Germany															1					1		1		3
Norway		1		2																				3
Austria		1										1												2
Holland										1	1													2
Ireland							2																	2
Poland							1	1																2
South Africa									2															2
Czechoslovakia																				1				1
India													1											1

181

CHAMPIONSHIPS (WON) BY NATION

XI. MODERN OLYMPICS 1936

Nation	TOTAL	YACHTING	WRESTLING greco-roman	WRESTLING catch-as-catch-can	WEIGHT LIFTING	WATER POLO	SWIMMING (women)	SWIMMING (men)	SOCCER	SHOOTING	ROWING	POLO	GYMNASTICS	FIELD HOCKEY	FIELD HANDBALL	FENCING	EQUESTRIAN	CYCLING	CANOEING	BOXING	BASKETBALL	TRACK & FIELD (women)	TRACK & FIELD (men)	MODERN PENTATHLON	SLEDDING	SKIING	SPEED SKATING	FIGURE SKATING	ICE HOCKEY
																									WINTER GAMES				
Germany	36	1		1	1					1	5		6		1		6	2	2	2		1	3	1		2		1	
United States	25			1	1		2	4												1	1	2	12		1				
Hungary	10		1	2		1		1								3			1	1									
Finland	8		3	2									1										2						
Italy	8								1							4		3											
Norway	8	1																								2	4	1	
Sweden	6		3	1															1							1			
France	6		1	1	1													2	1	1									
Netherlands	6	1					4											1											
Japan	5							3															2						
Great Britain	4	1									1									1									1
Austria	4				1														2									1	
Czechoslovakia	2												1						1										
Argentina	2											1								1									
Egypt	2				2																								
Estonia	2		1	1																									
Switzerland	1																								1				
Canada	1																									1			
India	1													1															
New Zealand	1																						1						
Turkey	1		1																										

182

CHAMPIONSHIPS (WON) BY NATION

XIV. MODERN OLYMPICS 1948

Nation	ICE HOCKEY	FIGURE SKATING	SPEED SKATING	SKIING	SLEDDING	MODERN PENTATHLON	TRACK & FIELD (men)	TRACK & FIELD (women)	BASKETBALL	BOXING	CANOEING	CYCLING	EQUESTRIAN	FENCING	FIELD HOCKEY	GYMNASTICS	ROWING	SHOOTING	SOCCER	SWIMMING (men)	SWIMMING (women)	WATER POLO	WEIGHT LIFTING	WRESTLING catch-as-catch-can	WRESTLING greco-roman	YACHTING	TOTAL
United States		1		1	1		11	1	1		1		1				2	1		8	4		4	2		2	41
Sweden			1	3		1	5				4		1						1						5		21
France				2				2				3	1	3													11
Hungary							1	1		2				3		1		1						1			10
Italy					1		1			1		2		1			1					1			1		9
Switzerland				2	1								1			3		1									8
Finland				1			1									4								1			7
Czechoslovakia							1			1	3					1											6
Turkey																								4	2		6
Denmark											1						1				2					1	5
Netherlands								4													1						5
Norway			3	1																						1	5
Argentina							1			2																	3
Belgium		1					1					1															3
Great Britain																	2									1	3
Australia							1										1										2
Austria				1				1																			2
Canada	1	1																									2
Egypt																							2				2
Mexico													2														2
South Africa										2																	2
India															1												1
Jamaica							1																				1
Peru																		1									1

183

Nation	Bobsledding	Figure Skating	Ice Hockey	Skiing	Speed Skating	Modern Pentathlon	Track & Field (men)	Track & Field (women)	Basketball	Boxing	Canoeing	Cycling	Equestrian	Fencing	Gymnastics	Rowing	Shooting	Soccer	Swimming (men)	Swimming (women)	Water Polo	Weight Lifting	Wrestling catch-as-catch-can	Wrestling greco-roman	Yachting	Field Hockey	TOTAL
United States		1			1		14	2	1	5	1					2	1		6	2		4	1		2		44
Russia		1		2	1		1	1		1	1				9		1			4		3	2	4			22
Hungary						1	1			1				2	2		1	1			1			2			16
Sweden						1					4		4		2									1	1		12
Norway				4	3		1			1	1						2							1			10
Finland				3						1	1						1		1					1	1		9
Italy				1								2		3				1	1								9
Czechoslovakia							3	3						2													7
Australia							1				1	2				1				1							6
France											1			2													3
Germany		2																						1			2
Austria		1		2																							2
Belgium												2															2
Canada			1					1		1	1						1										2
Denmark		1								1	1																2
Great Britain	2																										2
Jamaica							2																				2
South Africa										1																	2
Switzerland															2												1
Turkey				2																			2				1
Argentina										1																	1
Brazil							1																				1
Japan																1			1								1
Luxemburg							1																				1
New Zealand																1											1
Poland											1																1
Rumania																	1										1
Yugoslavia																									1		1
India																										1	1

184

BOXING

FLYWEIGHT

1904—George V. Finnegan, U.S.A., 105 lbs
1920—Frank Genaro, U.S.A.
1924—Fidel La Barba, U.S.A.
1928—Anton Kocsis, Hungary
1932—Stephen Enekes, Hungary

1936—Willi Kaiser, Germany
1948—Pascuel Perez, Argentina
1952—Nate Brooks, U.S.A.
1956—

BANTAMWEIGHT

1904—O. L. Kirk, U.S.A. ......115 lbs.
1908—H. Thomas, Gr. Britain
1920—Walker, So. Africa
1924—W. H. Smith, So. Africa
1928—Vittorio Tamagnini, Italy

1932—Horace Gwynne, Canada
1936—Ulderico Sergo, Italy
1948—T. Csik, Hungary
1952—Pentti Hamalainen, Finland
1956—

FEATHERWEIGHT

1904—O. L. Kirk, U.S.A.
1908—R. K. Gunn, Gr. Britain
1920—Fritsch, France
1924—Jack Fields, U.S.A.
1928—L. Van Klaveren, Holland
1932—Carmelo Ambrosio Robledo,
        Argentina

1936—Oscar Casanovas, Argentina
1948—Ernesto Formenti, Italy
1952—Jan Zachara, Czechoslovakia
1956—

LIGHTWEIGHT

1904—H. J. Spanger, U.S.A.
1908—F. Grace, Gr. Britain
1920—Samuel Mosberg, U.S.A.
1924—Harold Nielsen, Denmark
1928—Carlo Orlandi, Italy

1932—Lawrence Stevens, So. Africa
1936—Imre Harangi, Hungary
1948—Jerry Dreyer, So. Africa
1952—Aureliano Bolognesi, Italy
1956—

LIGHT WELTERWEIGHT

1952—Charles Adkins, U.S.A.

1956—

WELTERWEIGHT

1904—Al Young, U.S.A.
1920—Schneider, Canada
1924—J. S. DeLarge, Belgium
1928—Edward Morgan, New Zealand
1932—Edward Flynn, U.S.A.

1936—Sten Suvio, Finland
1948—Julius Torma, Czechoslovakia
1952—Zygmunt Chychia, Poland
1956—

LIGHT MIDDLEWEIGHT

1952—Laszlo Papp, Hungary

1956—

MIDDLEWEIGHT

1904—Charles Mayer, U.S.A.
1908—J. W. N. T. Douglas, Gr. Britain
1920—H. W. Mallin, Gr. Britain
1924—H. W. Mallin, Gr. Britain
1928—Piero Toscani, Italy

1932—Carmen Barth, U.S.A.
1936—Jean Despeaux, France
1948—Laszlo Papp, Hungary
1952—Floyd Patterson, U.S.A.
1956—

LIGHT HEAVYWEIGHT

1920—Edward Eagan, U.S.A.
1924—H. J. Mitchell, Gr. Britain
1928—Victoria Avendano, Argentina
1932—David E. Carstens, So. Africa

1936—Roger Michelot, France
1948—George Hunter, So. Africa
1952—Norvel Lee, U.S.A.
1956—

HEAVYWEIGHT

1904—Sam Berger, U.S.A.
1908—A. L. Oldham, Gr. Britain
1920—Rawson, Gr. Britain
1924—Otto Von Porath, Norway
1928—A. Rodriguez Jurado, Argentina

1932—Santiago A. Lovell, Argentina
1936—Herbert Runge, Germany
1948—Rafael Iglesias, Argentina
1952—Edward Sanders, U.S.A.
1956—

1904—United States	1936—Germany
1908—Great Britain	1948—{ Italy
1920—Great Britain	{ South Africa
1924—United States	1952—United States
1928—Italy	1956—
1932—United States	

CANOEING

KAYAK SINGLES 1,000 METERS

1936—Gregor Hradetzky, Austria	1952—Gert Fredriksson, Sweden
1948—Gert Fredriksson, Sweden	1956—

KAYAK SINGLES 10,000 METERS

1936—Ernst Krebs, Germany	1952—Thorvald Stromberg, Finland
1948—Gert Fredriksson, Sweden	1956—

CANADIAN SINGLES 1,000 METERS

1936—Francis Amyot, Canada	1952—Josef Holecek, Czechoslovakia
1948—Josef Holecek, Czechoslovakia	1956—

CANADIAN SINGLES 10,000 METERS

1948—F. Capek, Czechoslovakia	1956—
1952—Frank Havens, U.S.A.	

KAYAK PAIRS 1,000 METERS

1936—Austria (Adolf Kainz, Alfons Dorfner)
1948—Sweden (H. Berglund, L. Klingstroem)
1952—Finland (K. Wires, Y. Hietanen)
1956—

KAYAK PAIRS 10,000 METERS

1936—Germany (P. Wevers, Ludwig Lamden)
1948—Sweden (G. Akerlund, H. Wetterstroem)
1952—Finland (K. Wires, Y. Hietanen)
1956—

CANADIAN PAIRS 1,000 METERS

1936—Czechoslovakia (V. Syrovatka, F. Jan Brzak)
1948—Czechoslovakia (J. Brzak, B. Kudrna)
1952—Denmark (B. Rasch, F. Haunstoft)
1956—

CANADIAN PAIRS 10,000 METERS

1936—Czechoslovakia (V. Mottle, Z. Skrdlant)
1948—U.S.A. (S. Lysak, S. Macknowski)
1952—France (G. Turlier, J. Laudet)
1956—

(UNOFFICIAL) TEAM CHAMPIONS

1924—Canada	1952—Finland
1936—Austria	1956—
1948—Sweden	

CANOEING (WOMEN)

KAYAK SINGLES 500 METERS

1948—K. Hoff, Denmark	1956—
1952—Sylvia Saimo, Finland	

CYCLING

ROAD RACE (INDIVIDUAL)

1896—Konstantinidis, Greece
1906—Vast and Bardonneau (tie), France
1912—R. Lewis, South Africa
1920—H. Stenquist, Sweden
1924—A. Blanchonnet, France
1928—H. Hansen, Denmark

1932—Attilio Pavesi, Italy
1936—R. Charpentier, France
1948—J. Bayaert, France
1952—Andrae Noyelle, Belgium
1956—

ROAD RACE (TEAM)

1912—Sweden
1920—France
1924—France
1928—Denmark
1932—Italy

1936—France
1948—Belgium
1952—Belgium
1956—

1,000 METER SCRATCH

1896—Emile Masson, France
    (2,000 meters)
1900—Taillendier, France
1906—Francesco Verri, Italy
1908—Void, time limit exceeded
1920—Maurice Peeters, Holland
1924—Lucien Michard, France

1928—R. Beaufrand, France
1932—Jacobus van Edmond, Holland
1936—Toni Merkens, Germany
1948—Mario Ghella, Italy (920 meters)
1952—Enzo Sacchi, Italy
1956—

2,000 METER TANDEM

1906—Great Britain (Matthews, Rushen)
1908—France, (Schilles, Auffray)
1920—Great Britain (Ryan, Lance)
1924—France (Choury, Cugnot)
1928—Holland (Leene, van Dijk)

1932—France (Perrin, Chaillot)
1936—Germany, (Ihbe, Lorenz)
1948—Italy (Teruzzi, Perona)
1952—Australia (Cox, Mockridge)
1956—

4,000 METER TEAM PURSUIT

1908—Great Britain (1,980 yards)
1920—Italy
1924—Italy
1928—Italy
1932—Italy

1936—France
1948—France
1952—Italy
1956—

1,000 METER TIME TRIAL

1928—W. Falck-Hansen, Denmark
1932—E. L. Gray, Australia
1936—Arie Gerrit van Vliet, Holland

1948—J. Dupont, France
1952—Russell Mockridge, Australia
1956—

(UNOFFICIAL) TEAM CHAMPIONS

1896—France
1900—France
1904—None
1906—Great Britain
1908—Great Britain
1912—Sweden
1920—Great Britain

1924—France
1928—Holland
1932—Italy
1936—France
1948—France
1952—Italy
1956—

EQUESTRIAN EVENTS

3 DAY EVENT (INDIVIDUAL)

1912—Lt. A. Nordlander, Sweden
1920—Lt. De Moerner, Sweden
1924—A. D. C. Van Der Voort Van Zijp,
    Holland
1928—Lt. C. F. Pahud de Mortanges,
    Holland

1932—Lt. C. F. Pahud de Mortanges,
    Holland
1936—Ludwig Stubbendorff, Germany
1948—Capt. B. Chevallier, France
1952—Hans von Blixen-Finecke, Sweden
1956—Lt. Petrus Kasterman, Sweden

3 DAY EVENT (TEAM)

1912—Sweden (Nordlander, Aldercreutz, Casparsson)
1920—Sweden (H. Morner, Lundstrom, von Braun)
1924—Holland (van Zijp, de Mortanges, G. P. De Kruyff)
1928—Holland (de Mortanges, G. P. De Kruyff, van Zijp)

187

1932—U.S.A. (Earl Thomson, Edwin Argo, Harry Chamberlin)
1936—Germany (Ludwig Stubbendorff, Rudolph Lippert, Konrad Freiherr von Wangenheim)
1948—U.S.A. (F. S. Henry, C. H. Anderson, Earl Thomson)
1952—Sweden (von Blixen-Finecke, Stahre, Frolen)
1956—Great Britain (Lt. Col. F. Weldon, Arthur Rook, Albert Hill)

DRESSAGE (INDIVIDUAL)

1912—Capt. C. Bonde, Sweden
1920—Capt. Lundblad, Sweden
1924—E. v. Linder, Sweden
1928—C. F. von Langen, Germany
1932—F. Lesage, France

1936—H. Pollay, Germany
1948—Capt. H. Moser, Switzerland
1952—Major Henri St. Cyr, Sweden
1956—Major Henri St. Cyr, Sweden

DRESSAGE (TEAM)

1928—Germany (Von Langen, Linkenback, Von Lotzbeck)
1932—France (Lesage, Marion, Jousseaume)
1936—Germany (Pollay, Gerhard, Von Oppeln-Bronikowski)
1948—Sweden (Boltenstern St. Cyr, Persson)
1952—Sweden (St. Cyr, Stahre, Frolen)
1956—Sweden (St. Cyr, G. Persson, G. Boltenstern)

PRIX DES NATIONS (INDIVIDUAL)

1912—Capt. J. Cariou, France, 186 points
1920—Lt. Lequio, Italy, 2 faults
1924—Lt. Gemuseus, Switzerland, 6 faults
1928—F. Ventura, Czechoslovakia, no faults
1932—Takeichi Nishi, Japan, 8 faults

1936—Kurt Hasse, Germany, 4 faults
1948—H. Cortes, Mexico, 6¼ faults
1952—Pierre d'Oriola, France, 8 faults
1956—Hans Winkler, Germany, 4 faults

PRIX DES NATIONS (TEAM)

1912—Sweden (Lewenhaupt, Kilman, von Rosen), 545 points
1920—Sweden (von Rosen, Koenig, Norling), 14 faults
1924—Sweden (Thelning, Stahle, Lundstrom), 42.25 faults
1928—Spain (de los Truxillos, Morenes, Fernandez), 4 faults
1932—All teams participating disqualified.
1936—Germany (v. Barnekow, Hasse, Brandt), 44 faults
1948—Mexico (Cortes, Uriza, Valdes), 34¼ faults
1952—Great Britain (D. N. Stewart, W. W. White, H. M. Llewellyn), 40.75 faults
1956—Germany (H. Winkler, A. Lutke-Westhues, F. Thiedemann), 40 faults

(UNOFFICIAL) TEAM CHAMPIONS

1912—Sweden
1920—Sweden
1924—Sweden
1928—Holland
1932—United States

1936—Germany
1948—United States
1952—Sweden
1956—Germany

FENCING

INDIVIDUAL FOIL

1896—E. Gravelotte, France
1900—E. Coste, France
1904—Ramon Fonst, Cuba
1906—Dillon-Cavanagh, France
1912—Nedo Nadi, Italy
1920—Nedo Nadi, Italy
1924—Roger Ducret, France

1928—Lucien Gaudin, France
1932—Gustavo Marzi, Italy
1936—Giulio Gaudini, Italy
1948—Jean Buhan, France
1952—Christian d'Oriola, France
1956—

TEAM FOIL

1904—Cuba
1920—Italy
1924—France
1928—Italy
1932—France

1936—Italy
1948—France
1952—France
1956—

INDIVIDUAL EPEE

1896—E. Gravelotte, France
1900—Ramon Fonst, Cuba
1904—Ramon Fonst, Cuba
1906—Comte de la Falaise, France
1908—G. Alibert, France

1924—C. Delporte, Belgium
1928—Lucien Gaudin, France
1932—G. Cornaggia-Medici, Italy
1936—Franco Riccardi, Italy
1948—Luigi Cantone, Italy

1912—Paul Anspach, Belgium
1920—A. Massard, France

1952—Eduardo Mangiarotti, Italy
1956—

TEAM EPEE

1906—France
1908—France
1912—Belgium
1920—Italy
1924—France
1928—Italy

1932—France
1936—Italy
1948—France
1952—Italy
1956—

INDIVIDUAL SABER

1896—I. Georgiadis, Greece
1900—Comte de la Falaise, France
1904—M. de Diaz, Cuba
1906—G. Georgiadis, Greece
1908—E. Fuchs, Hungary
1912—E. Fuchs, Hungary
1920—Nedo Nadi, Italy

1924—Alexandre Posta, Hungary
1928—E. Tersctyanszky, Hungary
1932—George Piller, Hungary
1936—Endre Kabos, Hungary
1948—Aladar Gerevich, Hungary
1952—P. Kovacs, Hungary
1956—

TEAM SABER

1906—Germany
1908—Hungary
1912—Hungary
1920—Italy
1924—Italy
1928—Hungary

1932—Hungary
1936—Hungary
1948—Hungary
1952—Hungary
1956—

(UNOFFICIAL) TEAM CHAMPIONS

1896 France
1900—France
1904—Cuba
1906—France
1908—France
1912—Hungary
1920—Italy

1924—France
1928—France
1932—Italy
1936—Italy
1948—Italy *
1952—Italy
1956—

* French claim victory but 1 point behind according to usual scoring system.

FENCING (WOMEN)

INDIVIDUAL FOIL

1924—E. O. Osiier, Denmark
1928—Helene Mayer, Germany
1932—Elen Preis, Austria
1936—Ilona Elek, Hungary

1948—Ilona Elek, Hungary
1952—Irene Camber, Italy
1956—

GYMNASTICS (MEN)

FLYING RINGS

1896—Mitropoulos, Greece
1904—Herman T. Glass, U.S.A.
1924—F. Martino, Italy
1928—L. Stukelj, Yugoslavia
1932—George Gulack, U.S.A.

1936—A. Hudec, Czechoslovakia
1948—K. Frei, Switzerland
1952—G. Chaguinian, Russia
1956—

LONG HORSE (VAULTS)

1896—Karl Schumann, Germany
1904—Anton Heida
George Eyser, U.S.A. (tie)
1924—Frank Kriz, U.S.A.
1928—E. Mack, Switzerland

1932—S. Guglielmetti, Italy
1936—K. Schwarzmann, Germany
1948—P. J. Aaltonen, Finland
1952—V. Tchoukarine, Russia
1956—

1900—Sandras, France
1904—Anton Heida, U.S.A.
1906—Payssee, France
1908—Alberto Braglia, Italy
1912—Alberto Braglia, Italy
1920—G. Zampori, Italy
1924—L. Stukely, Yugoslavia

1928—G. Meiz, Switzerland
1932—Romeo Neri, Italy
1936—K. Schwarzmann, Germany
1948—V. Huhtanen, Finland
1952—V. Tchoukarine, Russia
1956—

ALL-AROUND TEAM EVENT

1896—Germany
1904—U.S.A.
1906—Norway
1908—Sweden
1920—Italy
1924—Italy

1928—Switzerland
1932—Italy
1936—Germany
1948—Finland
1952—Russia
1956—

SIDE HORSE

1896—Zutter, Switzerland
1904—Anton Heida, U.S.A.
1924—J. Wilhelm, Switzerland
1928—H. Hanggi, Switzerland
1932—Stephen Pelle, Hungary

1936—Konrad Frey, Germany
1948—P. J. Aaltonen, Finland
1952—V. Tchoukarine, Russia
1956—

HORIZONTAL BAR

1896—H. Weingartner, Germany
1904—Anton Heida
    E. A. Hennig, U.S.A. (tie)
1924—L. Stukely, Yugoslavia
1928—George Miez, Switzerland

1932—Dallas Bixler, U.S.A.
1936—A. Saarvala, Finland
1948—Josef Stalder, Switzerland
1952—J. Gunthard, Switzerland
1956—

PARALLEL BARS

1896—Alfred Flatow, Germany
1904—George Eyser, U.S.A.
1924—A. Guttinger, Switzerland
1928—L. Vacha, Czechoslovakia
1932—Romeo Neri, Italy

1936—Konrad Frey, Germany
1948—M. Reusch, Switzerland
1952—Hans Eugstar, Switzerland
1956—

FREE EXERCISES

1932—Stephen Pelle, Hungary
1936—George Meiz, Switzerland
1948—F. Putaki, Hungary

1952—Karl Thoresson, Sweden
1956—

(UNOFFICIAL) TEAM CHAMPIONS

1896—Germany
1900—France
1904—United States
1906—France
1908—Italy
1912—Sweden
1920—Italy

1924—Italy
1928—Switzerland
1932—United States
1936—Germany
1948—Switzerland
1952—Russia
1956—

GYMNASTICS (WOMEN)

ALL-AROUND

	Points	
1952—M. Gorokhovskaja, Russia	76.78	1956—

BEAM

	Points	
1952—N. Botcharova, Russia ..	19.22	1956—

FLOOR EXERCISE

	Points	
1952—A. Keleti, Hungary	19.36	1956—

190

LONG HORSE VAULT

	Points	
1952—E. Kalinthouk, Russia ..	19.20	1956—

PARALLEL BARS

	Points	
1952—Margit Korondi, Hungary	19.40	1956—

TEAM DRILL

	Points	
1952—Sweden	74.20	1956—

ALL-AROUND TEAM EVENT

	Points		
1928—Holland	316.75	1952—Russia	528.46
1936—Germany	506.50	1956—	
1948—Czechoslovakia	445.45		

MODERN MILITARY PENTATHLON

INDIVIDUAL *

1912—G. Lilliehook, Sweden
1920—J. Dryssen, Sweden
1924—O. Lindman, Sweden
1928—S. A. Thofelt, Sweden
1932—J. G. Oxenstierna, Sweden

1936—G. Handrick, Germany
1948—W. Grut, Sweden
1952—Lars Hall, Sweden
1956—

* All military personnel but titles omitted.

(UNOFFICIAL) TEAM CHAMPIONS

1912—Sweden
1920—Sweden
1924—Sweden
1928—Sweden
1932—Sweden

1936—Germany
1948—Finland
1952—Hungary *
1956—

* Event became official team affair with official scoring system.

ROWING

SINGLE SCULLS

1900—Barralet, France 7:35.6	1928—Henry R. Pearce, Australia 7:11
1904—Frank B. Greer, U.S.A. ———	1932—Henry R. Pearce, Australia 7:44.4
1908—H. T. Blackstaffe, Gr. Brit. ———	1936—Gustav Schaefer, Germany. 8:21.5
1912—W. D. Kinnear, Gr. Britain 7:47.6	1948—Mervyn T. Wood, Australia 7:24.4
1920—John B. Kelly, U.S.A. ... 7:35	1952—Jurig Tjukalov, Russia ... 8:12.8
1924—J. Beresford Jr., Gr. Brit. 7:49.2	1956—

DOUBLE SCULLS

1904—United States (Atlanta Boat Club)	1936—J. Beresford, Leslie South-wood, Gr. Britain 7:20.8
1920—John B. Kelly, Paul V. Costello, U.S.A. 7:09	1948—B. H. Bushnell, R. D. Bur-nell, Gr. Britain 6:51.3
1924—John B. Kelly, Paul V. Costello, U.S.A. 6:34	1952—T. Cappozza, E. Guerrero, Argentina 7:32.2
1928—Paul V. Costello, Charles J. McIlwaine, U.S.A. 6:41.4	1956—
1932—Kenneth Myers, W. E. Gar-rett Gilmore, U.S.A. .. 7:17.4	

PAIR-OARED SHELL WITH COXSWAIN

1900—R. Klein, F. A. Brandt, Holland 7:34.2	1932—Joseph A. Schauers, Charles M. Kieffer, U.S.A. 8:25.8
1906—Italy, Meters (1,600).... ———	1936—Gerhard Gustmann, Herbert Adamski, Germany 8:36.9
1906—Italy, Meters (1,000).... ———	

191

1920—M. Olgeni, G. Scatturin,
Italy 7:56
1924—M. Candeveau, A. Felber,
Switzerland 8:39
1928—H. W. Schochlin, C. F.
Schochlin, Switzerland. 7:42.6

1948—F. Pedersen, T. Henriksen,
Denmark 8:00.5
1952—R. Salles, G. Mercier,
France 8:28.6
1956—

PAIR-OARED SHELL WITHOUT COXSWAIN

1904—United States, Sewanhaka
Boat Club 10:57
1908—J. Fenning, G. Thomson,
Gr. Britain 9:41
1924—W. H. Rosingh, A. C.
Beynen, Holland 8:19.4
1928—K. Moeschter, B. Muller,
Germany 7:06.4
1932—Lewis Clive, H. R. Arthur
Edwards, Gr. Britain .. 8:00

1936—Willi Eichhorn, H. Strauss,
Germany 8:16.1
1948—J. H. T. Wilson, W. G. R.
M. Laurie, Gr. Britain . 7:21.1
1952—Charles Logg Jr., Thomas
Price, U.S.A. 8:20.7
1956—

FOUR-OARED SHELL WITH COXSWAIN

1900—Germany .... ———
1906—Italy .... ———
1912—Germany 6:59.4
1920—Switzerland 6:54
1924—Switzerland 7:18.4
1928—Italy 6:47.8

1932—Germany 7:19.2
1936—Germany 7:16.2
1948—United States 6:50.3
1952—Czechoslovakia 7:33.4
1956—

FOUR-OARED SHELL WITHOUT COXSWAIN

1904—United States, Century Boat
Club .... ———
1908—Great Britain .... ———
1924—Great Britain .... ———
1928—Great Britain .... ———

1932—Great Britain 6:58.2
1936—Germany 7:01.8
1948—Italy 6:39
1952—Yugoslavia 7:16
1956—

EIGHT-OARED SHELL

1900—United States, Vespers Boat
Club 6:07.8
1904—United States, Vespers Boat
Club .... ———
1908—Great Britain, Leander Club ———
1912—Great Britain, Leander Club 6:15
1920—United States, Navy 6:02.6
1924—United States, Yale 6:33.4
1928—United States, University
of California 6:03.2

1932—United States, University
of California 6:37.4
1936—United States, University
of Washington 6:25.4
1948—United States, University
of California 5:56.7
1952—United States, Navy 6:25.9
1956—

(UNOFFICIAL) TEAM CHAMPIONS

1900—France
1904—United States
1906—Italy
1908—Great Britain
1912—Great Britain
1920—United States
1924—United States

1928—United States
1932—United States
1936—Germany
1948—Italy
1952—United States
1956—

SHOOTING

FREE RIFLE
50 Meters

1908—A. A. Carnell, Great Britain
1912—F. S. Hird, United States
1920—L. Nusslein, United States
1924—Charles deLisle, France
1932—Bertil Ronnmark, Sweden

1936—Willy Rogeberg, Norway
1948—Arthur Cook, United States
1952—Anatoli Bogdanov, Russia
1956—

ANY TARGET PISTOL
50 Meters

1896—S. Paine, United States
1900—Roedern, Switzerland
1906—G. Orphanidis, Greece
1912—A. P. Lane, United States
1920—Karl Frederick, United States

1936—Torsten Ullman, Sweden
1948—E. Vasquez Cam, Peru
1952—Huelet Benner, United States
1956—

RUNNING DEER

1900—L. Debret, France	1924—J. K. Boles, United States
1908—O. Swahn, Sweden	1952—John Larsen, Norway
1912—Alfred G. A. Swahn, Sweden	1956—
1920—O. Olsen, Norway	

CLAY BIRD (TRAP)
Individual

1900—R. de Barbarin, France	1920—M. Arie, United States
1906—Gerald Merlin, Great Britain	1924—Jules Halasy, Hungary
(single shot)	1952—George Genereux, Canada
1908—W. H. Ewing, Canada	1956—
1912—James R. Graham, United States	

SILHOUETTE PISTOL

1952—Karoly Takacs, Hungary	1956—

SMALL-BORE RIFLE
All-Around

1952—Erling Kongshaug, Norway	1956—

SMALL-BORE RIFLE
Prone

1952—Josef Sarbu, Rumania	1956—

(UNOFFICIAL) TEAM CHAMPIONS

1896—Greece	1924—United States
1900—France	1928—United States
1904—None	1932—Italy
1906—France	1936—Germany
1908—Great Britain	1948—Sweden
1912—Sweden	1952—Norway
1920—United States	1956—

SWIMMING (MEN)

100 METER
World's Record

1954—R. Cleveland, U.S.A., New Haven, Conn. 54.8s

Olympic Record (*)

1896—Alfred Hajos, Hungary...	1:22.2	1928—John Weissmuller, U.S.A.	58.6s
1900—Jarvis, Gr. Britain......	1:16.4	1932—Y. Miyazaki, Japan.....	58.2s
1904—Z. de Holomay, Hungary.	1:02.8#	1936—Ferenc Czik, Hungary....	57.6s
1906—Charles Daniels, U.S.A...	1:13.4	1948—Walter Ris, U.S.A......	57.3s*
1908—Charles Daniels, U.S.A...	1:05.6	1952—Clarke Scholes, U.S.A...	57.4s
1912—D. P. Kahanamoku, U.S.A.	1:03.4	1956—	
1920—D. P. Kahanamoku, U.S.A.	1:01.4	#100 yards	
1924—John Weissmuller, U.S.A.	59 s		

400 METER
World's Record

1954—Ford Konno, U.S.A., New Haven, Conn. 4m.26.7s

Olympic Record (*)

1900—Jarvis, Gr. Britain......	—	1928—Albert Zorilla, Argentina.	5:01.6
1904—Charles Daniels, U.S.A..	6:16.2#	1932—Clarence Crabbe, U.S.A...	4:48.4
1906—Otto Sheff, Austria......	6:23.8#	1936—Jack Medica, U.S.A.....	4:44.5
1908—H. Taylor, Gr. Britain...	5:36.8	1948—Bill Smith, U.S.A......	4:41
1912—G. R. Hodgson, Canada..	5:24.4	1952—Jean Boiteux, France....	4:30.7*
1920—Norman Ross, U.S.A....	5:26.8	1956—	
1924—John Weissmuller, U.S.A.	5:04.2	#440 yards	

200 METER BREASTSTROKE
World's Record

1955—M. Furukawa, Japan, Tokyo 2m.31.0s

Olympic Record (*)

1908—F. Holman, Gr. Britain..	3:09.2	1932—Y. Tsuruta, Japan......	2:45.4
1912—Walter Bathe, Germany..	3:01.8	1936—Detsuo Hamuro, Japan ...	2:42.5

193

1920—H. Malmroth, Sweden...	3:04.4	1948—Joe Verdeur, U.S.A.....	2:39.3
1924—R. D. Skelton, U.S.A....	2:56.6	1952—John Davies, Australia..	2:34.4*
1928—Y. Tsuruta, Japan......	2:48.8	1956—	

800 METER RELAY
World's Record

1952—Yale University, U.S.A., New Haven, Conn.   8m.29.4s
    (W. Moore, J. McLane, D. Sheff, R. Thoman)

Olympic Record (*)

1908—Great Britain	10:55.6	1932—Japan	8:58.4
1912—Australia	10:11.6	1936—Japan	8:51.5
1920—United States	10:04.4	1948—United States	8:46
1924—United States	9:53.4	1952—United States	8:31.1*
1928—United States	9:36.2	1956—	

100 METER BACKSTROKE
World's Record

1955—G. Bozon, France, Troyes 1m.02.1s

Olympic Record (*)

1904—Walter Brock, Germany..	1:16.8#	1932—M. Kiyokawa, Japan....	1:08.6
1908—A. Bieberstein, Germany..	1:24.6	1936—Adolph Kiefer, U.S.A...	1:05.9
1912—Harry Hebner, U.S.A....	1:21.2	1948—Allen Stack, U.S.A.....	1:06.4
1920—Warren Kealoha, U.S.A..	1:15.2	1952—Y. Oyakawa, U.S.A.	1:05.4*
1924—Warren Kealoha, U.S.A..	1:13.2	1956—	
1928—George Kojac, U.S.A.....	1:08.2	#100 yards	

1,500 METER
World's Record

1949—H. Furuhashi, Japan, Los Angeles 18m.19s
1956—G. Breen, U.S.A., New Haven .... 18m.05.9s (pending)

Olympic Record (*)

1908—H. Taylor, Gr. Britain..	22:48.4.	1932—K. Kitamura, Japan....	19:12.4
1912—G. R. Hodgson, Canada..	22:00	1936—Norboru Terada, Japan.	19:13.7
1920—Norman Ross, U.S.A..	22:23.2	1948—Jimmy McLane, U.S.A..	19:18.5
1924—A. M. Charlton, Australia	20:06.6	1952—Ford Konno, U.S.A.....	18:30 *
1928—Arne Borg, Sweden....	19:51.8	1956—	

SPRINGBOARD DIVE

1904—Dr. G. E. Sheldon, U.S.A.	12⅔ points	1928—Pete Desjardins, U.S.A.	185.04 points
1906—Gottlob Walz, Germany	156 points	1932—Michael Galitzen, U.S.A.	161.38 points
1908—A. Zurner, Germany	85½ points	1936—Dick Degener, U.S.A.	163.57 points
1912—Paul Gunther, U.S.A.	6 points	1948—Bruce Harlan, U.S.A.	163.64 points
1920—L. E. Kuehn, U.S.A.	6 points	1952—David Browning, U.S.A.	205.29 points
1924—A. C. White, U.S.A.	7 points	1956—	

PLAIN HIGH DIVE

1908—H. Johanssen, Sweden.	83.70 points	1920—A. Wallman, Sweden.	7 points
1912—Erik Adlerz, Sweden..	7 points	1924—R. Eve, Australia....	13½ points

PLATFORM DIVE

1928—Pete Desjardins, U.S.A.	98.74 points	1948—Dr. Sammy Lee, U.S.A.	130.05 points
1932—Harold Smith, U.S.A.	124.80 points	1952—Dr. Sammy Lee, U.S.A.	156.28 points
1936—Marshall Wayne, U.S.A.	113.58 points	1956—	

WATER POLO

1900—Great Britain	1928—Germany
1904—United States	1932—Hungary
1908—Great Britain	1936—Hungary
1912—Great Britain	1948—Italy
1920—Great Britain	1952—Hungary
1924—France	1956—

1896—Greece	1924—United States
1900—Great Britain	1928—United States
1904—United States	1932—Japan
1906—Great Britain	1936—United States
1908—Great Britain	1948—United States
1912—Germany	1952—United States
1920—United States	1956—

SWIMMING (WOMEN)

100 METER
World's Record

1936—W. Den Ouden, Netherlands, Amsterdam 1m.4.6s

Olympic Record (*)

1912—Fanny Durack, Australia	1:22.2	1936—Rika Mastenbroek,	
1920—Ethelda Bleibtrey, U.S.A.	1:13.6	Netherlands	1:05.9*
1924—Ethel Lackie, U.S.A.	1:12.4	1948—Greta Andersen, Denmark	1:06.3
1928—Albina Osipowich, U.S.A.	1:11	1952—Katakin Szoke, Hungary	1:06.8
1932—Helene Madison, U.S.A.	1:06.8	1956—	

400 METER
World's Record

1940—R. Hveger, Denmark, Copenhagen 5m.0.1s

Olympic Record (*)

1924—Martha Norelius, U.S.A.	6:02.2	1948—Ann Curtis, U.S.A.	5:17.8
1928—Martha Norelius, U.S.A.	5:42.8	1952—Valerie Gyenge, Hungary	5:12.1*
1932—Helene Madison, U.S.A.	5:28.5	1956—	
1936—Rika Mastenbroek,			
Netherlands	5:26.4		

200 METER BREAST-STROKE
World's Record

1951—E. Novak, Hungary, Moscow 2m.48.5s

Olympic Record (*)

1924—Lucy Morton, Gr. Britain	3:33.2	1948—Nel van Vliet, Netherlands	2:57.2
1928—Hilde Schrader, Germany	3:12.3	1952—Eva Szekely, Hungary	2:51.7*
1932—Clare Dennis, Australia	3.06.3	1956—	
1936—Hideko Maehata, Japan	3:03.6		

100 METER BACKSTROKE
World's Record

1939—Cor Kint, Netherlands, Rotterdam 1m.10.9s

Olympic Record (*)

1924—Sybil Bauer, U.S.A.	1:23.2	1948—Karen Harup, Denmark	1:14.4
1928—Marie Braun, Netherlands	1:22	1952—Joan Harrison, So. Africa	1:14.3*
1932—Eleanor Holm, U.S.A.	1:19.4	1956—	
1936—Dina Senff, Netherlands	1:18.9		

400 METER RELAY
World's Record

1952—National Team, Hungary, Helsinki 4m.24.4s
(I. Novak, J. Temes, E. Novak, E. Szoeke)

Olympic Record (*)

1912—Great Britain	5:52.8	1936—Netherlands	4:36
1920—United States	5:11.6	1948—United States	4:29.2
1924—United States	4:58.8	1952—Hungary	4:24.4*
1928—United States	4:47.3	1956—	
1932—United States	4:38		

PLAIN HIGH DIVE

1912—G. Johansson, Sweden. 39.9 points	1924—Caroline Smith, U.S.A. 9 points
1920—Miss Fryland, Denmark 6 points	

PLATFORM DIVE

1928—E. B. Pinkston, U.S.A.	31.60 points		1948—Vicky Draves, U.S.A...	68.87 points
1932—D. Poynton, U.S.A...	40.26 points		1952—P. McCormick, U.S.A..	79.37 points
1936—D. Poynton, U.S.A...	33.93 points		1956—	

FANCY SPRINGBOARD DIVE

1920—A. Riggin, U.S.A...	9 points	1936—M. Gestring, U.S.A.	89.27 points
1924—E. Becker, U.S.A...	8 points	1948—Vicky Draves, U.S.A.	108.74 points
1928—Helen Meany, U.S.A.	76.62 points	1952—P. McCormick, U.S.A.	147.30 points
1932—G. Coleman, U.S.A...	87.52 points	1956—	

TEAM GAMES

SOCCER

1900—Great Britain	1928—Uruguay
1904—Great Britain	1932—None
1906—Denmark	1936—Italy
1908—Great Britain	1948—Sweden
1912—Great Britain	1952—Hungary
1920—Belgium	1956—
1924—Uruguay	

BASEBALL

1900—United States (demonstration)	1936—United States (demonstration)
1912—United States (demonstration)	1952—United States (demonstration)

BASKETBALL

1904—United States (demonstration)	1952—United States
1936—United States	1956—
1948—United States	

FIELD HOCKEY

1908—Great Britain	1936—India
1920—Great Britain	1948—India
1928—India	1952—India
1932—India	1956—

TRACK and FIELD (MEN)

100 METER DASH
World's Record

1936—Jesse Owens, U.S.A., Chicago, Ill. 10.2s
1941—Harold Davis, U.S.A., Compton, Cal.
1948—L. Labeach, Panama, Fresno, Cal.
1948—Norwood H. Ewell, U.S.A., Evanston, Ill.
1951—E. McD. Bailey, Great Britain, Belgrade
1954—H. Futterer, Germany, Yokohama
1956—Bobby Murrow, U.S.A., Los Angeles, Cal. (pending)
1956—Ira Murchison, U.S.A., Los Angeles, Cal. (pending)

Olympic Record (*)

1896—Thomas E. Burke, U.S.A..	12 s	1924—H. Abrahams, Gr. Britain.	10.6s
1900—F. W. Jarvis, U.S.A.....	10.8s	1928—Percy Williams, Canada...	10.8s
1904—Archie Hahn, U.S.A......	11 s	1932—Eddie Tolan, U.S.A.......	10.3⅝*
1906—Archie Hahn, U.S.A......	11 s	1936—Jesse Owens, U.S.A.	10.3s
1908—Reggie Walker, So. Africa	10.8s	1948—Harrison Dillard, U.S.A...	10.3s*
1912—Ralph C. Craig, U.S.A....	10.8s	1952—Lindy Remigino, U.S.A..	10.4s
1920—Charles W. Paddock, U.S.A.	10.8s	1956—	

200 METER DASH
World's Record

1949—Melvin E. Patton, U.S.A., Los Angeles, Cal. 20.2s

Olympic Record (*)

1900—J. W. B. Tewksbury, U.S.A.	22.2s	1928—Percy Williams, Canada...	21.8s
1904—Archie Hahn, U.S.A.	21.6s	1932—Eddie Tolan, U.S.A.......	21.2s
1908—Bobby Kerr, Canada......	22.4s	1936—Jesse Owens, U.S.A......	20.7s*
1912—Ralph C. Craig, U.S.A...	21.7s	1948—Melvin E. Patton, U.S.A..	21.1s
1920—Allan Woodring, U.S.A...	22 s	1952—Andy Stanfield, U.S.A....	20.7s*
1924—Jackson V. Scholz, U.S.A.	21.6s	1956—	

110 METER HURDLES
World's Record

1950—Richard Attlesey, U.S.A., Helsinki 13.5s
1940—Fred Wolcott, U.S.A., Princeton 13.5s
1956—Jack Davis, U.S.A., Bakersfield, Cal. .... (pending) 13.4s

Olympic Record (*)

1896—Tom Curtis, U.S.A....... 17.6s	1924—D. C. Kinsey, U.S.A...... 15 s
1900—Alvin Kraenzlein, U.S.A.. 15.4s	1928—Sam Atkinson, So. Africa. 14.8s
1904—F. W. Schule, U.S.A.... 16 s	1932—George Saling, U.S.A..... 14.6s
1906—R. G. Leavitt, U.S.A.... 16.2s	1936—Forrest Towns, U.S.A.... 14.2s
1908—Forrest Smithson, U.S.A.. 15 s	1948—William Porter, U.S.A... 13.9s
1912—F. W. Kelly, U.S.A..... 15.1s	1952—Harrison Dillard, U.S.A.. 13.7s*
1920—Earl Thomson, Canada.... 14.8s	1956—

400 METER HURDLES
World's Record

1953—J. Lituyev, U.S.S.R., Budapest 50.4s
1956—Glenn Davis, U.S.A., Los Angeles, Cal. .... (pending) 49.5s

Olympic Record (*)

1900—J. W. B. Tewksbury, U.S.A. 57.6s	1932—Robert Tisdall, Ireland... 51.8s
1904—Harry Hillman, U.S.A.... 53 s	1936—Glenn Hardin, U.S.A.... 52.4s
1908—Charles Bacon, U.S.A.... 55 s	1948—Roy Cochran, U.S.A.... 51.1s
1920—Frank Loomis, U.S.A.... 54 s	1952—Charles Moore, Jr., U.S.A.. 50.8s*
1924—F. Morgan Taylor, U.S.A.. 52.6s	1956—
1928—L. D. Burghley, Gr. Britain 53.4s	

400 METER RUN
World's Record

1955—Lou Jones, U.S.A., Mexico City 45.4s
1956—Lou Jones, U.S.A., Los Angeles, Cal. .. .. (pending) 45.2s

Olympic Record (*)

1896—Thomas E. Burke, U.S.A... 54.2s	1924—Eric Liddell, Gr. Britain.. 47.6s
1900—Maxey Long, U.S.A.,.... 49.4s	1928—Ray Barbuti, U.S.A.... 47.8s
1904—Harry Hillman, U.S.A.... 49.2s	1932—William A. Carr, U.S.A... 46.2s
1906—Paul Pilgrim, U.S.A.... 53.2s	1936—Archie Williams, U.S.A.... 46.5s
1908—Wyndham Halswelle,	1948—Arthur Wint, Jamaica.... 46.2s
Gr. Britain (walkover).. 50 s	1952—George Rhoden, Jamaica.. 45.9s*
1912—Charles Reidpath, U.S.A.. 48.2s	1956—
1920—Bevil Rudd, So. Africa.... 49.6s	

800 METER RUN
World's Record

1955—Roger Moens, Belgium, Oslo 1m.45.7s

Olympic Record (*)

1896—E. H. Flack, Australia.. 2:11	1924—Douglas Lowe, Gr. Britain 1:52.4
1900—A. E. Tysoe, Gr. Britain. 2:01.4	1928—Douglas Lowe, Gr. Britain 1:51.8
1904—Jim D. Lightbody, U.S.A. 1:56	1932—Tom Hampson, Gr. Britain 1:49.8
1906—Paul Pilgrim, U.S.A..... 2:01.2	1936—John Woodruff, U.S.A.... 1:52.9
1908—Mel Sheppard, U.S.A.... 1:52.8	1948—Mal Whitfield, U.S.A... 1:49.2*
1912—Ted Meredith, U.S.A..... 1:51.9	1952—Mal Whitfield, U.S.A... 1:49.2*
1920—A. G. Hill, Gr. Britain.. 1:53.4	1956—

1500 METER RUN
World's Record

1955—Laszlo Tabori, Hungary, Oslo 3m40.8s
1955—Gunnar Nielsen, Denmark, Oslo

Olympic Record (*)

1896—E. H. Flack, Australia... 4:33.2	1924—Paavo Nurmi, Finland.... 3:53.6
1900—C. Bennett, Gr. Britain.. 4:06	1928—Harry Larva, Finland.... 3:53.2
1904—Jim D. Lightbody, U.S.A. 4:05.4	1932—Luigi Beccali, Italy 3:51.1
1906—Jim D. Lightbody, U.S.A. 4:12	1936—J. Lovelock, New Zealand. 3:47.8
1908—Mel Sheppard, U.S.A..... 4:03.4	1948—Henri Eriksson, Sweden.. 3:49.8
1912—A. Jackson, Gr. Britain.. 3:56.8	1952—J. Barthel, Luxembourg .. 3:45.2*
1920—A. G. Hill, Gr. Britain... 4:01.8	1956—

400 METER RELAY
World's Record

1936—United States, Berlin (Owens, Metcalfe, Draper, Wykoff) 39.8s

Olympic Record (*)

1912—Great Britain	42.4s		1936—United States		39.8s*
1920—United States	42.2s		1948—United States		40.6s
1924—United States	41 s		1952—United States		40.1s
1928—United States	41 s		1956—		
1932—United States	40 s				

1600 METER RELAY
World's Record

1952—Jamaica National Team, Jamaica, Helsinki 3m.3.9s
(A. Wint, L. Laing, H. H. McKenley, V. G. Rhoden)

Olympic Record (*)

1908—United States	3:27.2	1932—United States	3:08.2
1912—United States	3:16.6	1936—Great Britain	3:09
1920—Great Britain	3:22.2	1948—United States	3:10.4
1924—United States	3:16	1952—Jamaica, B. W. I.	3:03.9*
1928—United States	3:14.2	1956—	

5000 METER RUN
World's Record

1955—Sandor Iharos, Hungary, Budapest 13m.40.6s
1956—Gordon Pirie, Great Britain, Bergen .... (pending) 13m.36.8s

Olympic Record (*)

1912—H. Kolehmainen, Finland.	14:36.6	1936—Gunnar Hoeckert, Finland.	14:22.2
1920—J. Guillemont, France....	14:55.6	1948—Gaston Reiff, Belgium....	14:17.6
1924—Paavo Nurmi, Finland...	14:31.2	1952—E. Zatopek, Czechoslovakia	14:06.6*
1928—Willie Ritola, Finland..	14:38	1956—	
1932—Lauri Lehtinen, Finland..	14:30		

10,000 METER RUN
World's Record

1954—Emil Zatopek, Czechoslovakia, Brussels 28m.54.2s

Olympic Record (*)

1912—H. Kolehmainen, Finland.	31:20.8	1936—Ilmari Salminen, Finland.	30:15
1920—Paavo Nurmi, Finland...	31:45.8	1948—E. Zatopek, Czechoslovakia	29:59.6
1924—Willie Ritola, Finland..	30:23.2	1952—E. Zatopek, Czechoslovakia	29:17 *
1928—Paavo Nurmi, Finland..	30:18.8	1956—	
1932—Janusz Kusocinski, Poland	30:11.4		

3,000 METER STEEPLECHASE
World's Record

1955—J. Chromik, Poland, Budapest 8m.40.2s

Olympic Record (*)

1920—P. Hodge, Gr. Britain..	10:02.4	1936—V. Iso-Hollo, Finland...	9:03.8
1924—Willie Ritola, Finland..	9:33.6	1948—T. Sjoestrand, Sweden..	9:04.6
1928—Toivo Loukola, Finland..	9:21.8	1952—H. Ashenfelter, U.S.A...	8:45.4*
1932—V. Iso-Hollo, Finland...	10:33.4#	1956—	

#ran extra lap by mistake

10,000 METER WALK
World's Record

1945—Verner Hardmo, Sweden, Kumla 42m.39.6s

Olympic Record (*)

1912—G. H. Goulding, Canada.	46:28.4	1948—J. Mikaelsson, Sweden..	45:13.2
1920—Ugo Frigerio, Italy.....	48:06.2	1952—J. Mikaelsson, Sweden..	45:02.8*
1924—Ugo Frigerio, Italy.....	47:49	1956—	

50,000 METER WALK
World's Record

1953—J. Ljunggren, Sweden, Fristad 4h.29m.58s
1956—Ladislav Moc, Czechoslovakia, Prague .... (pending) 4h.21m.07s.

Olympic Record (*)

1932—T. W. Green, Gr. Britain	4:50:10	1952—G. Dordoni, Italy	4:28:07.8*
1936—H. Whitlock, Gr. Britain	4:30:41.4	1956—	
1948—J. Ljunggren, Sweden..	4:41:52		

RUNNING BROAD JUMP
World's Record

1935—Jesse Owens, U.S.A., Ann Arbor .... 26ft.8¼in.

1896—Ellery Clark, U.S.A. .... 20 ft. 9¾ in.
1900—Alvin Kraenzlein, U.S.A. .... 23 ft. 6⅞ in.
1904—Myer Prinstein, U.S.A. .... 24 ft. 1 in.
1906—Myer Prinstein, U.S.A. .... 23 ft. 7½ in.
1908—Frank Irons, U.S.A. .... 24 ft. 6½ in.
1912—A. L. Gutterson, U.S.A. .... 24 ft. 11¼ in.
1920—William Petterssen, Sweden .... 23 ft. 5½ in.
1924—Dehart Hubbard, U.S.A. .... 24 ft. 5⅛ in.
1928—Edward B. Hamm, U.S.A. .... 25 ft. 4¾ in.
1932—Edward Gordon, U.S.A. .... 25 ft. ¾ in.
1936—Jesse Owens, U.S.A. .... 26 ft. 5-5/16 in.*
1948—Willie Steele, U.S.A. .... 25 ft. 8 in.
1952—Jerome Biffle, U.S.A. .... 24 ft. 10.03 in.
1956—

POLE VAULT
World's Record

1942—Cornelius Warmerdam, U.S.A., Modesto, Cal. .... 15 ft. 7¾ in.
1943—Cornelius Warmerdam, U.S.A., Chicago, Ill. (board runway) . 15 ft. 8½ in.

Olympic Record (*)

1896—William W. Hoyt, U.S.A. .... 10 ft. 9¾ in.
1900—I. K. Baxter, U.S.A. .... 10 ft. 9-9/10 in.
1904—C. E. Dvorak, U.S.A. .... 11 ft. 6 in.
1906—Gouder, France .... 11 ft. 6 in.
1908—A. C. Gilbert, E. T. Cook (Tie), U.S.A. .... 12 ft. 2 in.
1912—H. J. Babcock, U.S.A. .... 12 ft. 11½ in.
1920—Frank Foss, U.S.A. .... 13 ft. 5 in.
1924—Lee Barnes, U.S.A. .... 12 ft. 11½ in.
1928—Sabin W. Carr, U.S.A. .... 13 ft. 9⅜ in.
1932—William Miller, U.S.A. .... 14 ft. 1⅞ in.
1936—Earle Meadows, U.S.A. .... 14 ft. 3¼ in.
1948—Guinn Smith, U.S.A. .... 14 ft. 1¼ in.
1952—Robert Richards, U.S.A. .... 14 ft. 11¼ in.*
1956—

RUNNING HOP STEP AND JUMP
World's Record

1953—L. Scherbakov, Russia, Moscow .... 53 ft. 2¾ in.

Olympic Record (*)

1896—James B. Connolly, U.S.A. .... 45 ft.
1900—Myer Prinstein, U.S.A. .... 47 ft. 4¼ in.
1904—Myer Prinstein, U.S.A. .... 47 ft.
1906—P. O'Connor, Ireland .... 46 ft. 2 in.
1908—T. J. Ahearne, Gr. Britain .... 48 ft. 11¼ in.
1912—G. Lindblom, Sweden .... 48 ft. 5⅛ in.
1920—V. Tuulos, Finland .... 47 ft. 6⅞ in.
1924—A. W. Winter, Australia .... 50 ft. 11⅛ in.
1928—Mikio Oda, Japan .... 49 ft. 10-13/16 in.
1932—Chuhei Nambu, Japan .... 51 ft. 7 in.
1936—Naoto Tajima, Japan .... 52 ft. 5⅞ in.
1948—Arne Ahman, Sweden .... 50 ft. 6¼ in.
1952—Adhemar da Silva, Brazil .... 53 ft. 2½ in.*
1956—

RUNNING HIGH JUMP
World's Record

1953—Walter Davis, U.S.A., Dayton, Ohio .... 6 ft. 11½ in.
1956—Charles Dumas, U.S.A., Los Angeles, Cal. .... (pending) 7 ft. ½ in.

Olympic Record (*)

1896—Ellery Clark, U.S.A. .... 5 ft. 11¼ in.
1900—I. K. Baxter, U.S.A. .... 6 ft. 2⅘ in.
1904—Sam Jones, U.S.A. .... 5 ft. 11 in.
1906—Con Leahy, Ireland .... 5 ft. 9⅞ in.
1908—H. F. Porter, U.S.A. .... 6 ft. 3 in.
1912—Alma Richards, U.S.A. .... 6 ft. 4 in.
1920—Dick Landon, U.S.A. .... 6 ft. 4¼ in.
1924—Harold Osborn, U.S.A. .... 6 ft. 5-15/16 in.
1928—Robert W. King, U.S.A. .... 6 ft. 4⅜ in.
1932—D. McNaughton, Canada .... 6 ft. 5⅝ in.
1936—Cornelius Johnson, U.S.A. .... 6 ft. 7-15/16 in.
1948—John Winter, Australia .... 6 ft. 6 in.
1952—Walter Davis, U.S.A. .... 6 ft. 8¼ in.*
1956—

16-LB. SHOT PUT
World's Record

1956—Parry O'Brien, U.S.A., New York City .... (pending) 61 ft. 5¼ in.

Olympic Record (*)

1896—Robert Garrett, U.S.A. .... 36 ft. 2 in.
1900—Richard Sheldon, U.S.A. .... 46 ft. 3⅛ in.
1904—Ralph Rose, U.S.A. .... 48 ft. 7 in.
1906—Martin Sheridan, U.S.A. .... 40 ft. 4⅘ in.
1908—Ralph Rose, U.S.A. .... 46 ft. 7½ in.
1912—Pat McDonald, U.S.A. .... 50 ft. 4 in.
1920—Willie Porhola, Finland .... 48 ft. 7⅛ in.
1924—Clarence Houser, U.S.A. .... 49 ft. 2⅜ in.
1928—John Kuck, U.S.A. .... 52 ft. 11/16 in.
1932—Leo Sexton, U.S.A. .... 52 ft. 6-3/16 in.
1936—Hans Woellke, Germany .... 53 ft. 1-13/16 in.
1948—Wilbur Thompson, U.S.A. .... 56 ft. 2 in.
1952—Parry O'Brien, U.S.A. .... 57 ft. 1½ in.*
1956—

DISCUS THROW
World's Record

1953—Fortune Gordien, U.S.A., Pasadena .... 194 ft. 6 in.

Olympic Record (*)

1896—Robert Garrett, U.S.A. .... 95 ft. 7½ in.
1900—Rudolph Bauer, Hungary .... 118 ft. 2-9/10 in.
1904—Martin Sheridan, U.S.A. .... 128 ft. 10½ in.
1906—Martin Sheridan, U.S.A. .... 136 ft. ⅓ in.
1908—Martin Sheridan, U.S.A. .... 134 ft. 2 in.
1912—A. R. Taipale, Finland .... 148 ft. 3.9 in.
1920—E. Niklander, Finland .... 146 ft. 7¼ in.
1924—Clarence Houser, U.S.A. .... 151 ft. 5¼ in.
1928—Clarence Houser, U.S.A. .... 155 ft. 2⅘ in.
1932—John Anderson, U.S.A. .... 162 ft. 4⅞ in.
1936—Kenneth Carpenter, U.S.A. .... 165 ft. 7-29/64 in.
1948—Adolfo Consolini, Italy .... 173 ft. 2 in.
1952—Simeon Iness, U.S.A. .... 180 ft. 6½ in.*
1956—

16-LB. HAMMER THROW
World's Record

1955—M. P. Krivonosov, U.S.S.R., Warsaw .... 211 ft. ½ in.
1956—Clift Blair, U.S.A., Needham, Mass. .... (pending) 216 ft. 5½ in.

Olympic Record (*)

1900—John Flanagan, U.S.A. .... 167 ft. 4 in.
1904—John Flanagan, U.S.A. .... 168 ft. 1 in.
1908—John Flanagan, U.S.A. .... 170 ft. 4¼ in.
1912—Matt McGrath, U.S.A. .... 177 ft. 7 in.
1920—Pat Ryan, U.S.A. .... 173 ft. 5⅝ in.
1924—Fred Tootel, U.S.A. .... 174 ft. 10⅛ in.
1928—Pat O'Callaghan, Ireland .... 168 ft. 7½ in.
1932—Pat O'Callaghan, Ireland .... 176 ft. 11⅛ in.

```
1936—Karl Hein, Germany .............................. 185 ft. 4-3/16 in.
1948—Imre Nemeth, Hungary ........................... 183 ft. 11½ in.
1952—Josef Csarmak, Hungary .......................... 197 ft. 11¾ in.*
1956—
```

JAVELIN THROW
World's Record

```
1955—F. Held, U.S.A., Modesto, Cal. ................... 268 ft. 2½ in.
1956—Soini Nikkinen, Finland, Kuhmoinen ........... (pending) 274 ft. 1¾ in
```

Olympic Record (*)

```
1906—E. Lemming,    Sweden  ............................ 175 ft. 6 in.
1908—E. Lemming,    Sweden  ............................ 178 ft. 7½ in.
1912—E. Lemming,    Sweden  ............................ 198 ft. 11¼ in.
1920—Jonni Myyra,   Finland ............................ 215 ft. 9¾ in.
1924—Jonni Myyra,   Finland ............................ 206 ft. 6¾ in.
1928—E. H. Lundquist, Sweden ........................... 218 ft. 6⅛ in.
1932—Matti Jarvinen, Finland ........................... 238 ft. 7 in.
1936—Gerhard Stoeck, Germany ........................... 235 ft. 8-13/32 in.
1948—Kaji Rautavaara, Finland .......................... 228 ft. 10½ in.
1952—Cy Young, U.S.A. .................................. 242 ft. ¾ in.*
1956—
```

DECATHLON
Olympic Record (*)

1912—H. Wieslander, Sweden 7,724.495	1936—Glenn Morris, U.S.A... 7,900#
1920—H. Loveland, Norway 6,804.35	1948—Bob Mathias, U.S.A... 7,139
1924—H. Osborn, U.S.A..... 7,710.775	1952—Bob Mathias, U.S.A... 7,887°
1928—Paavo Yrjola, Finland. 8,053.29	1956—
1932—James Bausch, U.S.A.. 8,462.235	

#scoring system revised   °scoring system revised again

MARATHON (MEN)

No World or Olympic Records, for while distance the same, course varies. Distance: 26 miles.

```
1896—Spiridion Loues, Greece. 2:55:20      1924—A. C. Stenroos, Finland 2:41:22.6
1900—Michel Teato, France.. 2:59           1928—El Ouafi, France .. 2:32:57
1904—T. J. Hicks, U.S.A..... 3:28:53       1932—Juan Zabala, Argentina 2:31:36
1906—W. J. Sherring, Canada 2:51:23.6      1936—Kitei Son, Japan .. 2:29:19.2
1908—John J. Hayes, U.S.A. 2:55:18         1948—Delfo Cabrera, Argentina 2:34:51.6
1912—K. K. McArthur,                       1952—Emil Zatopek,
        So. Africa ........ 2:36:54.8             Czechoslovakia ..... 2:23:03.2
1920—H. Kolehmainen, Finland 2:32:35.8     1956—
```

(UNOFFICIAL) TEAM CHAMPIONS

```
1896—United States                         1924—United States
1900—United States                         1928—United States
1904—United States                         1932—United States
1906—United States                         1936—United States
1908—United States                         1948—United States
1912—United States                         1952—United States
1920—United States                         1956—
```

TRACK and FIELD (WOMEN)

100 METER DASH
World's Record

```
1955—Shirley de La Hunty, Australia, Warsaw ......................... 11.3s
```

Olympic Record (*)

```
1928—Elizabeth Robinson, U.S.A. 12.2s      1952—Marjorie Jackson, Australia 11.5s*
1932—Stella Walsh, Poland..... 11.9s       1956—
1936—Helen Stephens, U.S.A..... 11.5s*
1948—Fannie Blankers-Koen,
        Netherlands ........... 11.9s
```

200 METER DASH
World's Record

```
1952—Marjorie Jackson, Australia, Helsinki ......................... 23.4s
```

Olympic Record (*)

```
1948—Fannie Blankers-Koen, Netherlands ............................. 24.4s
1952—Marjorie Jackson, Australia ................................... 23.7s*
1956—
```

80 METER HURDLES
World's Record
1955—G. Ermolenko, U.S.S.R., Leningrad 10.8s

Olympic Record (*)
1932—Mildred Didrikson, U.S.A.. 11.7s   1952—Shirley Strickland
1936—Trebisonda Villa, Italy.... 11.7s   de La Hunty, Australia. 10.9s*
1948—Fannie Blankers-Koen,   1956—
      Netherlands 11.2s

400 METER RELAY
World's Record
1953—Russian National Team, Budapest (Sofronova, Dvalishvili-Hnikina,
     Turnova, Kalashnikova) 45.6s

Olympic Record (*)
1928—Canada .... 48.4s   1948—Netherlands 47.5s
1932—U.S.A. .... 47.s   1952—U.S.A. 45.9s*
1936—U.S.A. .... 46.9s   1956—

RUNNING BROAD JUMP
World's Record
1954—Y. Williams, New Zealand, Sydney .... 20 ft. 7½ in.
1955—G. Vinogradova, U.S.S.R., Moscow .... 20 ft. 7½ in.

Olympic Record (*)
1948—Olga Gyarmati, Hungary .... 18 ft. 8½ in.
1952—Yvette Williams, New Zealand .... 20 ft. 5¾ in.*
1956—

RUNNING HIGH JUMP
World's Record
1954—A. Chudina, U.S.S.R., Kiev .... 5 ft. 7¾ in.

Olympic Record (*)
1928—Ethel Catherwood, Canada .... 5 ft. 3 in.
1932—Jean Shiley, U.S.A. .... 5 ft. 5¼ in.
1936—Ibolya Csak, Hungary .... 5 ft. 3 in.
1948—Alice Coachman, U.S.A. .... 5 ft. 6⅛ in.*
1952—Esther Brand, So. Africa .... 5 ft. 5¾ in.
1956—

SHOT PUT
World's Record
1955—Galina Zybina, U.S.S.R., Leningrad .... 53 ft. 5¼ in.

Olympic Record (*)
1948—Micheline Ostermeyer, France .... 45 ft.1½ in.
1952—Galina Zybina, U.S.S.R. .... 50 ft. 1½ in.*
1956—

DISCUS THROW
World's Record
1952—N. Dumbadze, U.S.S.R., Tbilisi .... 187 ft.1½ in.

Olympic Record (*)
1928—H. Konopacka, Poland .... 129 ft. 11⅞ in.
1932—Lillian Copeland, U.S.A. .... 133 ft. 2 in.
1936—Gisela Mauermayer, Germany .... 156 ft. 3-3/16 in.
1948—Micheline Ostermeyer, France .... 137 ft. 6½ in.
1952—Nina Romaschkova, U.S.S.R. .... 168 ft. 8½ in.*
1956—

JAVELIN THROW
World's Record
1954—N. Konjaeva, U.S.S.R., Kiev .... 182 ft.

Olympic Record (*)
1932—Mildred Didrikson, U.S.A. .... 143 ft. 4 in.
1936—Tilly Fleischer, Germany .... 148 ft. 2¾ in.
1948—H. Baume, Austria .... 149 ft. 6 in.
1952—Dana Zatopekova, Czechoslovakia .... 165 ft. 7 in.*
1956—

WEIGHT LIFTING

CURRENT RULE FOR WEIGHTS STANDARDIZED IN 1928
BANTAMWEIGHT

1948—Joe N. De Pietro, U.S.A. .... 677½ lbs.
1952—Ivan Udodov, Russia .... 694 lbs.*
1956—
  * Olympic Record

FEATHERWEIGHT

1920—E. de Haes, Belgium.. 484 lbs.	1948—M. S. J. Fayad, Egypt 732½ lbs.
1924—M. Gabetti, Italy.... 885½ lbs.	1952—R. Chimishkyan, Russia 743½ lbs.*
1928—F. Andrysek, Austria.. 632½ lbs.	1956—
1932—R. Suvigny, France... 632½ lbs.	* Olympic Record
1936—A. Terlazzo, U.S.A... 687½ lbs.	

LIGHTWEIGHT

1920—A. Neyland, Estonia.. 567.68 lbs.	1936—M. A. Mesbah, Egypt. 753½ lbs.
1924—E. Decottignies, France 968 lbs.	1948—I. Shams, Egypt .... 793¼ lbs.
1928—K. Helbig, Germany. 709½ lbs.	1952—Tommy Kono, U.S.A.. 798¾ lbs.*
H. Hass, Austria (tie)	1956—
1932—Rene Duverger, France 715 lbs.	* Olympic Record

MIDDLEWEIGHT

1920—Gance, France ...... 540.012 lbs.	1948—F. I. Spellman, U.S.A. 859½ lbs.
1924—C. Galimberti, Italy.. 083½ lbs.	1952—Peter George, U.S.A.. 881½ lbs.*
1928—F. Roger, France... 738.01 lbs.	1956—
1932—R. Ismayr, Germany.. 759 lbs.	* Olympic Record
1936—Khadr El Touni, Egypt 852½ lbs.	

LIGHT HEAVYWEIGHT

1920—E. Cadine, France.. 639.334 lbs.	1948—Stan Stanczyk, U.S.A. 920 lbs.
1924—C. Rigoulot, France.. 1105½ lbs.*	1952—T. Lomakin, Russia.. 920¼ lbs
1928—E. S. Nosseir, Egypt. 781 lbs.	1956—
1932—L. Hostin, France... 803 lbs.	* Olympic Record
1936—L. Hostin, France... 821 lbs.	

MIDDLE HEAVYWEIGHT

1952—N. Schemansky, U.S.A. 980¾ lbs.*   1956—
  * Olympic Record

HEAVYWEIGHT

1920—F. Bottini, Italy.... 595.24 lbs.	1936—J. Manger, Germany. 902 lbs.
1924—J. Tonani, Italy.... 1138½ lbs.	1948—John Davis, U.S.A... 997¼ lbs.
1928—J. Strassberger,	1952—John Davis, U.S.A.. 1013¾ lbs.*
Germany .... 819½ lbs.	1956—
1932—J. Skobla,	* Olympic Record
Czechoslovakia ... 836 lbs.	

(UNOFFICIAL) TEAM CHAMPIONS

1920—France	1936—Egypt
1924—Italy	1948—United States
1928—Germany	1952—United States
1932—France	1956—

WINTER GAMES
SPEED SKATING

500 METERS
Olympic Record (*)

1924—Charles Jewtraw, U.S.A.... 44s	1936—Ivar Ballangrud, Norway... 43.4s
1928—Clas Thunberg, Finland....	1948—Finn Helgesen, Norway..... 43.1s
Bernt Evensen, Norway.. 43.4s	1952—Ken Henry, U.S.A......... 43.2s
1932—John A. Shea, U.S.A...... 43.4s	1956—Evgeny Grishin, Russia.... 40.2s*

1,500 METERS
Olympic Record (*)

1924—Clas Thunberg, Finland... 2:20.8	1948—Sverre Farstad, Norway.. 2:17.6
1928—Clas Thunberg, Finland... 2:21.1	1952—Hjalmar Andersen, Norway 2:20.4

203

1932—John A. Shea, U.S.A....	2:57.5	1956—E. Grishin, Russia.......	2:08.6*
1936—C. Mathisen, Norway.....	2:19.2	Y. Mikhailov, Russia (tie)	

5,000 METERS
Olympic Record (*)

1924—Clas Thunberg, Finland..	8:39	1948—Reidar Liaklev, Norway...	8:29.4
1928—Ivar Ballangrud, Norway..	8:50.5	1952—Hjalmar Andersen, Norway	8:10.6
1932—Irving Jaffee, U.S.A.....	9:40.8	1956—Boris Shilkov, Russia....	7:48.7*
1936—Ivar Ballangrud, Norway..	8:19.6		

10,000 METERS
Olympic Record (*)

1924—Julien Skutnabb, Finland	18:04.8	1948—Ake Seyffarth, Sweden..	17:26.3
1928—Irving Jaffee, U.S.A..	18:36.5#	1952—H. Andersen, Norway...	16:45.8
1932—Irving Jaffee, U.S.A...	19:13.6	1956—Sigge Ericsson, Sweden..	16:35.9*
1936—Ivar Ballangrud, Norway	17:24.3		

Thawing of ice caused event to be canceled. Jaffee had best time.

FIGURE SKATING (MEN)

1908—Ulrich Salchow, Sweden	
1920—Gillis Grafstrom, Sweden	
1924—Gillis Grafstrom, Sweden	2575.25 points
1928—Gillis Grafstrom, Sweden	2698.25 points
1932—Karl Schafer, Austria	2602 points
1936—Karl Schafer, Austria	2959.0 points
1948—Richard Button, United States	191.177 points
1952—Richard Button, United States	192.256 points
1956—Hayes Jenkins, United States	166.4 points

PAIRS

1908—Miss Hubler, H. Burger, Germany	
1920—Mr. & Mrs. Jakobsson, Finland	
1924—H. Englemann, A. Berger, Austria	74.50 points
1928—Andree Joly, Pierre Brunet, France	100.50 points
1932—Andree & Pierre Brunet, France	76.7 points
1936—Maxie Herber, Ernst Baier, Germany	103.3 points
1948—Micheline Lannoy, Pierre Baugniet, Belgium	11.227 points
1952—Ria & Paul Falk, Germany	11.400 points
1956—S. Schwartz, K. Oppelt, Austria	14 points

SKIING (MEN)

JUMPING

1924—Jacob T. Thams, Norway	18.96 points
1928—Alfred Andersen, Norway	19.208 points
1932—Birger Ruud, Norway	228.1 points
1936—Birger Ruud, Norway	232.0 points
1948—Petter Hugsted, Norway	228.1 points
1952—Arnfinn Bergmann, Norway	226.0 points
1956—Antti Hyvarinen, Finland	227.0 points

18 KILOMETERS

1924—Thorleif Haug, Norway	1:14:31
1928—Johan Grottumsbraaten, Norway (19,700 meters)	1:37:1
1932—Sven Utterstrom, Sweden (18,214 meters)	1:23:7
1936—Erik-Aug. Larsson, Sweden	1:14:38
1948—M. Lundstrom, Sweden	1:13:50
1952—Hallgeir Brenden, Norway	1:01:34
1956—Hallgeir Brenden, Norway (15 km)	49:39

50 KILOMETERS

1924—Thorleif Haug, Norway	3:44:32
1928—P. Hedlund, Sweden	4:52:37
1932—Veli Saarinen, Finland	4:28
1936—Elis Viklund, Sweden	3:30:11
1948—Nils Karlsson, Sweden	3:47:48
1952—Veikko Hakulinen, Finland	3:33:33
1956—Sixten Jernberg, Sweden	2:50:27

SLALOM

1948—Edi Reinalter, Switzerland .... 2m. 10.3s.
1952—Othmar Schneider, Austria .... 2m. 0.0s.
1956—Toni Sailer, Austria .... 3m. 14.7s.

GIANT SLALOM

1952—Stein Eriksen, Norway .... 2m. 25.0s.
1956—Toni Sailer, Austria .... 3m. 00.1s.

DOWNHILL RACE

1948—Henri Oreiller, France .... 2m. 55.0s.
1952—Zeno Colo, Italy .... 2m. 30.8s.
1956—Toni Sailer, Austria .... 2m. 52.2s.

NORDIC COMBINED (18 KM. RACE AND JUMP)

1924—Thorleif Haug, Norway .... 18.906 points
1928—Johan Grottumsbraaten, Norway .... 17.833 points
1932—Johan Grottumsbraaten, Norway .... 446.00 points
1936—Oddbjorn Hagen, Norway .... 430.30 points
1948—Heikki Hasu, Finland .... 448.80 points
1952—Simon Slattvik, Norway .... 451.60 points
1956—Sverre Stenersen, Norway .... 445.00 points

ALPINE COMBINED (DOWNHILL AND SLALOM)

1936—Franz Pfnur, Germany .... 99.25 points
1948—Henri Oreiller, France .... 3.27 points

40 KILOMETER RELAY

1936—Finland .... 2:41:33   1952—Finland 2:20:16
1948—Sweden .... 2:32:08   1956—Russia 2:15:30

BOBSLEDDING

2 MAN

1932—United States .... 8:14.74   1952—Germany 5:24.54
1936—United States .... 5:29.29   1956—Italy 5:30.14
1948—Switzerland 5:29.20

4 MAN

1924—Switzerland .... 5:45.54   1948—United States 5:20.1
1928—United States (5-man) ... 3:20.5   1952—Germany 5:07.84
1932—United States .... 7:53.68   1956—Switzerland 5:10.44
1936—Switzerland 5:19.85

FIGURE SKATING (WOMEN)

1908—Madge Syers, Great Britain
1920—Julin, Sweden
1924—Mrs. O. von Szabo-Plank, Austria .... 2094.25 points
1928—Sonja Henie, Norway .... 2452.25 points
1932—Sonja Henie, Norway .... 2302.5 points
1936—Sonja Henie, Norway .... 2971.4 points
1948—Barbara Ann Scott, Canada .... 163.077 points
1952—Jeannette Altwegg, Great Britain .... 161.756 points
1956—Tenley Albright, United States .... 169.6 points

SKIING (WOMEN)

DOWNHILL RACE

1948—Hedi Schlunegger, Switzerland .... 2m. 28.3s.
1952—Trude Jochum-Beiser, Austria .... 1m. 47.1s.
1956—Madeleine Berthod, Switzerland .... 1m. 40.7s.

1952—L. Wideman, Finland .... 41m. 40s.
1956—L. Kozyreva, Russia .... 38m. 11s.

SLALOM

1948—Gretchen Fraser, U.S.A. .... 1m. 57.2s.
1952—Mrs. Andrea Mead Lawrence, U.S.A. .... 2m. 11.4s.
1956—Renee Colliard, Switzerland .... 1m. 52.3s.

GIANT SLALOM

1952—Mrs. Andrea Mead Lawrence, U.S.A. .... 2m. 06.8s.
1956—Ossi Reichert, Germany .... 1m. 56.5s.

ALPINE COMBINED (DOWNHILL AND SLALOM)

1936—Christel Cranz, Germany .... 97.06 points
1948—Trude Jochum-Beiser, Austria .... 7.04 points

ICE HOCKEY

1920—Canada	1936—Great Britain
1924—Canada	1948—Canada
1928—Canada	1952—Canada
1932—Canada	1956—Russia

(Unofficial) Team Champions for all Winter Sports

(See page 171)

WRESTLING
Catch-as-Catch-Can

FLYWEIGHT

1904—R. Curry, United States (105 lbs.)   1952—Hassen Gemici, Turkey
1948—V. L. Vitala, Finland

BANTAMWEIGHT

1904—G. N. Mehnert, U.S.A. (115 lbs.)   1936—Odon Zombory, Hungary
1908—G. N. Mehnert, U.S.A. (119 lbs.)   1948—Nassuh Akkam, Turkey
1924—Kustaa Pihalajamaki, Finland   1952—Shohachi Ishii, Japan
1928—K. Makinen, Finland   1956—
1932—Robert E. Pearce, U.S.A.

FEATHERWEIGHT

1896—Karl Schumann, Germany   1932—Herman Pihlajamaki, Finland
1904—I. Niflot, United States   1936—Kustaa Pihlajamaki, Finland
1908—G. S. Dole, United States   1948—Gazanfer Bilge, Turkey
1920—Charles E. Ackerly, United States   1952—Bayram Sit, Turkey
1924—Robin Reed, United States   1956—
1928—Allie Morrison, United States

LIGHTWEIGHT

1904—B. J. Bradshaw, United States   1932—Charles Pacome, France
1908—G. de Relwyskow, Great Britain   1936—Karoly Karpati, Hungary
1920—Kalle Antilla, Finland   1948—Celal Atik, Turkey
1924—Russell Vis, United States   1952—Olle Anderberg, Sweden
1928—O. Kapp, Estonia   1956—

WELTERWEIGHT

1904—O. F. Roehm, United States   1936—Frank Lewis, United States
1924—Herman Gehri, Switzerland   1948—Yasar Dogu, Turkey
1928—A. J. Haavisto, Finland   1952—William Smith, United States
1932—Jack F. Van Bebber, United States   1956—

MIDDLEWEIGHT

1904—Charles Erickson, United States
1908—S. V. Bacon, Great Britain
1920—E. Leino, Finland
1924—Fritz Haggmann, Switzerland
1928—E. Kyburg, Switzerland

1932—Ivar Johansson, Sweden
1936—Emile Poilve, France
1948—Glenn Brand, United States
1952—David Gimakuridze, Russia
1956—

LIGHT HEAVYWEIGHT

1920—Anders Larsson, Sweden
1924—John Spellman, United States
1928—T. S. Sjostedt, Sweden
1932—Peter J. Mehringer, United States

1936—Knut Fridell, Sweden
1948—Henry Wittenberg, United States
1952—Wiking Palm, Sweden
1956—

HEAVYWEIGHT

1904—B. Hansen, United States
1908—G. C. O'Kelly, Great Britain
1920—Roth, Switzerland
1924—Harry Steele, United States
1928—Johan C. Richthoff, Sweden

1932—Johan C. Richthoff, Sweden
1936—Kristjan Palusalu, Estonia
1948—George Bobis, Hungary
1952—Arsen Mekokishvili, Russia
1956—

(UNOFFICIAL) TEAM CHAMPIONS

1904—United States
1908—Great Britain
1920—United States
1924—United States
1928—Finland

1932—United States
1936—United States
1948—Turkey
1952—Russia
1956—

Greco-Roman

FLYWEIGHT

1948—Pietro Lombardi, Italy
1952—Boris Gourevitch, Russia

1956—

BANTAMWEIGHT

1924—Edward Putsep, Estonia
1928—K. Leucht, Germany
1932—Jakob Brendel, Germany
1936—Martin Lorincz, Hungary

1948—K. A. Peterson, Sweden
1952—Imre Hodos, Hungary
1956—

FEATHERWEIGHT

1912—Kalle Koskelo, Finland
1920—Friman, Finland
1924—Kalle Antilla, Finland
1928—V. Wali, Estonia
1932—Giovanni Gozzi, Italy

1936—Yasar Erkan, Turkey
1948—M. Octav, Turkey
1952—Jakov Pounkine, Russia
1956—

LIGHTWEIGHT

1906—Watzl, Austria
1908—E. Porro, Italy
1912—E. E. Ware, Finland
1920—E. E. Ware, Finland
1924—Oskari Friman, Finland
1928—L. Keresztes, Hungary

1932—Erik Malmberg, Sweden
1936—Lauri Koskela, Finland
1948—K. Freij, Sweden
1952—Chasame Safine, Russia
1956—

WELTERWEIGHT

1920—Ivar Johansson, Sweden
1932—Ivar Johansson, Sweden
1936—Rodolf Svedberg, Sweden

1948—Gosta Andersson, Sweden
1952—Miklos Szilvasi, Hungary
1956—

MIDDLEWEIGHT

1906—Weckman, Finland
1908—F. M. Martenson, Sweden
1912—C. E. Johansson, Sweden
1920—Westergren, Sweden
1924—Edward Westerlund, Finland
1928—Vaino Kokkinen, Finland

1932—Vaino Kokkinen, Finland
1936—Ivar Johansson, Sweden
1948—R. Gronberg, Sweden
1952—Alex Gronberg, Sweden
1956—

LIGHT HEAVYWEIGHT

1908—W. Weckman, Finland
1912—A. O. Ahlgren, Sweden ⎫
    J. Boling, Finland ⎭ tie

1932—Rudolph Svensson, Sweden
1936—Axel Cardier, Sweden
1948—Karl Nilsson, Sweden

1920—Claes Johansson, Sweden
1924—Karl Westergren, Sweden
1928—S. Moustafa, Egypt

1952—Kolpo Grondahl, Finland
1956—

HEAVYWEIGHT

1896—Schumann, Germany
1906—J. Jensen, Denmark
1908—R. Weisz, Hungary
1912—U. Saarela, Finland
1920—Lindfors, Sweden
1924—Henri Deglane, France

1928—J. R. Svensson, Sweden
1932—Karl Westergren, Sweden
1936—Kristjan Palusalu, Estonia
1948—Armet Kirecci, Turkey
1952—Ionganes Kotkas, Russia
1956—

(UNOFFICIAL) TEAM CHAMPIONS

1912—Finland
1920—Finland
1924—Finland
1928—Germany
1932—Sweden

1936—Sweden
1948—Sweden
1952—Russia
1956—

YACHTING

6 METER CLASS

1900—Lerina, Switzerland
1908—Dormy, Great Britain
1912—Mac Miche, France
1920—Jo (new), Norway
    Edelweiss II (old), Belgium
1924—Elisabeth V, Norway

1928—Norna, Norway
1932—Bissbi, Sweden
1936—Lalage, Great Britain
1948—Llanoria, United States
1952—Llanoria, United States
1956—

STAR CLASS

1932—Jupiter, United States
1936—Wannsee, Germany
1948—Hilarius, United States

1952—Merope, Italy
1956—

DRAGON CLASS

1948—Pan, Norway
1952—Pan, Norway

1956—

5.5 METER CLASS

1952—Complex II, United States

1956—

FINN CLASS

1952—Denmark

1956—

MONOTYPE

1920—Orange, Holland
  { Boreas, Holland
  { Beatriss III, Holland
    (12 ft.—tied)
1924—L. Huybrechts, Belgium
1928—S. G. Thorell, Sweden

1932—Lebrun, France
1936—D. Kagchelland, Holland
1948—P. Elvstrom, Denmark (Firefly class)
1952—P. Elvstrom, Denmark (Finn class)
1956—(Finn class)—

FIREFLY

1948—P. Elvstrom, Denmark

1952—

8 METER CLASS

1900—Olle, Great Britain
1908—Cobweb, Great Britain
1912—Taifun, Norway
1920—Sildra (new), Norway
    Jerne (old), Norway

1924—Bera, Norway
1928—L'Aigle, France
1932—Angelita, United States
1936—Italia, Italy
1956—

SHARPIE (12 SQ. METER)
(UNOFFICIAL) TEAM CHAMPIONS

1900—France
1904—None
1906—None
1908—Great Britain
1912—Sweden
1920—Norway
1924—Norway

1928—Sweden
1932—United States
1936—Germany
1948—United States
1952—United States
1956—

Discontinued Olympic Sports and Events

ARCHERY

DOUBLE YORK ROUND, MEN
1904—Phil Bryant, U.S.A.
1908—W. Dodd, Great Britain

DOUBLE AMERICAN ROUND, MEN
1904—Phil Bryant, U.S.A.

TEAM ROUND, MEN
1904—U.S.A.

CONTINENTAL ROUND, MEN
1908—M. Grisot, France

BIRD SHOOTING
1920—van Meer, Belgium (standing target)
van Innes, Belgium (moving target)
Team—Belgium
1904—Albertson Van Zo Post, U.S.A.

NATIONAL ROUND, WOMEN
1908—Miss Q. Newall, Great Britain

DOUBLE NATIONAL ROUND, WOMEN
1904—Mrs. M. C. Howell, U.S.A.

DOUBLE COLUMBIA ROUND, WOMEN
1904—Mrs. M. C. Howell, U.S.A.

WOMEN'S TEAM CHAMPIONSHIP
1904—U.S.A.

BOBSLEDDING

SKELETON
1928—John Heaton, U.S.A. ..... 3:01.8   1948—Nino Bibbia, Italy 5:23.2

CANOEING

CANOE RACE, SINGLES
1906—Delaplane, France

FOUR OARED INRIGGERS RACE
1912—Denmark

FOLDING KAYAK SINGLES
1936—G. Hradetzky, Austria

FOLDING KAYAK DOUBLES
1936—S. Johansson, E. Bladstrom, Sweden

CYCLING

333.3 METER TIME TRIAL
1896—Emile Masson, France
1906—Francesco Verri, Italy

660 YARD SPRINT
1896—Emile Masson, France
1906—V. L. Johnson, Great Britain

5 KILOMETERS
1906—Francesco Verri, Italy
1908—Ben Jones, Great Britain

10 KILOMETERS
1896—Emile Masson, France

20 KILOMETERS
1906—W. J. Pett, Great Britain
1908—C. Kingsbury, Great Britain

50 KILOMETERS
1920—H. George, Belgium
1924—J. Willems, Holland

100 KILOMETERS
1896—C. Flameng, France
1908—C. Bartlett, Great Britain

12 HOUR RACE
1896—A. Schmall, Austria

FENCING

FOILS BETWEEN MASTERS
1896—Pirghos, Greece

INDIVIDUAL SWORDS
1900—Robert Ayat, France
1904—Ramon Fonst, Cuba

SINGLE STICKS
1904—Albertson Van Zo Post, U.S.A.

THREE CORNERED SABER
1906—Gustav Casimir, Germany

GOLF

1904—George S. Lyon, Canada

GYMNASTICS, MEN

ROPE CLIMBING

1896—Andriakopoulos, Greece ....
1904—George Eyser, U.S.A. ....7 sec. (25 ft.)
1906—G. Aliprantis, Greece ....11⅖ sec. (32 ft. 9.6 inches)
1924—B. Supcik, Czechoslovakia ....7⅕ sec.
1932—Raymond H. Bass, U.S.A. ....6.7 sec.

INDIAN CLUB SWINGING

1904—E. A. Hennig, U.S.A.. 13 points
1932—George Roth, U.S.A.. 26.9 points

TEAM COMPETITION, SWEDISH SYSTEM

1912—Sweden ....937.46 points
1920—Sweden ....1364 points

TEAM COMPETITION, SPECIAL CONDITIONS

1912—Italy ....53.15 points   1920—Denmark

TEAM COMPETITION, FREE CHOICE OF MOVEMENTS AND APPARATUS

1912—Norway .... 22.85 points

TUMBLING

1932—Rowland Wolfe, U.S.A. 56.7 points

ALL-AROUND, SIX EVENTS

1906—1st Class, Wilhelm Weber, Germany
      2nd Class, Lavielle, France

ALL-AROUND, FIVE EVENTS

1906—1st Class, Lavielle, France
      2nd Class, Anastassaglous, Greece

HANDBALL

1936—Germany

LACROSSE

1904—Canada   1932—U.S.A. (demonstration)
1908—Canada

POLO

1908—Great Britain   1924—Argentina
1920—Great Britain   1936—Argentina

RACKETS

MEN'S SINGLES
1908—E. B. Noel, Great Britain

MEN'S DOUBLES
1908—V. H. Pennell and
      J. J. Astor, Great Britain

ROQUE

1904—Charles Jacobus, U.S.A.

ROWING

2 JUNIOR OARSMEN
1900—Van Crombuge, De Sonville, Belgium

4 JUNIOR OARSMEN
1900—Tellier, Beauchamps, Henry, Hisser, France

16 OARED BARGE RACE 3,000 METERS
1906—Greece

SIX OARED MAN O' WAR GIGS, 2,000 METERS
1906—Italy

RUGBY FOOTBALL

1900—France
1908—Australia

1920—United States
1924—United States

SHOOTING

Due to the great number of different events in shooting, the discontinued events are listed by year rather than by event.

1896

MILITARY RIFLE, 200 METERS
Carassevdas, Greece

MILITARY RIFLE, 300 METERS
Orphanides, Greece

MILITARY REVOLVER, 25 METERS
J. Paine, U.S.A.

CHOICE REVOLVER, 30 METERS
S. Paine, U.S.A.

PISTOL, 25 METERS
Fragoudis, Greece

1900

MINIATURE RIFLE
C. Grosset, France

AUTOMATIC PISTOL OR REVOLVER
Roederer, Switzerland

TEAM PISTOL
Switzerland

RIFLE, 300 METERS
M. Kellenberger, Switzerland

1906

ANY RECOGNIZED ARMY RIFLE, 300 METERS, STANDING OR KNEELING
Richardet, Switzerland

GRAS ARMY RIFLE, 200 METERS, STANDING OR KNEELING
Capt. Moreaux, France

ANY RIFLE, 300 METERS, STANDING OR KNEELING
Meyer de Stadelhofen, Switzerland

INTERNATIONAL TEAMS, 5,300 METERS
Switzerland

GUN CHAMPIONSHIP
Skattebo, Norway

ANY RECOGNIZED ARMY REVOLVER, 20 METERS
Richardet, Switzerland

ARMY REVOLVER DESIGN No. 1873, 20 METERS
Fouconnier, France

ANY REVOLVER, 25 METERS
Lecoq, France

ANY REVOLVER, 50 METERS
G. Orthanidis, Greece

DUELING PISTOLS, 20 METERS, DELIBERATE AIM
Capt. Moreaux, France

Staehell, Switzerland

GUN CHAMPIONSHIP, PRONE POSITION
Skattebo, Norway

DUELING PISTOLS, 25 METERS,
AT COMMAND
Skarlatos, Greece

SPORTING SHOTGUN, CLAY PIGEONS,
DOUBLE SHOT
Sidney Merlin, Great Britain

1908

INTERNATIONAL MATCH
U.S.A.

300 METERS, TEAM
Norway

1,000, YARDS, INDIVIDUAL
Col. J. K. Millner, Great Britain

300 METERS, INDIVIDUAL
A. Helgerud, Norway

RUNNING DEER, 110 YARDS, TEAM
Sweden

RUNNING DEER, INDIVIDUAL,
110 YARDS, DOUBLE SHOT
W. Winans, U.S.A.

MINIATURE RIFLE, MOVING TARGET
A. F. Fleming, Great Britain

MINIATURE RIFLE,
DISAPPEARING TARGET
W. E. Styles, Great Britain

REVOLVER AND PISTOL
50 AND 100 YARDS, TEAM
U.S.A.

50 YARDS, INDIVIDUAL
P. van Aesbrock, Belgium

CLAY BIRD, TEAM
Great Britain

1912

ARMY RIFLE, TEAM,
200, 400, 500, and 600 METERS
U.S.A.

ARMY RIFLE, 600 METERS,
INDIVIDUAL
P. R. Colas, France

ARMY RIFLE, 300 METERS,
INDIVIDUAL
A. Prokopp, Hungary

ANY RIFLE, TEAM, 300 METERS
Sweden

ANY RIFLE, INDIVIDUAL, 300 METERS,
INTERNATIONAL TARGET
P. R. Colas, France

MINIATURE RIFLE, 50 METERS, TEAM
Great Britain

MINIATURE RIFLE, 25 METERS, TEAM
Sweden

MINIATURE RIFLE, 25 METERS,
INDIVIDUAL
W. Carlberg, Sweden

REVOLVER AND PISTOL, 50 METERS,
TEAM
U.S.A.

REVOLVER AND PISTOL, 50 METERS,
INDIVIDUAL
A. P. Lane, U.S.A.

REVOLVER AND PISTOL, 30 METERS
(DUEL SHOOTING), TEAM
Sweden

REVOLVER AND PISTOL, 30 METERS
(DUEL SHOOTING), INDIVIDUAL
A. P. Lane, U.S.A.

CLAY BIRD, TEAM
U.S.A.

RUNNING DEER, 100 METERS,
SINGLE SHOT, TEAM
Sweden

RUNNING DEER, 100 METERS,
DOUBLE SHOTS, INDIVIDUAL
Ake Lundberg, Sweden

1920

TRAPSHOOTING, TEAM
U.S.A.

PISTOL AND REVOLVER
Team, 50 Meters
U.S.A.

Team, 300 Meters, Prone
U.S.A.

Individual, 300 Meters, Prone
Lilloe Olsen, Norway

Individual, 50 Meters
Karl Frederick, U.S.A.

30 Meters, Revolver
U.S.A.

Individual, Revolver
Paraines, Brazil

RUNNING DEER, DOUBLE SHOTS
Norway

MATCHES FOR MILITARY RIFLES
Team, 300 Meters, Standing
Denmark

Individual, 300 Meters, Standing
Carl T. Osburn, U.S.A.

Team, 600 Meters, Prone
U.S.A.

Individual, 600 Meters, Prone
Johansson, Sweden

Team, 300 and 600 Meters, Prone
U.S.A.

MATCHES FOR RIFLES
OF ANY PATTERN
Five Man Team, 300 Meters
U.S.A.

300 Meters, Individual
Sgt. Morris Fisher, U.S.A.

Miniature Rifle Team, 50 Meters
U.S.A.

1924

RIFLE, INDIVIDUAL
Morris Fisher, U.S.A.

RIFLE, TEAM
U.S.A.

MINIATURE RIFLE, TEAM
France

REVOLVER, INDIVIDUAL
H. M. Bailey, U.S.A.

REVOLVER, TEAM
U.S.A.

RUNNING DEER, SINGLE SHOT, TEAM
Norway

RUNNING DEER, DOUBLE SHOT, TEAM
Great Britain

RUNNING DEER, DOUBLE SHOT,
INDIVIDUAL
Lilloe Olsen, Norway

CLAY PIGEON, TEAM
U.S.A.

1932

PISTOL
Renzo Morigi, Italy

1936

AUTOMATIC PISTOL OR REVOLVER,
25 METERS
Cornelius van Oyen, Germany

TARGET PISTOL, 50 METERS
Torsten Ullman, Germany

SWIMMING (MEN)

50 YARDS
1904—Z. de Halmay, Hungary 28s.

500 METERS
1896—P. Neumann, Austria   8 m. 12.6 s.

1200 METERS
1896—A. Hoyos Gutmann,
Hungary .... 18 m. 22.2 s.

880 YARDS
1904—E. Rausch, Germany. 13 m. 11.4 s.

1600 METERS
1906—H. Taylor, Gr. Britain 28 m. 28.0 s.

100 METERS FREE STYLE
BETWEEN SAILORS
1896—Malokinis, Greece

200, METER OBSTACLE RACE
1900—F. C. V. Lane,
Australia .... 2 m. 31.4 s.

1000, METER FREE STYLE
1900—J. A. Jarvis,
Great Britain...... 13 m. 40 s.

4,000, METER FREE STYLE
1900—J. A. Jarvis,
Great Britain...... 58 m. 24 s.

ONE MILE
1904—E. Rausch, Germany. 27 m. 18.2 s.

PLUNGE FOR DISTANCE
1904—W. E. Dickey, U.S.A... 62 ft. 6 in.

UNDERWATER
1900—Devendeville, France

1,000 METER RELAY
1906—Hungary ....17 m. 16.2 s.

FANCY HIGH DIVING
1904—G. E. Sheldon, U.S.A.. 12⅔ points
1912—Erik Adlerz, Sweden .. 7 points
1920—C. E. Pinkston, U.S.A. 7 points
1924—A. C. White, U.S.A. .. 9 points

200, METER BACKSTROKE
1900—P. Hoppenberg, Germany 2 m. 47 s.

RELAY RACE
1900—Germany

400, METER BREAST STROKE
1912—W. Bathe, Germany .. 6 m. 29.6 s.
1920—M. Malmroth, Sweden 6 m. 31.8 s.

440, YARD BREAST STROKE
1904—G. Zahanus, Germany. 7 m. 23.6 s.

220 YARDS
1904—C. M. Daniels, U.S.A.. 2 m. 44.2 s.

200 METERS
1900—F. C. Lane, Australia. 2 m. 25.5 s.

SWIMMING (WOMEN)

300 METERS
1920—Ethelda Bleibtrey, U.S.A. 4 m. 34 s.

TENNIS

Lawn Tennis

MEN'S SINGLES
1896—Boland, Great Britain
1900—L. Doherty, Great Britain
1904—Beals C. Wright, U.S.A.
1906—M. Decugis, France
1908—M. J. G. Ritchie, Great Britain
1912—C. L. Winslow, South Africa
1920—L. Raymond, South Africa
1924—Vincent Richards, U.S.A.

WOMEN'S SINGLES
1900—Miss Cooper, Great Britain
1906—Miss Semyriotou, Greece
1908—Mrs. L. Chambers, Great Britain
1912—Mlle. M. Broquedis, France
1920—Mlle. S. Lenglen, France
1924—Miss Helen Wills, U.S.A.

MEN'S DOUBLES
1896—Boland, Great Britain
      Traun, Germany
1900—Doherty brothers, Great Britain
1904—E. W. Leonard, Beals C. Wright, U.S.A.
1906—M. Decugis, M. Germot, France

1908—G. W. Hillyard, F. R. Doherty, Great Britain
1912—H. A. Kitson, C. Winslow, South Africa
1920—O. Turnbull, M. Woosnam, Great Britain
1924—Vincent Richards, F. T. Hunter, U.S.A.

WOMEN'S DOUBLES
1920—Mrs. J. McNair, Miss K. McKane, Great Britain
1924—Miss Helen Wills, Mrs. G. W. Wightman, U.S.A.

MIXED DOUBLES
1900—Miss, Cooper, F. Doherty, Great Britain
1906—M. and Mme. Decugis, France
1912—Fraulein D. Koring, H. Schomburgk, Germany
1920—Mlle. S. Lenglen, M. Decugis, France
1924—Mrs. G. Wightman, R. N. Williams, U.S.A.

Tennis, Covered Courts

MEN'S SINGLES
1896—Boland, Great Britain
1908—A. W. Gore, Great Britain
1912—A. H. Gobert, France

WOMEN'S SINGLES
1908—Miss G. Eastlake Smith, Great Britain
1912—Miss E. M. Hannam, Great Britain

MEN'S DOUBLES
1896—Boland, Great Britain
      Fritz Traun, Germany
1908—A. W. Gore, H. Roper Barrett, Great Britain
1912—A. H. Gobert, M. Germot, France
MIXED DOUBLES
1912—Mrs. E. Hannam and C. P. Dixon, Great Britian

Tennis Under English Rules

MEN'S SINGLES
1908—Jay Gould, U.S.A.

TRACK and FIELD (MEN)

60 METER RUN
1900—A. E. Kraenzlein, U.S.A.... 7 s.
1904—Archie Hahn, U.S.A......... 7 s.

FIVE MILE RUN
1906—H. Hawtrey, Gr. Brit. 26 m. 26.2 s.
1908—E. R. Voigt, Gr. Brit. 25 m. 11.2 s.
200 METER HURDLES
1900—A. C. Kraenzlein, U.S.A... 25.4 s.
1904—H. L. Hillman, U.S.A. .... 24.6 s.

2,500 METER STEEPLECHASE
1900—G. W. Orton, U.S.A. .. 7 m. 34 s.
1904—J. D. Lightbody,
U.S.A. .... 7 m. 39.6 s.

3,200 METER STEEPLECHASE
1908—A. Russell, Gr. Britain 10 m. 47.8 s.

4,000 METER STEEPLECHASE
1900—C. Rimmer, Gr. Brit. 12 m. 58.4 s.

8,000 METER CROSS COUNTRY
1912—H. Kolehmainen,
Finland .... 45 m. 11.6 s.

10,000 METER CROSS COUNTRY
1920—Paavo Nurmi,
Finland .... 27 m. 15 s.
1924—Paavo Nurmi,
Finland, ... 32 m. 54.8 s.

1,500 METER WALK
1906—George V. Bonhag,
U.S.A. .... 7 m. 12.6 s.

3,000 METER WALK
1920—Ugo Frigerio, Italy . 13 m. 14.2 s.

3,500 METER WALK
1908—G. E. Larner,
Great Britain...... 14 m. 55 s.

10 MILE WALK
1908—G. E. Larner,
Great Britain. 1 h. 15 m. 57.4 s.

TEAM RACE (RUNNING)
1900—Great Britain (5,000 meters)
1904—U.S.A. (3 miles)
1908—Great Britain (3 miles)
1912—U.S.A. (3,000 meters)
1920—U.S.A. (3,000 meters)
1924—Finland (3,000 meters)

CROSS COUNTRY TEAM RACE
1912—Sweden (8,000 meters)
1920—Finland (10,000 meters)
1924—Finland (10,000 meters)
ALL-AROUND CHAMPIONSHIP
1904—T. P. Kiely, Great Britain

STANDING HIGH JUMP
1900—R. C. Ewry, U.S.A... 5 ft. 5 in.
1904—R. C. Ewry, U.S.A... 4 ft. 11 in.
1906—R. C. Ewry, U.S.A... 5 ft. 1⅝ in.
1908—R. C. Ewry, U.S.A... 5 ft. 2 in.
1912—P. Adams, U.S.A.... 5 ft. 4¼ in.

STANDING BROAD JUMP
1900—R. C. Ewry, U.S.A. 10 ft. 6⅖ in.
1904—R. C. Ewry, U.S.A. 11 ft. 4⅞ in.
1906—R. C. Ewry, U.S.A. 10 ft. 10 in.
1908—R. C. Ewry, U.S.A. 10 ft. 11¼ in.
1912—C. Tsicilitiras,
Greece .... 11 ft. ¾ in.

STANDING, HOP, STEP AND JUMP
1900—R. C. Ewry, U.S.A... 34 ft. 8½ in.
1904—R. C. Ewry, U.S.A... 34 ft. 7¼ in.

56-LB. WEIGHT
1904—E. Desmarteau,
Canada .... 34 ft. 4 in.
1920—P. J. McDonald,
U.S.A. .... 36 ft. 11½ in.

DISCUS THROW—GREEK STYLE
1906—W. Jaervinen, Finland 115 ft. 4 in.
1908—M. J. Sheridan, U.S.A. 124 ft. 8 in.

PENTATHLON
1906—H. Mellander, Sweden.. 24 points
1912—F. R. Bie, Norway .... 16 points
1920—E. R. Lehtonen, Finland. 14 points
1924—E. R. Lehtonen, Finland.. 16 points
16-LB. SHOTPUT (BOTH HANDS)
1912—R. Rose, U.S.A...... 90 ft. 5½ in.

DISCUS THROW (BOTH HANDS)
1912—A. R. Taipale,
Finland ...... 271 ft. 10¼ in.

JAVELIN THROW (BOTH HANDS)
1912—J. Saaristo,
Finland ...... 358 ft. 11⅞ in.

JAVELIN THROW (FREE STYLE)
1908—E. Lemming,
Sweden ...... 179 ft. 10½ in.

TRACK and FIELD (WOMEN)

800 METERS FLAT
1928—Lina Radke, Germany . 2 m. 16.8 s.

TUG OF WAR

1904—United States
1906—Germany
1908—Sweden—Great Britain*

1912—Sweden
1920—Great Britain
  * Records Disagree

WEIGHT LIFTING

TWO HANDS

1896—V. Jensen, Denmark... 245.75 lbs.
1904—P. Kakousis, Greece.... 246 lbs.
1906—D. Tofolas, Greece .... 317.64 lbs.

ONE HAND

1896—L. Elliot, Great Britain 156.50 lbs.
1904—O. C. Osthoff, U.S.A. .. 48 points
1906—J. Steinbach, Austria . 168.60 lbs.

WINTER SPORTS

FREE FIGURE SKATING (MEN)
1912—N. Panin, Russia

SPEED SKATING (WOMEN)
1932—500 meter—Jean Wilson, Canada
  1000 meter—Eliz. Dubois, U.S.A.
  1500 meter—Kit Klein, U.S.A.

CURLING
1924—Great Britain
1932—Canada
1936—Austria

MILITARY SKI PATROL
1924—Switzerland
1928—Norway
1936—Italy
1948—Switzerland

SLED DOG RACING
1932—St. Goddard, Canada
MEN'S SPEED SKATING (4 EVENTS)
1924—Clas. Thunberg, Finland

YACHTING

BOATS FROM ½ TO 10 TONS
1900—Aschembrodel, Germany

BOATS ABOVE 10 TONS
1900—Esterel, France

7 METER CLASS
1908—Heroine, Great Britain
1920—Ancora (old), Great Britain

10 METER CLASS
1912—Kitty, Sweden
1920—Mosk II (new), Norway
  Eleda (old), Norway

TWO-TON BOAT
1900—de Pourtales, Switzerland

THREE-TON BOAT
1900—Exshaw, France

12 METER CLASS
1908—Hera, Great Britain
1912—Magda IX, Norway
1920—Heira II (new), Norway
  Atalanta (old), Norway

18 FEET
1920—Brat, Holland

30 METER CLASS
1920—Kullan, Sweden

40 METER CLASS
1920—Sif, Sweden